Lecture Notes in Computer Science   10059

Commenced Publication in 1973
Founding and Former Series Editors:
Gerhard Goos, Juris Hartmanis, and Jan van Leeuwen

More information about this series at http://www.springer.com/series/7409

Marinos Ioannides · Eleanor Fink
Antonia Moropoulou · Monika Hagedorn-Saupe
Antonella Fresa · Gunnar Liestøl
Vlatka Rajcic · Pierre Grussenmeyer (Eds.)

Digital Heritage

Progress in Cultural Heritage: Documentation, Preservation, and Protection

6th International Conference, EuroMed 2016
Nicosia, Cyprus, October 31 – November 5, 2016
Proceedings, Part II

 Springer

Editors

Marinos Ioannides
Cyprus University of Technology
Limassol
Cyprus

Eleanor Fink
Arlington, VI
USA

Antonia Moropoulou
National Technical University of Athens
Athens
Greece

Monika Hagedorn-Saupe
Institut für Museumsforschung
Berlin
Germany

Antonella Fresa
Promoter s.r.l.
Peccioli
Italy

Gunnar Liestøl
University of Oslo
Oslo
Norway

Vlatka Rajcic
University of Zagreb
Zagreb
Croatia

Pierre Grussenmeyer
INSA
Strasbourg
France

ISSN 0302-9743   ISSN 1611-3349   (electronic)
Lecture Notes in Computer Science
ISBN 978-3-319-48973-5   ISBN 978-3-319-48974-2   (eBook)
DOI 10.1007/978-3-319-48974-2

Library of Congress Control Number: 2016956494

LNCS Sublibrary: SL3 – Information Systems and Applications, incl. Internet/Web, and HCI

Printed on acid-free paper

This Springer imprint is published by Springer Nature
The registered company is Springer International Publishing AG
The registered company address is: Gewerbestrasse 11, 6330 Cham, Switzerland

Preface

Welcome to the proceedings of EuromedMed 2016, the biennial scientific event which this year was held in the capital city of Cyprus, the island that has always been a bridge to three continents in the world going back to the origins of civilization. It is a place where the fingerprints of several ancient cultures and civilizations on earth can be found, with a wealth of historical sites recognized and protected by UNESCO.

Several organizations and current EU projects (such as the Marie Sklodowska-Curie Fellowship project on Digital Heritage Marie Sklodowska-Curie FP7-PEOPLE ITN-DCH, the Marie Sklodowska-Curie FP7-IAPP 4D-CH-WORLD, the FP7-CIP ICT-PSP EuropeanaSpace, the H2020 Reflective 7 - INCEPTION, the H2020 CSA Virtual Museums ViMM, the Research Infrastructure DARIAH-EU ERIC and DARIAH-CY) as well as the Innovation in Intelligent Management of Heritage Buildings (i2MHB) decided to join EuroMed2016 and continue cooperating together in order to create an optimal environment for the discussion and explanation of new technologies, the exchange of modern innovative ideas, and in general to allow the transfer of knowledge between a large number of professionals and academics during one common event.

The main goal of the event is to illustrate the programs underway, whether organized by public bodies (e.g., UNESCO, European Union, National States, etc.) or by private foundations (e.g., Getty Foundation, World Heritage Foundation, etc.) in order to promote a common approach to the tasks of recording, documenting, protecting, and managing world cultural heritage. The 6th European-Mediterranean Conference (EuroMed 2016) was definitely a forum for sharing views and experiences, discussing proposals for the optimum approach as well as the best practice and the ideal technical tools to preserve, document, manage, present/visualize and disseminate the rich and diverse cultural heritage of mankind.

This conference was held during the mid-term of the new Framework Programme, Horizon 2020, which is the largest in the world in terms of financial support on research, innovation, technological development, and demonstration activities. The awareness of the value and importance of heritage assets has been reflected in the financing of projects since the first Framework Programme for Research & Technological Development (FP1, 1984–87) and continues into current HORIZON 2020 that follows FP7 (2007–13). In the past 30 years, a large community of researchers, experts, and specialists have had the chance to learn and develop the transferable knowledge and skills needed to inform stakeholders, scholars, and students. Europe has become a leader in heritage documentation, preservation, and protection science, with COST Actions adding value to projects financed within the FP and EUREKA programme and transferring knowledge to practice and supporting the development of SMEs.

The EuroMed 2016 agenda focused on enhancing and strengthening of international and regional cooperation and promoting awareness and tools for future innovative research, development, and applications to protect, preserve, and document the

European and world cultural heritage. Our ambition was to host an exceptional conference by mobilizing also policy makers from different EU countries, institutions (European Commission, European Parliament, Council of Europe, UNESCO, International Committee for Monuments and Sites ICOMOS, the International Committee for Documentation of Cultural Heritage CIPA, the International Society for Photogrammetry and Remote Sensing ISPRS, the International Centre for the study of the Preservation and Restoration of Cultural Property ICCROM, and the International Committee for Museums ICOM), professionals, as well as participants from all over the world and from different scientific areas of cultural heritage.

Protecting, preserving, and presenting our cultural heritage are actions that are frequently interpreted as change management and/or changing the behavior of society. Joint European and international research produce the scientific background and support for such a change. We are living in a period characterized by rapid and remarkable changes in the environment, in society, and in technology. Natural changes, war conflicts, and man-made changes, including climate, as well as technological and societal changes, form an ever-moving and colorful stage and a challenge for our society. Close cooperation between professionals, policy makers, and authorities internationally is necessary for research, development, and technologica advancements in the field of cultural heritage.

Scientific projects in the area of cultural heritage have received national, European Union, or UNESCO funding for more than 30 years. Through financial support and cooperation, major results have been achieved and published in peer-reviewed journals and conference proceedings with the support of professionals from many countries. The European Conferences on Cultural Heritage research and development and in particular the biennial EuroMed conference have become regular milestones on the never-ending journey in the search for new knowledge of our common history and its protection and preservation for the generations to come. EuroMed also provides a unique opportunity to present and review results as well as to draw new inspiration.

To reach this ambitious goal, the topics covered include experiences in the use of innovative technologies and methods and how to take best advantage to integrate the results obtained to build up new tools and/or experiences as well as to improve methodologies for documenting, managing, preserving, and communicating cultural heritage.

In these proceedings we present 105 papers, selected from 504 submissions, which focus on interdisciplinary and multidisciplinary research concerning cutting-edge cultural heritage informatics, physics, chemistry, and engineering and the use of technology for the representation, documentation, archiving, protection, preservation, and communication of cultural heritage knowledge.

Our Keynote speakers, Prof. Dr. Antonia Moropoulou (NTUA and Technical Chamber of Greece), Prof. Dr. Dieter Fellner (Director of FhD/IGD and TU Darmstadt, Germany), Prof. Dr. Wolfgang Kippes (University for Applied Arts Vienna and Donau University Krems, Austria), Prof. Dr. Sarah Whatley (Director of Centre for Dance Research, UK), Prof. Dr. Mustafa Erdik (Bogazici University of Instabul, Turkey), Mr. Jean-Pierre Massué (Senate Member of the European Academy of Sciences and Arts/COPRNM, France), Mr. Axel Ermert (Institute for Museum Research SMB/PK of Berlin, Germany), Mrs. Rosella Caffo (Director of the Central Institute for the Union

Catalogue of the Italian Libraries (ICCU), Italy), Mr. Vasco Fassina (President of the European Standardization Commission CEN/TC 346: Conservation of Cultural Heritage, Italy), Mrs. Maria P. Kouroupas (Director Cultural Heritage Center, US Department of State), Mrs. France Desmarais (ICOM), Dr. Thomas R. Klein (Counsel, Andrews Kurth LLP), Françoise Bortolotti (Criminal Intelligence Officer, Works of Art Unit, Interpol) and Prof. Dr. Markus Hilgert (Director, Vorderasiatisches Museum im Pergamonmuseum Staatliche Museen zu Berlin - Preußischer Kulturbesitz and Project Leader, ILLICID) are not only experts in their fields, but also visionaries for the future of cultural heritage protection and preservation. They promote the e-documentation and protection of the past in such a way for its preservation for the generations to come.

We extend our thanks to all authors, speakers, and those persons whose labor, financial support, and encouragement made the EuroMed 2016 event possible. The International Program Committee—whose members represent a cross-section of archaeology, physics, chemistry, civil engineering, computer science, graphics and design, library, archive and information science, architecture, surveying, history and museology—worked tenaciously and finished their work on time. The staff of the IT department at the Cyprus University of Technology helped with their local ICT and audio visual support, especially Mr. Filippos Filippou, Mr. Costas Christodoulou, and Mr. Stephanos Mallouris. We would also like to express our gratitude to all the organizations supporting this event and our co-organizers, the European Commission scientific and policy officers of the H2020 Marie Skłodowska-Curie Programme, the director general of Europeana, Mrs. Jill Cousins, the Getty Conservation Institute and World Monuments Fund, the Cyprus University of Technology, the Ministry of Energy, Commerce, Industry, and Tourism. Especially the permanent secretary and Digital Champion Dr. Stelios Himonas and Mr. Nikos Argyris, the Ministry of Education and Culture and particularly Minister Dr. Costas Kadis, the director of Cultural Services Mr. Pavlos Paraskevas, the Department of Antiquities in Cyprus, all the members of the Cypriot National Committee for E-Documentation and E-Preservation in Cultural Heritage, and finally our corporate sponsors, CableNet Ltd., the Cyprus Tourism Organization, the Cyprus Postal Services, the Cyprus Handicraft Center, and Dr. Kyriacos Themistocleous from the Cyprus Remote Sensing Society, who provided services and gifts in kind that made the conference possible.

We express our thanks and appreciation to Dr. Nikos Grammalides from CERTH in Greece and Dr. Sander Münster, the Dresden University of Technology, Germany, as well as the board of the ICOMOS Cyprus Section for their enthusiasm, commitment, and support for the success of this event. Most of all we would like to thank the organizations UNESCO, European Commission, CIPA, ISPRS, and ICOMOS Europa Nostra that entrusted us with the task of organizing and undertaking this unique event.

September 2016

Marinos Ioannides
Eleanor Fink
Antonia Moropoulou
Monika Hagedorn-Saupe
Antonella Fresa
Gunnar Liestøl
Vlatka Rajcic
Pierre Grussenmeyer

Acknowledgments and Disclaimer

The EuroMed 2016 conference was partly supported by the Republic of Cyprus, the Cyprus University of Technology, the Cyprus Tourism Organization, the CableNet Ltd., by CIPA (http://cipa.icomos.org/), ISPRS, ICOMOS, Europa Nostra the EU projects FP7 PEOPLE ITN2013 ITN-DCH and IAPP2012 4D-CH-WORLD, the DARIAH-EU ERIC and DARIAH-CY, the FP7-ICT-2011 i-Treasures, the CIP ICT-PSP EuropeanaSpace and H2020 INCEPTION and H2020-ViMM projects.

However, the content of this publication reflects only the authors' views; the European Commission, the Republic of Cyprus, CIPA, ISPRS, ICOMOS, Europa Nostra, Cyprus University of Technology and the EU projects FP7 PEOPLE ITN2013 ITN-DCH and IAPP2012 4D-CH-WORLD, the DARIAH-EU ERIC and DARIAH-CY, the FP7-ICT-2011 i-Treasures, the CIP ICT-PSP EuropeanaSpace and H2020-INCEPTION and H2020-ViMM are not liable for any use that may be made of the information contained herein.

Organization

Conference Chairs

Marinos Ioannides
Eleanor Fink
Antonia Moropoulou
Monika Hagedorn-Saupe
Antonella Fresa
Gunnar Liestøl
Vlatka Rajcic
Pierre Grussenmeyer

Paper Review Chair

Pavlos Chatzigrigoriou

Local Organizing Committee

Agapiou, Athos
Chatzigrigoriou, Pavlos
Eliades, Ioannis
Gkanetsos, Theodoros
Leventis, Georgios
Marina, Christodoulou
Nikolakopoulou, Vasiliki

Nobilakis, Elias
Papageorgiou, Eirini
Skriapas, Konstantinos
Yianni, Stephanie
Stylianou, Georgios
Themistocleous, Kyriacos
Athanasiou, Vasilios

International Scientific Committee

Agapiou, Athos	Cyprus	Caliandro, Rocco	Italy
Albertson, Lynda	Italy	Callet, Patrick	Italy
Angeletaki, Alexandra	Norway	Chatzigrigoriou, Pavlos	Greece
Balet, Olivier	France	Colla, Camilla	Italy
Barcelo, Juan	Spain	Corsi, Cristina	Italy
Bebis, George	USA	Cuca, Branca	Serbia
Belgiorno, Maria-Rosaria	Italy	Dallas, Costis	Canada
Bellini, Francesco	Italy	De Jong, Annemieke	Netherlands
Berni, Marco	Italy	De Kramer, Marleen	Austria
Bockholt, Ulrich	Germany	De Leeuw, Sonja	Netherlands
Bryan, Paul	UK	De Masi, Alessandro	Italy

De Niet, Marco	Netherlands	Liestøl, Gunnar	Norway
De Polo Saibanti, Andrea	Italy	Lobovikov Katz, Anna	Israel
Degraeve, Ann	Belgium	Lonnqvist, Minna	Lichtenstein
Dobreva, Milena	Malta	Lopez-Menchero Bendicho,	Italy
Domajnko, Matevz	Slovenia	Victor	
Doneus, Michael	Austria	Madija, Lidija	Serbia
Doulamis, Anastasios	Greece	Maietti, Federica	Italy
Doulamis, Nikolaos	Greece	Makantasis, Konstantinos	Greece
Drap, Pierre	France	Marcella, Stefano	Italy
Eppich, Rand	USA	Martins, Joao	Portugal
Farrag, Maged	Egypt	Masini, Nicola	Italy
Filin, Sagi	Israel	Mate, Toth	Hungary
Fouseki, Kalliopi	UK	Michail, Harris	Cyprus
Fresa, Antonella	Italy	Moropoulou, Antonia	Greece
Frick, Jürgen	Germany	Munster, Sander	Germany
Gebhardt, Andreas	Germany	Nanetti, Andrea	Singapore
Giannoulopoulos,	Spain	Nikolakopoulou, Vasiliki	Greece
Giannoulis Georgios		Nurminen, Antti	Finland
Giuliano, Angele	Italy	Nys, Karin	Belgium
Graf, Holger	Germany	Ouimet, Christian	Canada
Grammalidis, Nikos	Greece	Papageorgiou, Dimitris	Greece
Grosset, Marie	France	Papageorgiou, Eirini	Greece
Grussenmeyer, Pierre	France	Papagiannakis, George	Greece
Gutierrez, Mariano Flores	Spain	Petrelli, Daniela	UK
Gutiérrez Meana, Javier	Spain	Pietro, Liuzzo	Germany
Hagedorn-Saupe, Monika	Germany	Potsiou, Chryssy	Greece
Hanke, Klaus	Austria	Protopapadakis, Eftychios	Greece
Ibáñez, Francisco	Spain	Radoslav, Pavlov	Bulgary
Ioannidis, Charalambos	Greece	Rajcic, Vlatka	Hungary
Jabi, Wassim	UK	Rodriguez-Echavarria,	UK
Kersten, Thomas	Germany	Karina	
Klein, Michael	Austria	Roko, Zarnic	Slovenia
Klein, Reinhard	Germany	Ronchi, Alfredo	Italy
Kolias, Stefanos	Greece	Saleh, Fathi	Egypt
Koukios, Emmanuel	Greece	Sánchez Andreu, Joan	Spain
Koutsabasis, Panayiotis	Greece	Santana, Mario	Canada
Kuroczyński, Piotr	Germany	Santos, Pedro	Germany
Kyriakaki, Georgia	Greece	Schindler, Mathias	Germany
Landes, Tania	France	Sempere, Isabel Martínez	Spain
Lange, Guus	Belgium	Shang, Jin	China
Laquidara, Giuseppe	Italy	Snyders, Marius	Netherlands
Leissner, Johanna	Germany	Stork, Andre	Germany
León, Alfredo Grande	Spain	Tapinaki, Sevasti	Greece
Lerma, José Luis	Spain	Themistocleous, Kyriacos	Cyprus
Leventis, Georgios	Greece	Thwaites, Harold	MY
Liarokapis, Fotis	Greece	Tsai, Fuan	Taiwan

The Icons of the Chapel of Saint Jacob

The icon shown on the cover of LNCS 10058 (Part I) depicts the scene of the Enthroned Virgin Mary with Child together with Saint John the Evangelist, while the icon shown on the cover of LNCS 10059 (Part II) illustrates Jesus Christ on a throne together with Saint John the Baptist. The icons are dated back to 1620 A.D. and were painted by the artist Meletios from Crete. These icons were stolen from the iconostasis of the chapel of Saint Jacob in Trikomo (Famagusta district) after the Turkish invasion of 1974. Saint Jacob's chapel had no frescoes but it was decorated with colorful plates of traditional folk art.

The icon illustrating Jesus Christ and Saint John the Baptist is 110 × 128 cm in size and close to the feet of the latter there is the inscription "ΧΕΙΡ ΜΕΛΕΤΙΟΥ ΤΟΥ ΚΡΙΤΟΣ ΑΧΚ(= 1620) Χ(ριστο) Υ. Μ(ηνος) αυγούστου)," which includes the name of the artist as well as the date. The icon of Mary, Mother of Jesus, together with Saint John the Evangelist is 114 × 134 cm in size. Both of them were in the possession of the Russian–Jewish art dealer Alexander Kocinski, until their confiscation by the Swiss Police in Zurich in 2007. The only documentation available to recover these stolen icons from abroad was a paper published in the *Proceedings of the International Cretan Conference* in 1976 by the former director of the Department of Antiquities of Cyprus, Mr. Athanasios Papageorgiou.

The icons were tracked down in 2007 in Christie's Auction House in London, from where they were withdrawn after actions by Kykkos Monastery. Following information by the bishop of Kykkos Monastery, representatives of the monastery traveled to Zurich to meet the owner of the icons; however, it was not possible to persuade him to return the icons to the lawful owners and therefore the authorities of Cyprus were informed. A written complaint by the Byzantinologist of Kykkos Monastery, Dr. C. Chotzakoglou, to the Cypriot Police and to Interpol in Cyprus initiated the repatriation procedure of the icons, eventually leading to their confiscation by the Swiss Interpol.

By means of a new testimony from Dr. C. Chotzakoglou, in addition to a full documentation of the Cypriot origin of the icons and their looting after the Turkish invasion in northern Cyprus, the Supreme Court of Famagusta, based in Larnaca, took legal measures against the owner of the icons, who was convicted. The verdict of the Cypriot Supreme Court was subsequently used in the Swiss Court, leading to the signing of a compromise settlement between the Church of Cyprus and Kocinski for the return of the icons to Cyprus.

Dr. Ioannis A. Eliades,
Director,
Byzantine Museum and Art Galleries,
Archbishop Makarios III Foundation,
Arch. Kyprianos sqr., P.O. Box 21269,
CY-1505 Nicosia, CYPRUS

Contents – Part II

Innovative Methods on Risk Assessment, Monitoring and Protection of Cultural Heritage

Intangible Cultural Heritage Documentation

Digital Applications for Materials' Preservation and Conservation in Cultural Heritage

Visualisation, VR and AR Methods and Applications

The New Era of Museums and Exhibitions: Digital Engagement and Dissemination

Digital Cultural Heritage in Education, Learning and Training

Contents – Part I

Full Paper: Non-destructive Techniques in Cultural Heritage Conservation

Full Paper: Visualisation, VR and AR Methods and Applications

Full Paper: The New Era of Museums and Exhibitions: Digital Engagement and Dissemination

Full Paper: Digital Cultural Heritage in Education, Learning and Training

**Project Paper: Data Acquisition, Process and Management
in Cultural Heritage**

Project Paper: Data, Metadata, Semantics and Ontologies in Cultural Heritage

Project Paper: 3D Reconstruction and 3D Modelling

Project Paper: Heritage Building Information Models (HBIM)

Project Paper: Novel Approaches to Landscapes in Cultural Heritage

**Project Paper: Innovative Methods on Risk Assessment, Monitoring
and Protection of Cultural Heritage**

**Project Paper: Digital Applications for Materials' Preservation
and Conservation in Cultural Heritage**

Project Paper: Visualisation, VR and AR Methods and Applications

**Project Paper: The New Era of Museums and Exhibitions: Digital
Engagement and Dissemination**

Project Paper: Serious Games for Cultural Heritage

Project Paper: Digital Cultural Heritage in Education, Learning and Training

Data Acquisition, Process and Management in Cultural Heritage

Development of Photogrammetric Documentation of the Borough at Biskupin Based on Archival Photographs - First Results

D. Zawieska[✉] and J. Markiewicz

Faculty of Geodesy and Cartography, Institute of Photogrammetry,
Remote Sensing and Spatial Information Systems, Warsaw University of Technology,
Warsaw, Poland
{d.zawieska,j.markiewicz}@gik.pw.edu.pl

Abstract. This paper presents the initial results of research work carried out as part of a project entitled *"The design of development of the Lusatian culture settlement at Site 4 at Biskupin: pre-war research work"* financed by the Ministry of Culture and National Heritage, within the National Heritage 2016 Programme, "Conservation of archaeological monuments". The high quality of photographic documents results from the professional, technical and organizational facilities organized by the Biskupin Expedition during the period 1934-1939. A group of photographs acquired from various heights at that time were selected (an aeroplane, a barrage balloon, an observational balloon and terrestrial photographs); these were used for further processing. Using photographs, a true orthoimage, 3D vector models and a 3D visualization of photorealistic models were generated. This paper presents the methodology and stages of the technological process of generation of photogrammetric documentation based on archival data. The benefits and disadvantages of the conventional photogrammetric approach are discussed, and a modified approach involving the application of commonly-used computer vision algorithms is also presented.

Keywords: Archival photographs · Borough at Biskupin · 3D modelling · True-orthimages · Vector products · Automatic image processing

1 Introduction

Cultural heritage is evidence of the past, and historical objects are a very important part of this cultural legacy. A high level of participation from disciplines involved in spatial documentation is required within the field of heritage conservation. The approach used by numerous specialists towards conservation through documentation, initially understood as technical records of historical artefacts which it was impossible to maintain in physical form, has recently been considerably widened. Documentation has become an important tool for preventive conservation, as well as the basis for the media and social transfer of a historical object in the virtual space [1]. In general, geometric documentation is an inseparable part of the documentation of a historical object [2].

© Springer International Publishing AG 2016
M. Ioannides et al. (Eds.): EuroMed 2016, Part II, LNCS 10059, pp. 3–9, 2016.
DOI: 10.1007/978-3-319-48974-2_1

Photogrammetric documentation may form the basis for the reconstruction of a historical object, or, if the original documentation does not exist, may be used as a comparative material for reconstruction of a similar object. Cultural heritage objects have traditionally been archived in various forms, such as drawings or sketches; when technology developed, these were measured and documented with the use of analogue metric cameras (mono- or stereometric), and graphical or analytical documentation was generated. Using archival photographs and vector documents, as well as modern data processing techniques, models of non-existent cultural heritage objects may be generated and visualized.

2 Methodology

The conventional photogrammetric approach consists of the use of analogue photographs which create so-called-stereograms, used for stereodigitization and generation of vector maps. This approach is required to meet a series of geometric conditions (such as coverage and base/distance ratio) in order to achieve the required accuracy and the possibility of realizing a stereoscopic effect. Modern photogrammetric data processing is fully automated, using a combination of photogrammetric algorithms and computer vision (CV); this allows self-calibration, orientation of photographs and 3D reconstruction [3]. This method is based on searching for the same primitives within at least two photographs or groups of photographs of any geometry. A primary feature of the image-based method is the possibility of image correlation during the 3D reconstruction. This problem has been studied for more than 30 years; however, many problems still exist, such as the lack of full automation, occlusions, poor or non-textured areas and repetitive structures [4]. The CV algorithms are designed to give digital photographs of high radiometric quality and sufficient image resolution. The processing stage of digital photographs aimed at the development of 3D models consists of three basic steps. The first of these utilizes an automatic approach known as structure from motion (SfM), which allows the determination of interior and exterior orientation elements and, indirectly, the "scarce cloud of points". The second utilizes algorithms applied in multi-view stereo to automatically densify these clouds of points. The final step is the reconstruction of the surface and texturing [5, 6]. This approach is widely applied in digital photography; however, in analogue photography it generates many difficulties and therefore is not a fully automated process. This paper discusses issues concerning the processing of archival photographs with the use of modern image-processing tools.

3 Performed Experiments

This paper presents the initial results of research work carried out within a project entitled, "The design of development of the Lusatian culture settlement at Site 4 at Biskupin: pre-war research works" financed by the Ministry of Culture and National Heritage, within the National Heritage 2016 Programme "Conservation of archaeological monuments" (www.biskupin.pl).

3.1 Source Data Characteristics

The high quality of pre-war photographic documents is a result of the professional technical and organizational facilities organized by the Biskupin Expedition during the period 1934-1939, as well as from the involvement of Polish military assets for this purpose. As part of this project, 800 photographic glass plates were inventoried with the use of a photogrammetric scanner of resolution 3200 dpi. A group of photographs acquired from various heights were selected (an aeroplane, a barrage balloon, an observational balloon and terrestrial photographs). In addition, vector data processed during archaeological works (scale 1:10) were also utilized.

3.2 Completed Research Work

The effective use of archival data requires appropriate preparation and processing of photographs (Fig. 1).

Fig. 1. Diagram of processing archival photographs (a) mutual orientation and manual measurements of tie points on photographs; (b) the dense cloud of points; (c) the textured digital surface model (mesh); (d) true ortho-image

Division and selection of photographs. Available archival data included multitemporal photographs acquired from various heights. This required an initial division of photographs with regard to their locations and acquisition heights. For this purpose, a "top-down" approach was assumed (Fig. 2).

Fig. 2. Approximate locations of photographs: the "top-down" approach

The aerial photograph which covered the entire Biskupin Peninsula was taken as a reference image. Following this, photographs of particular parts of the settlement were searched for. This task was not straightforward, due to repeating elements in the construction of the settlement; this therefore required a deep analysis of the construction to be performed in cooperation with employees of the State Museum at Biskupin. Photographs were also divided according to the heights of acquisition; this simplifies the automatic processing of photographs by means of the "Chunck" functions in AgiSoft software.

Orientation of photographs (SfM). Ordered groups of points were used to orientate the photographs; these were processed using AgiSoft tools. During the first approach, automatic searching for tie points was applied without manual measurements. As a result, incorrectly orientated photographs were obtained. A scarce cloud of points almost correctly generated should create a plane; in this case, a parabolic surface was created. In order to achieve the correct orientation of photographs it was necessary to perform manual measurements of tie points, distributed according to the conventional von Gruber approach (Krauss, xxx). Selected tie points were distributed on various planes in order to ensure variations in depth. In the conventional approach, at least six tie points are required; however, the authors decided to increase the number of tie points to ten. This allowed improvements to the orientation of oblique photographs as compared with nadir photographs.

In order to geo-reference photographs in relation to archaeological stations, photogrammetric control was developed based on vector drawings at a scale of 1:10. The mean accuracy of the exterior orientation of photographs in the reference system was approximately 1 cm.

Generating a dense cloud of points (multi-view stereo) and the digital surface model. Following the orientation of photographs, the next step was the densification of the cloud of points, carried out with the use of algorithms applied in the multi-view stereo approach. When archival photographs are processed, several difficulties related to generation of the depth map may appear unless initial radiometric processing is performed. Archaeological excavations had been carried out over various periods within the investigated areas; it was therefore decided to generate spread point clouds for each excavation. The digital surface model in the TIN structure was generated based on the generated cloud of points. When the resulting clouds of points and the digital surface model were analysed, some incorrectness in the obtained dataset was noticed; the obtained cloud of points was characterized by a grainy surface structure. This resulted from searching for characteristic points in the penultimate level of the pyramid of images and the variations in quality and conditions of the processed photographs. An additional factor influencing the quality of the resulting digital surface model is the low value of depth of the processed elements. The lack of data is visible in the cloud of points, resulting from difficulties related to the restoration of the repeating structure of the elements of construction, which is difficult to process using MVS algorithms. In future experiments it will therefore be necessary to restore the missing elements of the terrain surface, based on manual measurements of the corresponding features of images using other software tools.

Orthorectification and mosaicking of photographs. The final stage of true-ortho generation was classification and mosaicking of photographs (Fig. 3). For this purpose, photographs acquired from the lowest possible height were selected, in order to ensure the smallest possible GSD value. In addition, photographs with slight blurring, which were used in the orientation process of the photographs, were eliminated at this final stage. For the southern and eastern fragments, a GSD value of close to 50 cm was calculated (Fig. 3A). This resulted from the scale of the photographs, which were mostly acquired from an aeroplane and the barrage balloon. The northern and eastern parts were projected using balloon photographs from a lower height, corresponding to a GSD value of approximately 10 cm (Fig. 3B).

Fig. 3. Examples of true-ortho (a) GSD 50 cm; (b) GSD 10 cm

Visualization and 3D modelling. When archival photographs are used in archaeological work, two approaches to 3D modelling may be applied. Due to the specific features of this work and the assumptions of the project, two types of models were proposed. A non-metric model was created, based on individual photographs and using Blender software (Fig. 4).

Fig. 4. Examples of visualization of models generated from individual photographs using Blender software

This model is used for the photointerpretation of the structure and the relationships between the elements of the settlement construction. It allows for the separation of the constructional layers created in different periods of the settlement's history. According to the opinions of archaeologists, many constructions exist in the analysed areas, and were created at different times. The final visualization allows for the confirmation or contradiction of the formulated hypothesis. The second approach in the 3D modelling of constructions allows for the geometric dimensioning of constructional elements. At this stage, Trimble Sketch Up software was used. Figure 5 presents the models, including the 3D model matched in the photographs, and a photorealistic 3D model of the fireplace and a fragment of the floor.

Fig. 5. A 3D model (a) matched in the photograph; (b) a photorealistic model of a fireplace and a floor fragment

4   Conclusions

Widely-used computer vision algorithms were used for data processing. In the authors' opinion, the use of those algorithms to process scanned photographs did not lead to successful results in several cases. The experiments carried out showed unreliability when full automation was used; it was therefore necessary to support the algorithms with manual measurements of tie points. All photogrammetric products will be entered into the planned HGIS database, and the designed and developed modules of the HGIS database will allow the display of objects processed at the stage of virtual reconstruction of relics of the settlement's development.

Acknowledgements. The authors would like to thank the Project Coordinator of the State Archaeological Museum at Biskupin, Jarosław Kopiasz, for making the photographs and archival materials available for this project. The authors would also like to thank Jowita Tazbir and Aleksandra Tobiasz for their assistance during the data processing phase.

References

1. Tomaszewski, A.: Towards a new philosophy of heritage. International Cultural Center (2013)
2. Markiewicz, J., Podlasiak, P., Zawieska, D.: A new approach to the generation of orthoimages of cultural heritage objects—integrating TLS and image data. Remote Sens. **7**(12), 16963–16985 (2015)
3. Moussa, W.: Integration of Digitall Photogrammetry and Terrstrial Laser Scanning for Cultural Heritage Data Recording. Verlag der Bayerischen Akademie der Wissenschaften in Kommission beim Verlag C.H.Beck Studgart, Germany (2014)
4. Remondino, F., Menna, F.: Image-based surface measurement for close range heritage documentation. Int. Arch. Photogram. Remote Sens. Spat. Inf. Sci. **XXXVIII**-5, 199–206 (2008)
5. Chiabrando, F., Donadio, E., Rinaudo, F.: SfM for orthophoto generation: a winning approach for cultural heritage knowledge. Int. Arch. Photogram. Remote Sens. Spat. Inf. Sci. **XL**-5, 91–98 (2015)
6. Giuliano, M.G.: Cultural heritage: an example of graphical documentation with automated photogrammetric systems. Int. Arch. Photogram. Remote Sens. Spat. Inf. Sci. **XL**-5, 251–255 (2014)

Capturing Our Cultural Intangible Textile Heritage, MoCap and Craft Technology

Eva Andersson Strand[1(✉)], Stefan Lindgren[2], and Carolina Larsson[2]

[1] Archaeological Department, Centre for Textile Research (CTR), SAXO Institute,
University of Copenhagen, Copenhagen, Denmark
evaandersson@hum.ku.dk
[2] Humanities Lab, Lund University, Lund, Sweden

Abstract. Textile craft and textile design have always had an important social, cultural and economic impact on both individuals and societies. The cultural heritage of textiles does not end with the preservation and collection of costumes and other textiles in museums. It also includes living traditions inherited from our ancestors. Furthermore, understanding craft and craft processes are crucial when considering both past societies and the cultural heritage of humankind. The study of intangible processes, hidden within archaeological objects, crafts, action and activities as well as cognitive processes, involves both practical and theoretical considerations. Today, computer applications such as Motion Capture can enhance our knowledge of the complexity and variety of artifacts, their production, and how various craft traditions develop over time, yielding new insights and perspectives applicable to ancient societies as well as to traditional craft today.

Keywords: Craft · Textile processes · Motion capture · Archaeology · Theories of practices

1 Introduction

How do we decide to make things? How do we learn to make things? The study of craft and craft production is fundamental for understanding the underlying causes for the complexity of ancient societies as well as traditional craft performed today. In the following we will *illuminate how the body and mind are involved in the production processes behind ancient and traditional textile technology and how this can be further explored by developing the use of 3-dimensional method, Motion Capture.* Craft and craft production can, in a broad sense, be said to meet the social and psychological needs of human beings, and facilitate social coherence (Costin, 2007, p. 146). In recent years, the assumed dichotomies between technology (practice) and theoretical knowledge are being questioned. Theories of practice are being developed, and how professionals think in action and how their skills are transmitted are investigated (e.g. Bourdieu, 1977; Schön, 1983; Latour, 1999; Ingold 2000; Bender Jørgensen 2012; Sutton, 2015). Combining theory and practice permits us to understand, e.g. how we learn craft, how we record the differences of skills and abilities of craftspeople and how old traditions

© Springer International Publishing AG 2016
M. Ioannides et al. (Eds.): EuroMed 2016, Part II, LNCS 10059, pp. 10–15, 2016.
DOI: 10.1007/978-3-319-48974-2_2

affect the possibility to learn new techniques and improve skills - questions pertinent to craft transmission and developments in past societies. Thus, it is essential to develop methodologies through which tacit or embodied knowledge can be translated into a form that goes beyond mere textual analysis but which can also be observed and described from an anthropological perspective (Bender Jørgensen, 2012).

2 Experimental Archaeology and Documentation of Crafts

A combination of craft knowledge with experimental archaeology has already proved to be a significant method enabling new interpretations and perspectives on the archaeologically invisible parts of ancient societies (e.g. Andersson, 2003; Renfrew and Bahn, 2004; Grömer, 2010; Olofsson et al., 2015). However, this method has also been criticized. One of the post-processual arguments was that designs of experiments were influenced by subjective values of the present, which would have affected the outcome of any experiment (Brattli and Johnsen, 1989). Yet even though debated, this method has been, and is still, used today (e.g. Olofsson et al., 2015; Belanová-Štolcova and Grömer, 2010). The performance of experiments and *traditional textile craft* is often photographed and/or filmed and the objects produced are sometimes documented and preserved. However, using these methods to obtain a full 3-dimensional coverage of the process, would require a multiple video camera setup, preferably using cameras with a higher frame rate than ordinary cameras. Such a setup would produce a large amount of data which would prolong the post-processing significantly.

3 Motion Capture: A New Method in Documenting Textile Craft

New innovative methods are necessary and also available in order to come closer to both ancient societies and the people themselves. Motion capture (MoCap) is the process of recording the movement of objects or people in 3D. A MoCap system also uses a multiple camera setup, but the cameras only work in the infrared spectrum, and they only record markers placed on the subject or the tools used by the subject. The markers are placed to get a good representation of the subject studied, which means it is possible to focus only on the parts of interest. Since it is only the markers being recorded, the amount of data is not particularly large, which makes the post-processing relatively simple. Movements are sampled c. 250 times per second to capture all types of movements with high precision.

In the commercial sphere, MoCap is famously used to develop videogames and movies. But it is a useful method in several different research fields as well. In medicine it is used to study rehabilitation of different types of injuries. In the humanities, it is used to study body language and gestures. We believe this method permits new innovations when conducting and studying different craft experiments and recording craft processes. MoCap can enhance our knowledge of the complexity and variety of artifacts, their production, and how various craft traditions develop over time, yielding new insights and perspectives applicable *to ancient societies* as well as to *traditional craft today*.

The possibilities of combining MoCap and textile experimental archaeology, and determining how far these results can be used in our interpretation of intangible craft production, will be explored in this research project via systematic experiments in collaboration with textile technicians.

4   The First Tests

Our aim is to document, measure and study various textile activities and parameters. In order to test MoCap, its possibilities and limitations, we have so far conducted two spinning tests with suspended spindles copied from Viking Age originals. The reason for choosing spinning with this type of spindle is that the production of yarn has been of the highest importance and one of the most time-consuming tasks in all ancient societies. For example, to produce two Viking Age costumes, one male and one female in a general quality, more than 40 000 m of yarn, which took c. 800 h to spin, was used. To produce a sail used on one of the Viking Age longships, one would need to spin more than 200 000 meters of yarn (Andersson, 2003; Andersen and Nørgård, 2009). Furthermore, spinning tools are frequently found on archaeological excavations, and spindles have been used at least since the Neolithic era all over the world. It is also essential to note that hand spinning is a technique which is still used in some places by craftspeople producing traditional textiles, for example, Peru and Jordan. However, in many places such as Turkey and Scandinavia, machine spun yarn is frequently used and the knowledge of how to spin is rapidly disappearing.

Fifty-six markers were put on the spinner's body, and additional markers were put on the spindle which gave us the possibility to also see the spindle's movement. After the tests, the spun yarn was analyzed which gave another and comparative perspective, as it was then possible to see how the yarn was affected by a certain movement. It is our expectation that this new knowledge will be applicable on archaeological textiles, and bring information on the craftsmanship in ancient societies and the spinner's skills and abilities.

The first test results clearly demonstrated the movements of the spinner, how fast the spindle was moving, and when it started to wobble. The data consists of the 3D-position of all of the markers relative to each other in every single time frame. By choosing the interesting parameters, for example the z-coordinate of a marker on the spinner's hand, it was possible to see the up and down movement of the arm. The recordings showed how regularly the spinners were working. By looking only at the 3D-position of the marker placed on the spindle, it was possible to see if it started to wobble. Two parameters strongly affect the outcome of the spun yarn; if the spindle is wobbling, and if the spinner does not work regularly, the yarn will be unevenly spun. By looking at several markers at the same time, it was, for example possible to see how the movement of the hand affected the spindle.

Certainly it is necessary to be able to connect the measurement to the resulting yarn, so it is possible to assess what effect a particular motion in the recording has on the produced yarn. To do that, it is just a matter of adding the distances that the hand travels in each pull in the recording, which gives a reasonable value of the length of the yarn.

In the second test, two spinners were conducting simulations with the same tool and raw material. While the preliminary results show that the working positions/spinning techniques were slightly different, even so and in this case, the yarn spun by the two spinners were similar and could be used in the same fabric. This is important as it suggests that several spinners, given the same tools and raw material, could spin a yarn used in the same fabric which is necessary if one wants a homogenous fabric, for example a sail cloth.

5   Expectations of New MoCap Recordings and Future Research

Thanks to MoCap, we can study the movements in detail. Also other textile tools, for example different types of looms will be tested, e.g. how the weaver beats the weft, how much work is done in any given length of time, how/if the weaving speed changes, how different movements influence the final result - the produced object, and what separates and connects skilled spinners or weavers. With the use of MoCap we will be able to see how different textile technicians use the textile tools and how this affects the outcome, but also their bodies, for example, the joints in the arms and hands. What are the differences between a professional craftspeople and a beginner, an adult and a child, how does the age affect the result etc. are other interesting questions. It will, furthermore, be possible to compare how different raw materials such as wool, flax and silk influence spinning and weaving techniques, for example, the choice of spinning tool, which will allow more secure interpretations on the types of fibre material that were used in specific places- something which is frequently debated today. These results can make an important contribution to the discussion on the use of different types of textile tools, whether it is a cultural tradition and if the type of tool really affects the outcome.

Additionally, MoCap is not only a method which can be used in textile experimental archaeology. With MoCap as a method, it is possible to record the details in, for example, flint-knapping, bronze casting and many other crafts. It is clear that this application, combined with the traditional experiments, enables us to develop an innovative method to compare data from different experiments involving different actors. This provides new possibilities for analyses of the recorded data and for experiments, thereby raising new research questions to pursue. All this new information will be applicable to the archaeological material and will help us study the tools and the processes with new eyes and give new information on craft and craft traditions.

6   MoCap and Traditional Craftsmanship

Finally and perhaps more importantly, is how MoCap can help us to preserve, document and also develop traditional craftsmanship. Today, there is a consciousness of the importance not only of preserving craft objects but also of encouraging craftspeople to produce and to pass on their skill to others (see for example the UNESCO convention on traditional craftsmanship: UNESCO. 2016. *Traditional craftsmanship*. [Online]. [Accessed 14 October 2016]. Available from: http://www.unesco.org/culture/ich/en/traditional-craftsmanship-00057). This is a challenge. Thanks to the industrial revolution, textiles have never been as cheap or as easily mass produced, with the sad consequence that traditional textile craft skills and knowledge are not always valued. The skills required for the complexity of textile craft are partly forgotten. It is, indeed, very time consuming to produce a textile by hand, and such textiles have become expensive with few people being able to afford them. Thus, the market for them becomes ever more restricted with the result that it becomes less advantageous for craftspeople to maintain their skills. Old (traditional) designs go out of fashion and it can be difficult for the craftspeople to use traditional techniques to produce new designs. There is a negative circle of cause and effect which results in the diminution of traditional textile craft and a loss of knowledge. This loss is often invisible and has so far been definitive. However, many designers are now exploiting the potential of traditional craft in their work and revitalizing practices. It is essential to preserve this knowledge and skill, and also to make its importance more visible and available to a wider audience. A digital MoCap library will make old textile techniques accessible for a large audience interested in learning, studying, and practicing.

7   Conclusion and Further Remarks

The first results have clearly demonstrated its potential, but much more has to be done in order to develop the methodology and improve the use of the MoCap techniques. Still, there are many questions to be asked, for example: What are the possibilities and what are the limitations? How can we bring the MoCap method out to the workshops? As there is an endless number of possibilities, how do we decide what to record and analyse? Which parameters could be combined and compared in each process and craft? How long time do we need to record in order to get a reliable result? etc.

However, it is our expectations that MoCap, combined with experimental archaeology and craft technology, will enable us to record movements of craftspeople today for a new understanding of tacit craft knowledge and craft practice in producing objects both ancient and modern.

Acknowledgement. This project is a collaboration between Lund University Humanities Lab Sweden, the Danish National Research Foundation's Centre for Textile Research and the Archaeological department, SAXO Institute, University of Copenhagen. The recordings were made at Lund University Humanities Lab Sweden. The article is written with the support of DNRF64 and Lund University Humanities Lab.

References

Andersen, E., Nørgård, A.: Et uldsejl til Oselven. Vikingeskibsmuseet, Roskilde (2009)

Andersson, E.: Tools for Textile Production – From Birka and Hedeby (Birka Studies 8). Stockholm (2003)

Belanová-Štolcova, T., Grömer, K.: Loom weights, spindles and textiles - textile production in central Europe from the Bronze and Iron age. In: NESAT X, pp. 9–20. Oxbow, Oxford (2010)

Bender Jørgensen, L.: Introduction to part II: technology as practice and spinning faith. In: Sørensen, M.L.S., Rebay-Salisbury, K. (eds.) Embodied Knowledge: Perspectives on Belief and Technology, pp. 91–94 and 128–136. Oxbow Books, Oxford (2012)

Bourdieu, P.: Outline of a Theory of Practice. Cambridge University Press, Cambridge (1977)

Costin, C.L.: Thinking about production: phenomenological classification and lexical semantics. Archaeological Papers of the American Anthropological Association **17**(1), 143–162 (2007)

Ingold, T.: The Perception of the Environment: Essays on Livelihood, Dwelling and Skill. Routledge, London, New York (2000)

Latour, B.: Pandora's Hope: Essays on the Reality of Science Studies. Harvard University Press, Cambridge (1999)

Olofsson, L., Andersson Strand, E., Nosch, M.-L.: Experimental testing of Bronze age textile tools. In: Andersson Strand, E., Nosch, M.-L. (eds.) Tools, Textiles and Contexts: Investigating Textile Production in the Aegean and Eastern Mediterranean Bronze Age, pp. 75–100. Oxbow Books, Oxford (2015)

Renfrew, C., Bahn, P.: Archaeology: Theories, Methods, and Practice. Thames & Hudson Ltd., New York (2004)

Schön, D.A.: The Reflective Practitioner: How Professionals Think in Action. Maurice Temple Smith, London (1983)

Sutton, J., Keene, N.: Cognitive history and material culture. In: Gaimster, D., Hamling, T., Richardson, C. (eds.) The Ashgate Research Companion to Material Culture in Early Modern Europe (2015)

CH Digital Documentation and 3D Survey to Foster the European Integration Process: The Case Study of Geguti Palace in Kutaisi, Georgia

Marco Medici[1(✉)], Federico Ferrari[1], Nana Kuprashvili[2], Tamar Meliva[2], and Nino Bugadze[2]

[1] Department of Architecture, University of Ferrara, Ferrara, Italy
{marco.medici,federico.ferrari}@unife.it
[2] Tbilisi State Academy of Arts, Tbilisi, Georgia
nana.kuprashvili@art.edu.ge, tamarameliva@gmail.com,
n_bugadze@yahoo.com

Abstract. The European integration process brings countries closer to each other, breaking down barriers to mobility and fostering cooperation. As a result of these long-term processes, the European societies feature a large diversity of values and lifestyles, views and beliefs, identities and cultures that influence on daily basis the European economy, society, politics and law. Studies contributing to the understanding of Europe's intellectual basis, creative capacity, cultural identity and history rely more and more on digital expressions of culture and identity. Advanced research and modelling and preservation technologies maximize the value of tangible and intangible heritage and of collections in libraries, archives, museums, galleries and other public institutions.

Keywords: CH digital documentation · 3D survey · Cultural identity

1 Introduction

As stated by European Commission, "Europe is characterized by a variety of different peoples, traditions, regional and national identities as well as by different levels of economic and social development. It has a very rich intellectual and historical basis with many European and non-European influences that have shaped it over the centuries and continue to do so today."[1]

At the same time, looking at the territory that defines a fluid European cultural border, it is easy to find clear mutual influences that need to be explored in order to better understand our culture, breaking down barrier and fostering the cooperation.

In these efforts of understanding common intellectual basis, advanced researches on tangible cultural heritage, based on digital technologies, will give the chance of explore

---

[1] European Commission, "Europe in a changing world: inclusive, innovative and reflective societies" in HORIZON 2020 – WORK PROGRAMME 2014-2015, p. 32.

© Springer International Publishing AG 2016
M. Ioannides et al. (Eds.): EuroMed 2016, Part II, LNCS 10059, pp. 16–21, 2016.
DOI: 10.1007/978-3-319-48974-2_3

valuable assets, preserve them from different kind of threat and enhance a more accessible enjoyment by Information and Communication Technologies and innovative digital tools [1].

This work-in-progress joint research, developed by the Department of Architecture of the University of Ferrara and the Tbilisi State Academy of Arts, in collaboration with the National Agency for Cultural Heritage Preservation of Georgia, refers to main aims of the previously illustrated framework. The documentation of an important Georgian monument – the complex of Geguti Palace, located at the border of European territory and symbol of cultural identity - is a great opportunity to better understand the relationship between our countries and cultures, and our common roots. The project has been arranged in order to develop memory conservation processes and actions aimed at the valorization and preservation of cultural heritage assets and, on the other hand, to share interdisciplinary skills between two research centers.

2   Case Study Context

Geguti Palace, a medieval royal palace, dates back in XII-XIV centuries and was built as the summer residence of the Georgian Kings. The earliest structure of the Palace is believed to be built even earlier, in 8th century. The Palace is frequently mentioned as a beloved place of the Georgian royalty [2].

The palace, now in ruins, is located 7 km south of the city Kutaisi, along the river Rioni. The complex includes the palace itself and the church. Also, there are archaeological excavations in course on the territory, which proves the existence of the previous structures. The palace spreads on about 2,000 sqm and is composed by the huge central hall and small additional rooms around it.

Bricks are the main building material, but depending on the different building periods: river stones, lime stones and different kind of bricks are used. The palace is distinguished with its history and architecture. It is important to be mentioned the multi-layered nature of the structure, as it shows the different layers of the history which is connected with the important persons and periods of the Country. And, furthermore, it is the only royal palace preserved till today in Georgia.

The Monument is categorized as the National Importance by the Georgian state.[2]

Since XVIII cen. the palace was abandoned. In the 30ies of XX cen. the monument has become the interesting for the researchers and several campaign of fieldwork was realized, including the archaeological and reconstruction work.

---

[2] "On the basis of a recommendation of the Ministry, cultural properties may be granted the grade of national importance by an ordinance of the Government of Georgia if such cultural property has special artistic or aesthetic value, or if it is associated with an event or a person of special historical significance, or if it is related to a stage of national development, and if it has distinctive general and national values." Georgian law on cultural heritage, Article 18, Law of Georgia No 1330 of 25 September 2013.

3   Aims and Objectives

The research needs to be defined as a cross-disciplinary process involving different skills by the partners, aiming at a better interpretation and understanding for a sustainable development of the site and its accessibility. To reach the above mentioned overall goal, the research will be developed in two main phases:

- interdisciplinary survey and documentation of the asset in order to create a comprehensive database for research purposes, future interventions and knowledge dissemination;
- development of a valorization strategy for the site involving both physical (building preservation and restoration, site enjoyment facilities, permanent and temporary exhibitions, etc.) and digital aspects (digital end-users applications, abroad accessing by Virtual Reality, on-site understanding by Augmented Reality, etc.).

4   Methodology

Over last years, methods and processes for data collection have faced a fast and effective improvement, allowing the possibility a growing number of interdisciplinary applications thanks to a lot of valuable research project on this topic [3].

The vision of an integrated digital documentation for cultural heritage assessment is becoming even more a real opportunity, thanks to improved instrument features and technical skills on 3D survey. The 3D laser scanner technology allows to create a high definition database by capturing a set of X, Y, Z coordinates able to define a metric and morphologic model of the surveyed building or site. This database, with its own specific degree of accuracy depending by the instrumental performance and survey procedures, according to the complexity of the object, could become the starting point for the creation of a valuable digital archive, providing extremely useful information in cultural heritage field.

Starting from the concept of "geometric memory" [4], it is possible to enhance the knowledge and the understanding of Cultural Heritage assets in order to pursue a sustainable preservation.

Operating within a context of several millions of organized three-dimensional coordinates allows to extract many different data for the enhancement of documentation for conservation, diagnostics, monitoring and restoration project.

Moreover, the promotion and valorization phase should take the opportunity to exploit the captured technical data for the digital cultural heritage accessibility, making contents and resources available for as many people as possible by using ICT functionalities and applications. From researchers and scholars to visitors and tourists, new digital technologies allow to develop user-oriented narratives and to access the site from abroad, preserving its memory and disseminating its value all over the world. By this, an inclusive and flexible valorization strategy will be arranged. The access to the digital model could be also provided directly on site, in order to enrich the monument enjoyment.

5 Preliminary Results and Future Developments

Until now, the joint research activities have been performed by the direct funding of the two universities. The main preliminary results refer to the 3D survey activities performed in the summer of 2016. The survey project has been also positively evaluated by the Young Researchers commission by the University of Ferrara, receiving a special funding.[3]

While the survey project has been developed by the Department of Architecture of the University of Ferrara, the field work has been performed by an interdisciplinary team that consist of researchers by both the research institution, in order to ensure a valuable understanding of the site.

Fig. 1. 3D point cloud: top view of the complex

From technical side, the following instruments has been used:

- Geomax Zoom 300, a time-of-flight laser scanner provided for free by Geomax AG, for metrical survey;
- NCTech iStar 360, a spherical camera by NCTech, for 360° virtual tour;
- Samsung WB690 compact camera for photo-modelling source and photographic documentation.

During a one-week field work, the following result have been achieved:

- Creation of the high density 3D point cloud composed by the 200 millions of points taken from 60 stations. The dataset was registered with ICP method, average error - 3, 8 cm, using JRC 3D Reconstructor by Gexcel (Figs. 1, 2);

---

[3] The Young Researcher fund consists on a percentage (0.5 %) freely devolved by Italian taxpayers to the University of Ferrara from their annual income tax return (year 2013).

Fig. 2. 3D point cloud: general view on the palace

- Capturing of 60 HDR 360° spherical photos in order to develop an exhaustive visualization for VR (Virtual Reality) viewers (Fig. 3);
- Creation of 3D models for 17 archaeological excavation areas by the photo SFM modelling in order to create and easy updatable documentation of excavation processes (Fig. 4).

Fig. 3. 360° spherical photo: general view on the palace

These performed actions are the basis on which will be developed, in next few months, the comprehensive database for research purposes, future interventions and knowledge dissemination, as planned in objectives definition.

Fig. 4. 3D photo modelling: archaeological excavation area with ceramic vessel

At the same time, according to specific agreements with the National Agency for Cultural Heritage Preservation of Georgia, in 2017 an answer to the second planned objective will be provided, developing an integrated strategy for valorization.

References

1. Di Giulio, R.: Towards sustainable access, enjoyment and understanding of cultural heritage and historic settings. In: Borg, R.P., Gauci, P., Staines, C.S., (eds.) Proceedings of the International Conference "SBE Malta 2016, Europe and the Mediterranean: Towards a Sustainable Built Environment", Valletta, Malta, 16th-18th March 2016, pp. 269–277. Gutenberg Press, Malta (2016). ISBN 9 789995 709358
2. Beridze, V.: Dzveli Kartuli Khurotmodzghvreba (transcript)/old Georgian architecture (translation) ძველი ქართული ხუროთმოძღვრება. Tbilisi, pp. 64–165 (1974)
3. Ioannides, M., Magnenat-Thalmann, N., Fink, E., Žarnić, R., Yen, A.-Y., Quak, E. (eds.): EuroMed 2014. LNCS, vol. 8740. Springer, Heidelberg (2014). doi: 10.1007/978-3-319-13695-0
4. Maietti, F., Ferrari, F., Medici, M., Balzani, M.: 3D integrated laser scanner survey and modelling for accessing and understanding european cultural assets. In: Borg, R.P., Gauci, P., Staines, C.S., (eds.) Proceedings of the International Conference "SBE Malta 2016, Europe and the Mediterranean: Towards a Sustainable Built Environment", Valletta, Malta, 16th-18th March 2016, pp. 317–324. Gutenberg Press, Malta (2016). ISBN 9 789995 709358

Data, Metadata, Semantics and Ontologies in Cultural Heritage

Applying Deep Learning Techniques to Cultural Heritage Images Within the INCEPTION Project

Jose Llamas[1]([⊠]), Pedro M. Lerones[1], Eduardo Zalama[2], and Jaime Gómez-García-Bermejo[2]

[1] CARTIF Foundation, Parque Tecnológico de Boecillo, Valladolid, Spain
joslla@cartif.es
[2] ITAP-DISA, University of Valladolid, Valladolid, Spain

Abstract. The digital documentation of cultural heritage (CH) often requires interpretation and classification of a huge amount of images. The INCEPTION European project focuses on the development of tools and methodologies for obtaining 3D models of cultural heritage assets, enriched by semantic information and integration of both parts on a new H-BIM (Heritage - Building Information Modeling) platform. In this sense, the availability of automated techniques that allow the interpretation of photos and the search using semantic terms would greatly facilitate the work to develop the project. In this article the use of deep learning techniques, specifically the convolutional neural networks (CNNs) for analyzing images of cultural heritage is assessed. It is considered that the application of these techniques can make a significant contribution to the objectives sought in the INCEPTION project and, more generally, the digital documentation of cultural heritage.

Keywords: Deep learning · CNN · Semantic information · Cultural heritage

1 Introduction

The digital documentation of cultural heritage requires integration of different kinds of information: 3D models, photographs, thermographs, multispectral images, historical documents, among others. The semantic information is crucial to understanding optimally every element under consideration: its parts, its evolution, the conservation status, interventions, historical context, etc.

Specifically, the use of all kinds of images is one of the most common sources of documentation, and its interpretation is a complex and tedious task, both for the variety of items to interpret as the huge amount that is necessary to handle in these cases. It is very common to have hundreds and even thousands of photographs of each building, so the development of tools to facilitate their interpretation would be highly desirable.

In this paper the use of convolutional networks that allow extract useful information automatically from images of assets is studied. This task will be an important part of the INCEPTION European project. The main aim of INCEPTION project is to realize innovation in 3D modelling of cultural heritage through an inclusive approach for

© Springer International Publishing AG 2016
M. Ioannides et al. (Eds.): EuroMed 2016, Part II, LNCS 10059, pp. 25–32, 2016.
DOI: 10.1007/978-3-319-48974-2_4

time-dynamic 3D reconstruction of artefacts, built and social environments. These 3D models generated through INCEPTION methods and tools will be accessible for all types of user [1]. Semantic enrichment will result in 'intelligent' models for multiple purposes depending on the needs and level of knowledge of the end-users. For instance, the 3D semantic models contain geometric information for 3D visualization, historical information for narration, and geo-technical as well as structural information for material conservation, maintenance and refurbishment.

The end-users will be able to access information utilizing a standard browser, and they will be able to query the database using keywords and an easy search method, similar to Google. The search result will display a list of H-BIM models, description, historic information, the corresponding images and geographic location.

INCEPTION semantic modelling approach will resolve the existing barriers between data collection and documentation, as well as between model creation and analysis/interpretation.

Implementation will also implement a Historical model search engine. This web application will allow to search with specific keywords contained in the semantic information. As part of 3D integrated survey applied to Cultural Heritage, the digital representation is gradually emerging as effective support of a lot of data (images, photos, texts, video, non-destructive diagnostic analysis, multi-resolution images, historical data, etc.) in addition to the shape, morphology and dimensional data.

To achieve most of these objectives, the use of techniques such as those presented here will be extremely useful.

2   Implementation of Deep Learning Applied to Cultural Heritage Images

Deep learning is a branch of machine learning based on a set of algorithms that attempt to model high-level abstractions in data by using model architectures, with complex structures or otherwise, composed of multiple non-linear transformations. Deep learning is part of a broader family of machine learning methods based on learning representations of data. One of the great progressions of deep learning is replacing handcrafted features with efficient algorithms for unsupervised or semi-supervised feature learning and hierarchical feature extraction. Deep learning is based on the supervised or unsupervised learning of multiple levels of features or representations of the data. Higher level features are derived from lower level features to form a hierarchical representation [2]. The present paper is focused on image classification for the so particular as innovative case of built heritage.

In last years, deep Convolutional Neural Networks and most recently, Residual Networks have become the most popular architecture for large-scale image recognition tasks. The field of computer vision has been pushed to a fast, scalable and end-to-end learning framework, which can provide outstanding performance results on object recognition, object detection, scene recognition, semantic segmentation, action recognition, object tracking and many other tasks [2].

Table 1. Dataset of CH images used.

With the availability of large scale datasets such as ImageNet and MIT Places, researchers have resorted to transfer learning techniques for efficient training of relatively smaller related datasets [3].

We have used the Inception-v3 model (which is, coincidentally, the same name as our project) which is trained for the ImageNet Large Visual Recognition Challenge using the data from 2012. Our training loads the pre-trained model and replaces the final layer of the network by means of a new training using the categories we have considered. In this way, the lower layers that have been pre-trained can be reused for our recognition task with no need to modify them [4].

In this initial phase of the project ten categories of elements have been identified in the considered images. It has not been used a strict criteria to select those categories. Only it seeks to establish a base to go hereinafter expanding the number of categories to study incorporating those considered most useful to the project.

The categories considered are as follows with some examples (in brackets the number of images used in training and validation of each category is included) (Table 1):

In all we have used over 10,000 images (10092), all of them have been collected from Flickr, with no known copyright restrictions. About 8000 images were used for training, 1000 for validation and the remaining 1000 for additional testing.

3 Results

What is to be achieved is a system that not only automatically classifying all images incorporated into the database, but in this way allows to search the database of images semantically.

We have been tested different learning rates and different numbers of iterations (up to 100000) and obtained promising results: accuracy, at best, 92 %. All training was performed using the Tensorflow library from Google (Core in C++ with different front ends for specifying/driving the computation: Python and C++ today) [5].

We have tested several combinations of the parameters of the neural network to be tuned. Different numbers of iterations have been tried: from 4000 to 100000 and has been observed that from 8500 iterations, the achieved accuracies were similar (between 89 % and 92 %). Other parameters have been also tried such as learning rate (different values have been considered from 0.0001 to 0.02) being its effect on the final result not too noticeable (it is considered that its influence, in the case of the used image dataset, it is less than 2 %).

The following image is displayed, as example, showing the variation in the accuracy achieved during training iterations (9000 steps in this train). Training accuracy is displayed in green and the validation accuracy is indicated in blue colour. A fast of accuracy at the start of training and then a slower convergence to the final result is observed, as expected in this kind of trainings (Fig. 1).

Once the convolutional neural network has been trained and validated, we can proceed to check its performance using previously unused images. The program used shows the five most significant results corresponding to the five categories that yield higher probability index according to the calculated parameters.

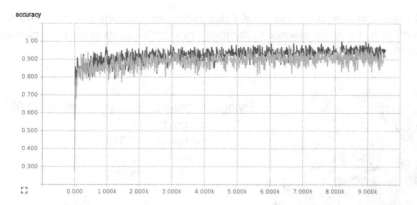

Fig. 1. Accuracy results of CNN: training (green) and validation (blue). (Color figure online)

Some examples with test images using the CNN Obtained are the following.

In the first case, where the facade of a church appears, the network correctly identifies a portal and a bell tower, with a low probability identifies flying buttresses and with a very low probability other elements that do not appear in the image as apse and vault.

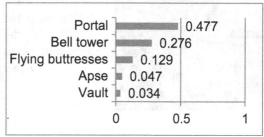

In the second example it is clearly identified a vault and the system detects (albeit with low probability) the presence of a portal. This is because the system has not been trained to detect an altar that may be similar in some ways to a portal.

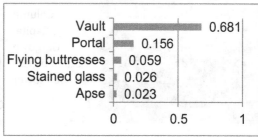

In the third case the presence of flying buttresses is clearly detected. This high probability is due to the absence in the image of other elements that can be classified (or confused) in other categories.

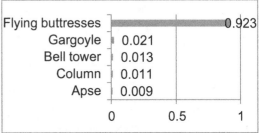

In the fourth case the system acceptably detects the vault and a stained glass. As in the second case, a small probability of portal is obtained. Training the system with new categories as an altar or inner apse could improve these results.

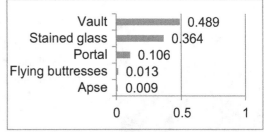

Finally, in the fifth case, it has been tested an image of a car to check its results with an image that does not correspond to any element of the trained categories. As it expected anything is detected with high probability, but the probability values should be lower if we had used a larger number of images in training (Fig. 2).

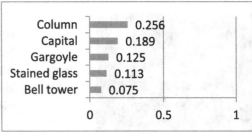

Fig. 2. Some examples of test images and corresponding results using the CNN.

4   Conclusion and Future Works

In this paper the results obtained training and tuning a pre-trained network are shown. For this purpose 10 categories of elements with cultural heritage interest have been defined and more than 10,000 images have been employed for such training. The results have been very promising and continuing this line of research is considered worth. Automatic classification of new images will speed up the digital documentation of cultural heritage and incorporating this information into databases will allow performing powerful searches based on semantic terms. The correct interpretation of images is a great added value to our project, since the problem is not having a lot of data but to extract the maximum amount of information from them.

This is a work in progress and this is just the beginning of the planned tasks to be done. In the near future are considered, among others, the following further steps:

Development of a specific CNN from scratch for these tasks to try to improve the results obtained so far, specifically, considering the use of residual networks, which are currently the state of the art in these issues.

Network training incorporating new categories of elements (arches, altar, frescos…) and also the training of other networks including new kinds of categories, e.g., artistic styles, historical periods, etc. This requires more computational power and a bigger data set [6].

Using these networks for automatic detection of interventions or pathologies of the building.

Calculations, for now, have been made using only conventional CPUs (PC running Linux/Ubuntu operating system). In the following phases of the project when the tasks will be more complex, GPUs that accelerate significantly the time required will be used. Training on a GPU Instead of a CPU will be relatively faster, as many optimization techniques are in place [7].

The presented applied deep learning techniques could be easily reached out in the Middle East countries where CH is in serious danger (especially in Syria and Iraq) due to the use of already existing images of the built heritage before its destruction for proper reconstruction and contextualization of elements.

The ultimate goal of this part of the project is to define all the categories considered most appropriate to the global objectives and connect the deep learning system developed with specific datasets of cultural heritage images (such as Europeana) to get a really useful tool for researchers and historians allowing also a better understanding of our common cultural heritage to the general public [8].

Acknowledgements. This research project has received funding from the EU's H2020 Reflective framework programme for research and innovation under grant agreement no. 665220. This work was also supported by the Ministry of Science and Innovation, fundamental research project ref. DPI2014-56500 and Junta de Castilla y León ref. VA036U14.

References

1. Sebastian, R., Bonsma, P., Bonsma, I., Ziri, A.E., Parenti, S., Lerones, P.M., Llamas, J., Maietti, F., Turillazzi, B., Iadanz, E.: Roadmap for IT research on a heritage-BIM interoperable platform within INCEPTION. In: SBE 16 MALTA, Europe and the Mediterranean Towards a Sustainable Built Environment (2016)
2. Szegedy, C., Liu, W., Jia, Y., Sermanet, P., Reed, S., Anguelov, D., Erhan, D., Vanhoucke, V., Rabinovich, A.: Going deeper with convolutions. In: Proceedings of the IEEE Conference on Computer Vision and Pattern Recognition (2015)
3. Shankar, S., Robertson, D., Ioannou, Y., Criminisi, A., Cipolla, R.: Refining architectures of deep convolutional neural networks. In: Conference on Computer Vision and Pattern Recognition (2016)
4. Szegedy, C., Vanhoucke, V., Ioffe, S., Shlens, J., Wojna, Z.: Rethinking the inception architecture for computer vision (2015). arXiv preprint arXiv:1512.00567
5. Abadi, M., Agarwal, A., Barham, P., Brevdo, E., Chen, Z., Citro, C., Corrado, G.S., Davis, A., Dean, J., Devin, M., Ghemawat, S., Goodfellow, I., Harp, A., Irving, G., Isard, M., Jozefowicz, R., Jia, Y., Kaiser, L., Kudlur, M., Levenberg, J., Mané, D., Schuster, M., Monga, R., Moore, S., Murray, D., Olah, C., Shlens, J., Steiner, B., Sutskever, I., Talwar, K., Tucker, P., Vanhoucke, V., Vasudevan, V., Viégas, F., Vinyals, O., Warden, P., Wattenberg, M., Wicke, M., Yu, Y., Zheng, X.: TensorFlow: large-scale machine learning on heterogeneous systems (2015). Software tensorflow.org
6. Sharma, P., Schoemaker, M., Pan, D.: Automated Image Timestamp Inference Using Convolutional Neural Networks. Stanford University Report (2016)
7. Simonyan, K., Zisserman, A.: Very deep convolutional networks for large-scale image recognition. arXiv technical report (2014)
8. Makantasis, K., Doulamis, A.D., Doulamis, N.D., Ioannides, M.: In the wild image retrieval and clustering for 3D cultural heritage landmarks reconstruction. Multimed. Tools Appl. **75** (7), 3593–3629 (2016)

Reaching the World Through Free Licenses and Wikimedia's Crowdsourced Platforms

John Andersson[(✉)]

Wikimedia Sverige, Stockholm, Sweden
john.andersson@wikimedia.se

Abstract. Wars and disasters, negligence and poor maintenance mean that much of our immovable cultural heritage is at risk of being lost forever. Interest and knowledge is needed to avoid its destruction. The Connected Open Heritage project will work to gather as much information as possible about cultural heritage from countries all over the world and connect it in a standardized and structured form on Wikidata, a project that is operated by the Wikimedia movement. It will connect the structured data with historical images from digitized collections from archives and museums and with freely licensed modern images and other types of media gathered by volunteers and other organizations. The Connected Open Heritage is a project by Wikimedia Sverige, UNESCO, Cultural Heritage without Borders and Wikimedia Italia, and financed by the Culture Foundation of the Swedish Postcode Lottery.

Keywords: Wikimedia · Wikipedia · Wikidata · Wikimedia commons · Connected data · Linked data · Open data · Cultural heritage data

1 Introduction

Every year the world sees the destruction of a huge amount of important immovable cultural heritage. The recent destruction of Palmyra in Syria, and natural catastrophes such as the massive earthquakes in Nepal and Chile, where a large amount of the cultural heritage was destroyed, has put the risks in the spotlight. However, destruction of cultural heritage is also happening in a number of other less extreme ways all over the world.

As Lars Amréus, Director-General of the National Heritage Board of Sweden stated: "The greatest threat towards the cultural heritage is lack of knowledge and disinterest. The best way to protect the cultural heritage is therefore knowledge and information that is easy to find and free" [1].

Partly because of this realization, that unintended destruction of cultural heritage can be prevented with better and more accessible information, there has been a shift in the availability of open data about cultural heritage globally. This has been coupled with the need to increase interest in cultural heritage in order to get political support to protect the sites. There have been numerous attempts to reach the general public. Some of which have been very costly. Some that have failed. Some only partly successful. One low cost

© Springer International Publishing AG 2016
M. Ioannides et al. (Eds.): EuroMed 2016, Part II, LNCS 10059, pp. 33–37, 2016.
DOI: 10.1007/978-3-319-48974-2_5

strategy that has however proven itself over and over for cultural heritage institutions all over the world is working with the Wikimedia movement.

The goal of the Wikimedia movement, which consists of thousands of volunteers and a number of non-profits under the umbrella of the Wikimedia Foundation, is to educate the public. This is a goal the movement shares with museums and archives and arguably the interests are very well aligned. This realization has led to a number of collaborations globally and the Wikimedia movement now has well developed methodologies in place, as well as a number of identified future possibilities that can be developed together with other institutions.

Now, through support from the Culture Foundation of the Swedish Postcode Lottery, Wikimedia Sverige, a Swedish non-profit association, has launched a major new project called *Connected Open Heritage*. In this project Wikimedia Sverige is working together with the wider Wikimedia movement, UNESCO and Cultural Heritage without Borders (CHWB) to bring online freely licensed information about cultural heritage at risk. The information will be in a structured and unified format, and connects the open data to different resources from museums, archives and from the general public [2].

This article will attempt to give an overview of what the Connected Open Heritage project aims to achieve regarding different types of digital material in order to inform the public and to gather and connect information that will benefit researchers, decision makers and content reusers.

2   The Connected Data

To be able to understand larger trends, see new patterns and get a better understanding of the world's immovable cultural heritage, there is a need to gather and connect information. The possibilities with databases have been acknowledged by researchers and experts for years, [3] and significant efforts and resources have been used to compile datasets for the immovable cultural heritage in different countries. The states have however not worked together to compile the information in a unified way. Hence, the datasets have not been connected and the possibilities to process information and find patterns have ended at the national border. The Connected Open Heritage project is working to change this. This is a continuation of a massive international effort that has taken place during the last 6 years.

In 2010 the Wikimedia movement for the first time organized the photo contest Wiki Loves Monuments (WLM) in the Netherlands. [4] The group organizing the contest decided that in order to make it easy for participants to know what to photograph, they would create well-structured lists of all the objects that were part of the contest. They approached the problem by processing data about the Dutch National Heritage Sites (Rijkmonuments). The Rijkmonuments include architecture and objects of general interest that have been recognized for their aesthetic, scientific, and/or cultural importance. This data was added into a database, called the *Monuments database*, [5] which was created specifically for the contest. The database is still run by a few volunteers in their spare time.

The contest was quickly scaled up and in 2011 there were 18 countries that participated, with 170,000 images of immovable cultural heritage uploaded. In each of the 18 countries data had been gathered from different authorities, or in a few cases from other sources, and was subsequently added into the Monuments database. Already in 2011 WLM became the largest photo contest in the world according to the Guinness Book of Records. [6] Next year the amount of photos more than doubled, to more than 350,000 photos from 33 countries. [7] Since then more than 300,000 images have been uploaded every year by people taking part in the contest and structured data from 56 countries has been gathered and added to the database [8].

The images that are taken by the public are linked to the different objects in the database, each having its own unique identification number. Because of this it is easy for national organizations working with cultural heritage to reuse the images. Which has been done by e.g. the National Heritage Board of Sweden. [9] To ensure usability the images uploaded during the WLM contest are uploaded through a special upload wizard that automatically adds available data from the official dataset about the cultural heritage to the metadata page for the image. This is dependent on the official datasets but can include up to 16 pieces of data. The uploader, other volunteers or interested parties (including researchers) can then add more information to the wiki if needed.

This massive amount of data is unique and the lists created on Wikipedia from the database are used widely, including by staff at IGOs such as UNESCO and ICOMOS.

One of the goals of the Connected Open Heritage project is to transfer the data (now in free text fields) into *Wikidata* in a structured format, and then link it to other resources. Wikidata is a project run by the Wikimedia Foundation and Wikimedia Deutschland that connects structured data in a way that is readable both for computers and people. When the Monuments-database was created Wikidata did not yet exist. Since its foundation in October 2012 Wikidata has however grown fast and now it has data about more than twenty-five million items, [10] all under the Creative Commons Zero (CC0) license [11].

By transferring the data, and at the same time creating the methodologies in order to scale it, the project is ensuring that the material will continue to be available and accessible. By having the data on Wikidata it will also be easier to include the data into the online encyclopedia Wikipedia in an automated way. In addition, storing the data on Wikidata will make it easier to continue to add more relevant data about immovable cultural heritage from other institutions, and link it all together. The linking between datasets can be done through a mixture of volunteers adding connections manually and by semiautomatic programs specifically designed to connect two distinct sets of data that have unique identifiers. These linked datasets allow new discoveries to be made as advanced queries can be performed.

Furthermore, the Connected Open Heritage project aims to add data from another 10 countries where the cultural heritage is at risk. The project team created a set of criterion for how to prioritize what countries to work with and by combining the number of sites listed on the *2016 and 2014 World Monuments Fund World Monuments Watch list* and the *UNESCO World Heritage sites in danger list*, the countries with most monuments in danger were identified. [12] Afterwards that relevant information about the different countries were collected in standardized country reports to see how the countries fulfilled the criterion. [13] This includes a number of countries in the Middle East but also Small Island Developing States (SIDS). However, initial contacts indicate that in many SIDS official lists seem to be completely missing. Data from some countries in the Middle East have already been added to the database and the project team is working with local Wikimedia movement affiliates, through UNESCOs and Cultural Heritage without Borders networks and with direct requests to decision makers about the possible inclusion of datasets from their countries. Also other groups that might hold well defined datasets pertaining to the rich cultural heritage in the Middle East will be approached when identified. Meetings with decision makers will take place in late 2016 and during the first half of 2017.

With the data about immovable cultural heritage in a structured format, it is possible to quickly identify what type of heritage that is missing information and work to fill in these gaps. One area that is targeted as part of the Connected Open Heritage project are images and other types of media that exist in collections held by museums and archives all over the world.

3   The Connected Images

Careful documentation of cultural heritage also makes it possible to recover damaged cultural heritage, and to continue to learn from it, even if it would be destroyed later on. The value and importance of documenting cultural heritage is well recognized internationally, and with a rapid technical development of different tools for depicting, measuring, sensing and other forms of data gathering, digital preservation of objects that are in danger is becoming easier and more efficient. [14] As explained before, Wikidata will allow different actors to easily identify what data that is missing and work to add it.

On top of *modern* media files and other information, also *historical* data that has been collected over the decades can add important knowledge when digitized and connected to other data and media. This type of material can enhance the understanding of cultural heritage and complements newly created media and information to form a deeper and more comprehensive picture. Connected Open Heritage is specifically targeting different museums and archives to help them with uploading their collections and connecting them to the datasets. The aim of the project is to add 100,000 images that can be added to the information on Wikidata and Wikipedia articles. [15] Before any image is uploaded the copyright situation has to be investigated by the museum/ archive and only material that they formally confirm is either in the public domain (because of age) or that they have the copyright for the images and have released them under a suitable free license will be uploaded to Wikimedia Commons and included in the project.

The Wikimedia movement has cooperated with a large amount of different archives and museums. This is to ensure and improve the quality of the thousands of articles on Wikipedia that are covering cultural heritage and to give a context to the cultural heritage that is around you. Through Connected Open Heritage the Wikimedia movement will be able to do more, and to be active in new parts of the world together with a myriad of local and international partners.

References

1. Amréus, L.: Aftonbladet. Riksantikvarien: Vi kan inte hålla kulturarvet hemligt (2013). www.aftonbladet.se/debatt/article16548578.ab

2. Meta.wikimedia.org, Connected Open Heritage. https://meta.wikimedia.org/w/index.php?title=Connected_Open_Heritage&oldid=15661601

3. Meyer, E., Grussenmeyer, P., Perrin, J.P., Durand, A., Drap, P.: A web information system for the management and the dissemination of cultural heritage data. J. Cult. Herit. **8**, 396–411 (2007). doi:10.1016/j.culher.2007.07.003

4. Malbos, V.: Libération. Le monumental concours de Wikimédia (2011). www.liberation.fr/ecrans/2011/09/09/le-monumental-concours-de-wikimedia_958415?page=article

5. Commons.wikimedia.org, Commons: monuments database. https://commons.wikimedia.org/w/index.php?title=Commons:Monuments_database&oldid=159553268

6. Wikilovesmonuments.org, Wiki Loves Monuments 2011 officially broke world record. www.wikilovesmonuments.org/wiki-loves-monuments-2011-officially-broke-world-record/

7. Wikilovesmonuments.org, Wiki Loves Monuments is over – but not entirely. www.wikilovesmonuments.org/wiki-loves-monuments-2012-is-over-but-not-entirely/

8. Commons.wikimedia.org, Commons: monuments database/statistics. https://commons.wikimedia.org/w/index.php?title=Commons:Monuments_database/Statistics&oldid=200327855

9. K-blogg.se, Nu har vi kopplat ihop Kringla och Wikipedia www.k-blogg.se/2012/11/08/nu-har-vi-kopplat-ihop-kringla-och-wikipedia/

10. Wikidata.org, Wikidata: News (2012–2016). https://www.wikidata.org/w/index.php?title=Wikidata:News&oldid=351922770

11. Wikidata.org, Wikidata: Introduction (2012–2016). https://www.wikidata.org/w/index.php?title=Wikidata:Introduction&oldid=236887346

12. Meta.wikimedia.org, Connected Open Heritage/Country selection criteria (2016). https://meta.wikimedia.org/w/index.php?title=Connected_Open_Heritage/Country_selection_criteria&oldid=15670541

13. Meta.wikimedia.org, Connected Open Heritage/Countries (2016). https://meta.wikimedia.org/w/index.php?title=Connected_Open_Heritage/Countries&oldid=15703501

14. Remondino, F., Rizzi, A.: Reality-based 3D documentation of natural and cultural heritage sites techniques, problems, and examples. Appl. Geomat. **2**, 85 (2010)

15. Meta.wikimedia.org, Connected open heritage/information for GLAM partners. https://meta.wikimedia.org/w/index.php?title=Connected_Open_Heritage/Information_for_GLAM_Partners&oldid=15644313

3D Reconstruction and 3D Modelling

Definition of a Workflow for Web Browsing of 3D Models in Archaeology

A. Scianna[✉], M. La Guardia, and M.L. Scaduto

ICAR-CNR (High Performance Computing and Networking Institute - National Research Council of Italy), GISLab, University of Palermo, Viale Delle Scienze, Edificio 8, 90128 Palermo, Italy
andrea.scianna@cnr.it, marcellolaguardia87@libero.it, ml.scaduto@gmail.com

Abstract. The Cultural Heritage (CH) is a fundamental element of promotion of territories and of tourism development. Publishing 3D models of archaeological sites and their three-dimensional reconstruction on the Web is one of the best ways to spread their knowledge. However, many recent scientific researches in this field have highlighted the limitations and difficulties related to the networking of interactive 3D models. The main difficulties are related to the complexity and the size of models, which influence the access speed, and the cost of software and hardware needed for the publication on the WEB. In light of this background, this article describes the further advances of research activities carried out at GISLAB CNR-UNIPA for creating interactive 3D models of archaeological sites, accessible and navigable with a Web browser, fully compliant with HTML5. This system includes also the surrounding landscape, essential to analyze and understand the close relationship between human settlements and the surrounding geographical contexts. Such models don't need specific app for navigation but are accessible on the WEB via the WebGL open source libraries, compliant with the most popular Web browsers (Firefox, Safari and Chrome). The system consists of a headboard multimedia platform tested on Mokarta archaeological site (Trapani, Sicily). The user can explore the 3D model of the archaeological site in its current state, its virtual reconstruction, and the historical documentation. This application has highlighted the great potential and the limits of the sharing of complex 3D models via the Web, opening new scenarios for the purpose of valorization of the archaeological heritage through the use of effective technologies and reduction of costs, opening new themes of further research.
This experimentation is also a real example of an open data application.

Keywords: 3D · Cultural heritage · Archaeological site · WebGL · HTML5 · Web-based visualization · Geospatial DB · Virtual reality

1 Introduction

The technologies used for the creation and publishing of digital models have evolved very fast in the last years. Initially developed for industrial applications, they are ideal to promote the CH giving significant added value, ensuring an impact similar to that represented by the advent of photography at the end of 19th Century.

© Springer International Publishing AG 2016
M. Ioannides et al. (Eds.): EuroMed 2016, Part II, LNCS 10059, pp. 41–52, 2016.
DOI: 10.1007/978-3-319-48974-2_6

Furthermore most of CH applications are available using various media or platforms: PCs, smartphones, museum kiosks, etc. [18].

In addition, in the panorama of most recent research, new strategies, procedures and technologies have emerged in order to create a Web-based application for user access and interactive exploration of three-dimensional models, through the integration of geometrical and non-geometrical information into an interface [7]. The main goal is to provide users with a new exploration experience based on a free interactive navigation interface of environment and CH, and on the opportunity to integrate different types of data. According to these policies, the Web represents the ideal mean for accessing information, managing documentation and disseminating CH values [4]. These researches are supported by recent advances in visual computing that have opened new opportunities about documenting CH through geospatial data integrations, graphical representations, multimedia contents and semantic metadata [5, 8, 10, 11, 14, 19].

Above the skills of creating models with good levels of detail, the central question regards the access and possibilities of use of these three-dimensional models for the community [4], made up of both sectoral experts and researchers, as well as other common stakeholders, such as students and tourists.

Unfortunately, the visualization of 3D models presents some issues related to the complexity of models, and also to the interaction with them. Indeed most of the users are not used to navigate 3D complex environments [3].

In order to solve these issues, the use of an intuitive interface for CH interactive 3D models with free and open source software into experimentations of Web-based application is becoming less rare [6].

Several projects of virtual CH reconstruction and diffusion on the WEB have been proposed between 2000 and 2010. Many of these systems have, however, never been released to wider public, and have only been used for academic studies [2]. But technology in these last six years has evolved very rapidly so that today there exist the possibilities to create new and more powerful systems able to diffuse more effectively the knowledge of ancient architecture and environment through the WEB.

Many experiments have been carried out at GISLAB in order to share 3D geospatial models on web though geospatial web services, pdf 3D, VRML.

This paper illustrates further developments of the work carried out for sharing information on archeological contexts with the aim to define a sufficiently standardized procedure. The experimentation has allowed testing of different kind of interfaces and navigation ways or exploration interfaces more effective and intuitive for users.

On these bases this paper illustrates the development of a WebGL based application, in order to overcome the proprietary plugins issues not always compliant with all available Web browsers, allowing to access directly to full 3D vector models and to navigate inside them, without the need to install apps or other kinds of extensions on the clients. It is also possible to obtain simple information on some objects present in the model with the ultimate aim of creating geospatial 3D information systems for CH.

The developed platform has been applied to the archaeological site of Mokarta (Trapani, Sicily) and to their neighboring landscapes.

During the progression of this work capabilities and limitations of the proposed method for Web sharing of 3D vector heritage models have been considered, such as:

- synchronic and diachronic representation possibilities
- multi-resolution data integration
- relations between Levels of Detail (LoD) of the model vs speed of access to geospatial 3D information and multi-resolution data integration.

2 The Main Ways to Share CH Models on Web

In the past, our research group has studied a method for sharing of 3D urban models based on 3D geospatial Web-services (3D WFS). This method could be applied also for full sharing on the Web 3D geometrical and semantic data of CH [12].

Unfortunately, there isn't a global standardized way to share models on Web suitable for every cultural good like BIM technologies [17].

For this reason, we oriented our research activities toward the definition of simplest ways of publishing and visualizing 3D models on Web.

In the course of time different combinations between Client-side and Webserver-side have been experimented, where Client usually needed specific plugins.

In order to simplify the access to 3D models by the users, recently we experimented a different option using Web Graphics Library (WebGL) technologies, based on Java-Script API.

According to it the Client requires only a Web browser installed on it without the need of any plugin, while the Server requires installing a Webserver, an RDBMS server, PHP extension, WebGL libraries and models (Fig. 1).

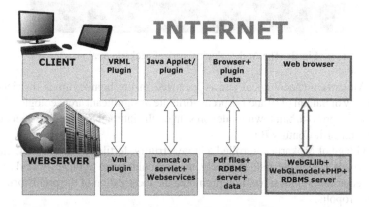

Fig. 1. Different options for sharing and browsing 3D geospatial models on Web (the adopted solution is underlined in red). (Color figure online)

In particular GISLAB working group has recently tested this option for virtual navigation in 3D models of ancient theaters with good results [13]. This paper presents the last development stage.

Moreover, in order to share CH models on the Web, a specific research is required about the system usability (regarding the ways of access, the navigation speed and the characteristics of the interface, the quality and quantity of contents should be diversified according to types of users, the type of CH, its structure).

3   The Archaeological Site of Mokarta

In order to test the experimental framework here described, a 3D CH information system has been developed and applied to the archaeological site of Mokarta (Trapani, Sicily) (Fig. 2).

Fig. 2. The Archaeological park of Mokarta (real view).

The Mokarta archaeological site is localized in the homonymous district of the municipality of Salemi (TP) and is a prehistoric site of significant archaeological interest, because of its proto-urban town model present on the internal Sicily reliefs between the late 13th and 11th Century B.C.

The village of Mokarta controlled a large territory, fertile and almost flat, and even the main roads around the area. Precisely, the particular value of the hilly landscape and advantageous geographical position promoted the localization of the prehistoric village and its necropolis.

The first investigations, carried out in the seventies of the last Century, have brought to light a necropolis on the hill "Cresta di Gallo", made up of about a hundred rock-cut tombs. They have a form of a "cave", with circular and sometimes small dromos (passageway) that hosted more burials with grave goods consisting of cups and bowls with high foot; unfortunately, over the years, lack of control and illegal excavations have caused the loss of most of finds.

A further and smaller necropolis was also discovered in the southwestern part of the hill, on top of which the ruins of the Arab-Norman castle age are still visible, yet not studied and known.

The excavations, conducted by the Superintendence for Archaeological Heritage of Trapani province, initially, began in 1994 and during further occasions have allowed unearthing housing facilities. In them there exist elements of tradition (the round hut) and innovative elements (the rectangular building).

Mokarta ceased to live around in the 11th Century B.C. (or in the 10th), following a destruction probably made by the Elimi [20, 21].

4   The Procedure Scheme

The methodological workflow for construction of an interactive navigation environment of a 3D model on the Web includes many steps regarding archaeologists, geomatics and computer science experts, as shown in Fig. 3.

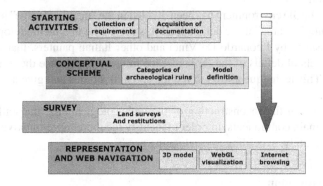

Fig. 3. The methodological workflow.

The first phase corresponds to the collection of requirements. It is a phase of primary importance that is placed behind the design of the system. The subsequent actions and the development strategy depend strongly from this stage. The requirements of the system in terms of content, interface, and method of exploration should emerge from it.

The second phase regards the acquisition of bibliographical and archival documentation required for diachronic and synchronic description of the archaeological site of Mokarta. Great contribution in this phase is provided by archaeologists from which the 3D model of the reconstruction hypothesis derives.

The others phases can be synthesized in these steps, and are detailed in the following subparagraphs:

- definition of a conceptual scheme
- land surveys and restitutions
- development of the 3D model
- construction of WebGL visualization system
- user interface construction
- browsing on internet.

4.1 Definition of the Elements Inside the Model

During the design of the conceptual model, the archaeological site of Mokarta was structured into different elements, in order to cope with the complexity of the geometric model and to define other semantic and geometric hierarchies. Parts to be modelled in 3D are different from other study cases typical of Greek and Roman architecture in which there are building with a well-defined structure compliant to an architectural style or period.

This model is not limited to reproduce the archeological site itself, but it's also extended to the surrounding landscape, in order to highlight the strong relationships between these elements. The description of surrounding environment is useful to understand the reason that led inhabitants to settle just in that site (i.e. prominent position in the territory, defense strategies, presence of water springs or waterways, presence of communication routes).

Therefore the 3D environment has been divided in the "near landscape" less detailed, and "archaeological area" more detailed; all this according to a methodology followed in the Renaissance by Leonardo Da Vinci and other Italian painters, that was used to reduce the levels of details of the far landscape in order to enhance the sense of depth in the scene. This technique allows to reduce uploading times and give a very realistic visualization.

Furthermore, in the reconstruction of the archaeological site, the settlement was divided in its main components, in order to identify the more representative units, to be described separately, according to cataloguing needs.

4.2 Data Acquisition

In the study case of the archaeological site of Mokarta, the model of the territorial context was realized through photogrammetry restitution and filming made with a UAV flight (flying wing) at different heights (110 m and 65 m, with 16 Mpixel calibrated camera).

The flight at 110 m, was exhaustive for the development of the "near landscape", but not sufficient for the definition of a more detailed model of the ruins.

In order to represent, with a high level of detail, the ruins of the archaeological area of Mokarta, a further lower flight was performed (h = 65 m).

The orthorectification and the development of the 3D model have been performed with free and open source software like Apero/MIC MAC, Visual SFM, Meshlab and Blender, adopting also, as geographic reference, some Ground Control Points collected from a GPS survey.

4.3 The Development of the 3D Model

Principal objects to build are (I) the "near landscape", or the landscape around the ruins; (II) the "archaeological area" that consists in the perimeter of the archaeological site of Mokarta; (III) the rebuilt huts.

To clean the point cloud and to separate objects according to the conceptual model previously defined, the rebuilt models from survey have been heavily processed.

For the simplification, we have used algorithms present in Meshlab and Blender software in order to delete clusters and outliers. During this process, any reference point has been lost for construction of meshes compliant to LoDs required for the artefacts to model.

Instead, the "far landscape" consists in a big sphere that incorporates the 3D loaded model, and the lights of the environment. On its inner surface is projected a 360° panoramic photo, in order to represent easily and efficiently the far landscape (Fig. 4).

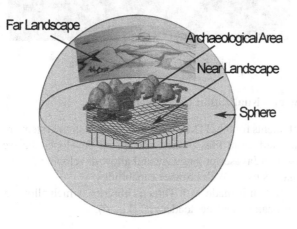

Fig. 4. Structure of 3D environment.

For the modeling of the near landscape, we proceeded with a photogrammetric reconstruction based on aerial photos taken by a fixed wing UAV flight, in order to obtain a point cloud of the entire affected area.

The main phase in the modeling is the building of the meshes, which consists in a three-dimensional model, rebuilt from point clouds.

Three-dimensional elements, like rebuilt parts, are imported inside the WebGL environment using .obj formats. Every model is built using three files: one.obj, one.mtl file and one.jpg.

The .obj file represents the core of the mesh, which lists all the geometrical elements including their coordinates in 3D space. This is the heaviest file, and it is essentially, what determines the loading time of .html pages. In addition, texture coordinates are associated to the geometry of the vertices, both present in the same file.

The .mtl file contains all information of surfaces, in order to manage every parameter like the lighting, reflection, opacity and color. This file also declares the texture associated with the model.

The .jpg file, finally, contains the texture associated with the model. It must be defined with a resolution in pixels corresponding to power of two (256 × 256, 512 × 512, 1024 × 1024, 2048 × 2048, etc.) in order to be correctly visualized in the WebGL environment. This change does not compromise the correct displaying of images, because the pixel positions are related to the coordinates of the model in .obj files (Fig. 5).

Fig. 5. Blender model of Mokarta.

4.4 The Browser Visualization Using WebGL

The necessary elements for the HTML5/WebGL visualization system are Apache server, Three.js libraries and .html files (which contain all developed Javascripts). Three.js libraries are based on Javascript language and allow developing 3D environments and interactive 3D games using Web browser capabilities.

The WebGL system is made with Three.js libraries, which allow setup of 3D visualization, controls, camera, scene, loader etc. (Fig. 6).

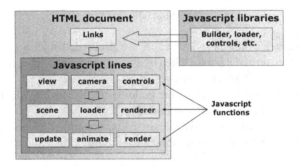

Fig. 6. Structure of the navigation .html page.

In particular, in this model Three.min.js library has been used as builder file, and other .js files like OrbitControls.js for calibrating the navigation and OBJMTLLoader.js for loading 3D model. The platform folder, that also contains Three.js libraries and Jquery.js libraries, is located inside Apache HTML folder. These are called inside.html pages, using JavaScript statements in order to load and visualize correctly the model.

Nevertheless, some of the visualization parameters cannot be managed inside the .html file, but can be changed only inside the Three.js libraries.

The far landscape and the real 3D model are inserted directly in the same .html page, using the JavaScript lines and the Three.js libraries.

The 3D model of the Archaeological Area is imported from Blender software application, and consists in the central element of the WebGL environment.

4.5 Describing the Interface

In order to enhance the interest of users, the main page of the site that allows access to 3D models permitting to choose different navigation options allowing also to obtain different kind of information.

Particularly, in this page the users can visualize the ortophoto of the entire area in high res, learn about the history of the artifact and its architectural features, go to the interactive navigation model or enjoy a virtual visit in the past with the reconstruction of the system of huts.

The interactive navigation interface was developed in order to allow different kinds of navigation, with different and simple commands and movements (using mouse buttons or arrow keys of the keyboard like some 3D pc games), in order to be very user friendly (Fig. 7).

Fig. 7. Interactive flight navigation inside the model of Mokarta in the past.

Users can also click on the lateral map in order to move to some way points in the archaeological site.

5 Results

The online platform of Mokarta is one of the first examples of a free navigation in an archaeological area comprising not only the model of interest but also the surrounding area. Our experience proves the possibility of creating complex 3D CH navigation systems using simplified methods compliant with HTML5-WebGL technologies and tools. Our experimentation, proposed in this paper, has produced:

- a 3D geospatial environment navigable on Web, accessible without any additional plugin or applet, and totally based on open source software
- an user-friendly interface that allows navigating and browsing interactively models inside of archeological site

– a new methodological approach in order to find the right balance between the LoD of 3D elements and textures and the speed features necessary for enjoying the geospatial 3D information, only based on geomatics processing.

This latter aspect depends surely on the typology of CH represented in the model, on the LoDs and also on the extension of the environment around CH.

These experimented technologies still have some limits caused by slow times of access to high-detailed models for mobile devices, such as smartphones and tablets. In order to solve this temporary problem (nowadays mobile devices are upgrading very quickly) the platform for mobile devices has been simplified and compressed, reducing texture resolution and number of polygons, but still maintaining a good visualization quality and an acceptable speed of access according to visualization features of smartphones and tablets.

Finally, the research work presented in this paper is an experimental example of how new open source technologies can be applied in order to promote CH and to network 3D models on Web.

6   Conclusions and Open Scenarios

Meanwhile the 3D representation of individual CH models has been proposed by many scholars [5, 11], the modeling of archaeological sites, considering the surrounding landscape, hasn't been really focused in these years. All this is important to know reasons of settlements in a specific area and the relations between settlements and their neighbours.

Many projects regarding virtual heritage, started far in the time, in the last years have produced some archives of CH remains; usually, little artifacts are published as WebGL models [1, 15] or, in some cases, entire ancient buildings and rarely wide archaeological and landscape contexts have been published [16]. Often visualization is optimized using proprietary, closed techniques, often model are published without textures in order to improve access speed.

Our workflow allows to publish CHs and surrounding environments at reasonable access speed with a visualization quality that could be acceptable for CH valorization.

Therefore the aim of this work is of developing a CH 3D archaeological model, navigable on the Web, created with open source technologies and based only on ultimate HTML5 capabilities.

The platform thus created allows users to identify individual elements of the model, in order to link the semantic information to it. This one could be considered a first step for the creation of a full 3D Geospatial Information System of CH.

Solutions for improving access speed to 3D models could be: (I) the development of a multiscale level of details (LoDs), depending on the distance of the objects in respect to the point of view; (II) the implementation of streaming technologies or Web services in order to carry segmented information of the 3D model to the browser as a function of display visualization; (III) the definition of specific methods that allows further compression of data maintaining requested LoDs.

Acknowledgements. This research work has been supported and founded by Municipality of Calatafimi (IT) within the HOLOGRAMME Project PS 2.2.003 P.O. Italy-Tunisia 2007 2013 - Program ENPI of Trans-frontier Cooperation Italy-Tunisia 2007-2013.

References

1. 3D Icons project. http://3dicons-project.eu/eng
2. Anderson, E.F., McLoughlin, L., Liarokapis, F., et al.: Developing serious games for cultural heritage: a state-of-the-art review. Virt. Reality **14**, 255 (2010). doi:10.1007/s10055-010-0177-3
3. Callieri, M., Dellepiane, M., Scopigno, R.: Remote visualization and navigation of 3D models of archaeological sites. In: The International Archives of the Photogrammetry, Remote Sensing and Spatial Information Sciences, vol. XL-5/W4, 2015 3D Virtual Reconstruction and Visualization of Complex Architectures, 25-27 February 2015, Avila, Spain (2015)
4. Benedetto, M., Ponchio, F., Malomo, L., Callieri, M., Dellepiane, M., Cignoni, P., Scopigno, R.: Web and mobile visualization for cultural heritage. In: Ioannides, M., Quak, E. (eds.) 3D Research Challenges in Cultural Heritage: A Roadmap in Digital Heritage Preservation. LNCS, vol. 8355, pp. 18–35. Springer, Heidelberg (2014). doi:10.1007/978-3-662-44630-0_2
5. Gomes, L., Pereira Bellon, O.R., Silva, L.: 3D reconstruction methods for digital preservation of cultural heritage: a survey. Pattern Recognit. Lett. **50**, 3–14 (2014)
6. Guarnieri, A., Pirotti, F., Vettore, A.: Cultural heritage interactive 3D models on the web: an approach using open source and free software. J. Cult. Herit. **11**, 350–353 (2010)
7. Manferdini, A.M., Remondino, F.: Reality-based 3D modeling, segmentation and web-based visualization. In: Ioannides, M., Fellner, D., Georgopoulos, A., Hadjimitsis, Diofantos, G. (eds.) EuroMed 2010. LNCS, vol. 6436, pp. 110–124. Springer, Heidelberg (2010). doi:10.1007/978-3-642-16873-4_9
8. Meyer, E., Grussenmeyer, P., Perrin, J.P., Durand, A., Drap, P.: A web information system for the management and the dissemination of cultural heritage data. J. Cult. Herit. **3**, 325–331 (2002)
9. Nicoletti, F., Tusa, S.: L'insediamento del tardo Bronzo di Mokarta (strutture e scavi 1994–97). In: Atti della XLI Riunione scientifica: dai ciclopi agli ecisti: società e territorio nella Sicilia preistorica e protostorica, San Cipirello (PA), 16-19 novembre 2006, pp. 905–916 (2006)
10. Noh, Z., Sunar, M.S., Pan, Z.: A review on augmented reality for virtual heritage system. In: Chang, M., Kuo, R., Kinshuk, Chen, G.-D., Hirose, M. (eds.) Edutainment 2009. LNCS, vol. 5670, pp. 50–61. Springer, Heidelberg (2009). doi:10.1007/978-3-642-03364-3_7
11. Remondino, F., Rizzi, A.: Reality-based 3D documentation of natural and cultural heritage sites-techniques, problems, and examples. Appl. Geomat. **2**, 85–100 (2010)
12. Scianna, A.: Experimental studies for the definition of 3D geospatial web services. Appl. Geomat. **5**(1), 59–71 (2013)
13. Scianna, A., La Guardia, M., Scaduto, M.L.: Sharing on Web 3D models of ancient theaters: a methodological workflow. In: The International Archives of the Photogrammetry, Remote Sensing and Spatial Information Sciences, vol. XLI-B2, 2016 XXIII ISPRS Congress, 12–19 July 2016, Prague, Czech Republic (2016)
14. Scianna, A., Sciortino, R.: Utilizzo di strumenti free e open source per la fruizione di modelli 3D di siti archeologici basati sul formato PDF. Archeologia e calcolatori **4**, 202–208 (2013)
15. Sketchfab online publishing site. https://sketchfab.com/models/categories/cultural-heritage

16. Zamaniproject. http://www.zamaniproject.org/index.php/algeria-3d-model-of-baptistry.html, http://www.zamaniproject.org/index.php/jordan-3d-model-of-the-treasury.html
17. Scianna, A., Gristina, S., Paliaga, S.: Experimental BIM applications in archaeology: a workflow. In: Ioannides, M., Magnenat-Thalmann, N., Fink, E., Žarnić, R., Yen, A.-Y., Quak, E. (eds.) EuroMed 2014. LNCS, vol. 8740, pp. 490–498. Springer, Heidelberg (2014). doi: 10.1007/978-3-319-13695-0_48
18. Scopigno, R., Callieri, M., Cignoni, P., Corsini, M., Dellepiane, M., Ponchio, F., Ranzuglia, G.: 3D models for cultural heritage: beyond plain visualization. IEEE Comput. **44**(7), 48–55 (2011)
19. Siotto, E., Callieri, M., Pingi, P., Scopigno, R., Benassi, L., Parri, A., La Monica, D., Ferrara, A.: From the archival documentation to standardised web database and 3D models: the case study of the Camaldolese Abbey in Volterra (Italy). In: International Conference on Cultural Heritage and New Technologies, Vienna (2013)
20. Tusa, S., Nicoletti, F.: L'epilogo sicano nella Sicilia Occidentale: il caso Mokarta - Capanna I. In: Atti delle Terze giornate internazionali di studi sull'area Elima, Gibellina - Erice - Contessa Entellina, 23–26 ottobre 1997, pp. 963–984 (2000)
21. Tusa, S.: Da Mokarta a Monte Polizzo: la transizione dall'età del Bronzo Finale all'età del Ferro. In: atti del V Convegno di Studi del "Progetto Mesogheia", Caltanissetta il 10–11 maggio 2008, pp. 27–52 (2009)

The VALMOD Project: Historical and Realistic 3D Models for the Touristic Development of the Château de Chambord

Xavier Brunetaud, Romain Janvier, Sarah Janvier-Badosa, Kévin Beck, and Muzahim Al-Mukhtar[✉]

PRISME Laboratory UPRES EA 4229, University of Orleans,
8 rue Leonard de Vinci, 45072 Orleans, France
{xavier.brunetaud,romain.janvier,sarah.janvier,kevin.beck,
muzahim.al-mukhtar}@univ-orleans.fr

Abstract. The VALMOD project is a French regional scientific program whose objective is to propose innovative scenarios for the tourist development of built heritage from the combined contribution of *in situ* 3D acquisitions, informatics, and history. This interdisciplinary approach aims to stage original historical content thanks to appropriate 3D models and the use of adequate media for the targeted public. This communication presents several examples selected among the applications developed during this program: the creation of a global model able to precisely describe the whole architecture of the Château de Chambord; a 3D print of the double staircase that can be unscrewed to separate the two stairways; replicas of pieces of the lapidary deposit to make them virtually easy to handle. The challenges concern both technical aspects such as the precise registration of thousands of multi-scale scans or the creation of manifold meshes from point clouds, and project management aspects such as making the interdisciplinary approach effective.

Keywords: 3D acquisition · Tourist development · Built heritage · Interdisciplinary approach

1 Introduction and Scientific Context

The VALMOD project is a scientific program founded by the region "Centre Val de Loire" of France for the period 2014-2017. It is led by the Civil Engineering research team of the PRISME laboratory at the University of Orléans. The partners are the CESR laboratory (history of the Renaissance), the LI laboratory (informatics), and the "Domaine national de Chambord". VALMOD is part of a group of 7 programs concerning the Château de Chambord, named "Chantier Chambord Château", which is itself part of a larger group of about 100 programs concerning regional heritage named "Intelligence des Patrimoines". Several completed or still ongoing programs constitute the scientific and collaborative basis of VALMOD: SACRE (PRISME 2008-2012); REPTURE (PRISME 2010-2013); MONUMENTUM (MAP/GAMSAU 2013-2017); RIHVAGE (CESR 2013-2014). The SACRE program (Degradation monitoring and restoration of limestone monuments) laid the methodological groundwork for the study of the origin of degradations, thanks to the

© Springer International Publishing AG 2016
M. Ioannides et al. (Eds.): EuroMed 2016, Part II, LNCS 10059, pp. 53–60, 2016.
DOI: 10.1007/978-3-319-48974-2_7

creation of a digital health record of the monument [1–9]. During this first program, laboratory and in-situ experiments, analysis of archives, and 3D acquisitions for the conservation of the Château of Chambord started. The REPTURE program (Restoration of damaged statues: transversal methodology of structural analysis) was devoted to developing a method to assess restoration options for broken statues, thanks to its mechanical simulation based on the 3D model resulting from laser scanning. The MONUMENTUM program (Numerical modeling and database management for the conservation of masonry structures) stems from the SACRE program, and focuses on breaking scientific barriers concerning the 3D acquisition pipeline and database management, to enable all actors in the conservation field to query the digital health record. Finally, the RIHVAGE program (Interdisciplinary research on the history of castles and courts in the Val de Loire during the medieval and renaissance period) established a database to organize and disseminate digital archives concerning Chambord.

A high potential for tourist development could be expected from all these research programs. However, this potential was underexploited due the disciplinary segmentation of the related scientific fields, each one generating hard to find, complex, and fragmented results. The VALMOD program is an attempt to promote the tourist development of scientific results based on the hypothesis that such a development can only be the result of a multidisciplinary approach, encompassing actors working in different media. More practically, the objective of the VALMOD program is to contribute to the tourist development of the Château de Chambord, an icon of regional, national and global heritage, through the use of 3D models resulting from in situ acquisitions in order to stage historical content. From the scientific point of view, the collection or acquisition of architectural and historical data, already started in previous research programs, is pursued with a systematic emphasis on the potential for tourist applications. The challenge is to promote a "have fun and learn" approach to scientifically validated results by using appropriate media to target different publics, while trying to minimize the usual weakening induced by outreach.

The VALMOD program can be divided into four main tasks:

The first task consists in completing the 3D acquisition campaigns of the Château de Chambord and other heritage constructions included in the Domaine national de Chambord, using photogrammetry based on multiple image correlation and laser scanning, added to a topographic survey. The processing of the resulting raw data involves the registration of multiple scale acquisitions and the fusion of data from laser scanning and photogrammetry. The results of this first task are the creation of different 3D models with varying resolution and spatial segmentation in order to optimize the viewing experience.

The second task consists in collecting historical and architectural archives, and creating a synthesis in order to highlight the most promising documents to be used for tourist applications. The main application concerns the construction and restoration steps. The definition of the chronological and spatial evolution of the monument based on archives such as iconographic documents and deeds is the main input for the creation of alternative chronological 3D restitutions.

The third task aims at proposing and testing different enhancement scenarios of the produced and collected data, taking into account both 3D acquisitions and historical inventories, and by cross-checking the opportunities for tourist applications with the

other programs of the "Chantier Chambord Château". This task is mostly interdisciplinary; the challenge is to promote the involvement of all partners in the creation of innovative, coordinated and scientifically validated products.

During the last task, the most promising and fully developed enhancement scenarios
will be tested at the Château of Chambord in the form of pilot actions. Here, the challenge
will be to propose the suitable medium for a targeted public. The relevance of the
resulting experiment will be assessed by analyzing the public's perception.

The objective of this communication is to present some examples selected among
the applications developed, halfway through the VALMOD program. According to the
structure of the program, these examples are candidates for task 3 (establishment of
enhancement scenarios). Attention is paid to explaining the challenges and the lessons
learned from this experience.

2 Protocol for 3D Acquisition of Architecture

Before presenting the examples of applications, and in order to clarify the scientific and
technological issues, a preamble about the common feature of all scenarios is the requirement of resorting to 3D acquisition. Two different technologies are used in the VALMOD
project: laser scanning and photogrammetry based on multiple image correlation.

For the laser scanning of architecture at the Domaine national de Chambord, we used
exclusively a Faro Focus 3D (phase shift laser scanner), whose precision and acquisition
speed are satisfactory when the working distance is between 1 and 30 meters. This
scanner has an embedded coaxial digital camera for the acquisition of color, so as to
provide colorimetric information on each point of the resulting scans. However, the color
information is inhomogeneous and sometimes approximate. The main processing task
consists in spatial registration, which can be automated thanks to the positioning of
spherical references, or conducted manually by the localization of reference points
directly in the scan [3].

For photogrammetry, we used a Canon 6D digital camera (21 MPixels; 24 × 36 mm
sensor) with various lenses (24 mm; 105 mm; fish-eye), with a tripod. We applied this
technique to several facades of the Château de Chambord and to some pieces of the
lapidary deposit in order to obtain a better color restitution compared to laser scanning.
To process the photographs in order to obtain 3D models, we used MicMac (open source
and free software), which is based on multiple image correlation. This software is
particularly efficient in creating accurate 3D models by taking into account control points
from topography.

3 Examples of Applications

3.1 Global Model of the Château

The creation of a global 3D model of the Château de Chambord from laser scanning is
the first application. This model can be used to present the results of 6 years of successive
3D acquisitions. Many students from the Civil Engineering department of Polytech

Orléans (Engineering School at the University of Orléans, France) have contributed to this progressive acquisition. For outdoor laser scanning, we used spherical references to facilitate the registration process, whereas for indoor laser scanning we performed only manual registration so as to avoid impacting the scanning with unnecessary outliers. We acquired the geometry of the whole outside facades of the château, except for some parts of the roof because we performed terrestrial laser scanning only. Moreover, we acquired some indoor scenes such as the double staircase, several restored attics, and one modular housing of the keep. Our ground resolution ranged between 2 mm for the most proximal points and 5 cm for the most distal ones. The registration of all the scans (about 400, i.e. 10 billion points before fusion) taken at different scales into one 3D model represents a real challenge, and the refinement of registration at the millimeter scale for some parts is still in progress. After fusion and resolution limitation, point cloud models of no more than several hundred million points can be obtained. These models can now be quite easily handled by recent software and computers to create real-time rendering (Fig. 1a). Additionally, this kind of 3D model can be processed to extract original architectural information such as vertical (Fig. 1b) or horizontal slides (Fig. 1c), planar and cylindrical projections to create high-resolution metric elevation. This global model has been used to illustrate two national television documentaries concerning the Château de Chambord [10, 11].

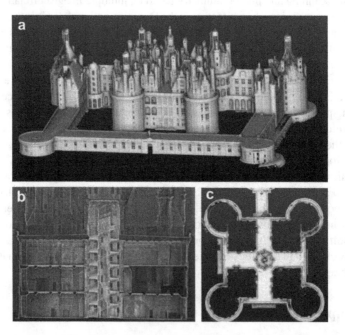

Fig. 1. (a) Rendering of the point clouds representing the Château de Chambord; (b) Vertical slide of the keep; (c) Horizontal slide of the keep.

3.2 3D Print of the Double Staircase

From the global model of the Château, the double staircase was segmented. One of the challenges here was to define a processing pipeline to create bridges between the formats of data from in-situ acquisitions (dense point clouds, Fig. 2a) to ready-to-print 3D sketches (light and manifold solid model, Fig. 2b). From the educational point of view, the most important point was to segment this double staircase into two separate helicoidal stairways so that it could be unscrewed (Fig. 3b). Finally, the 3D print of the double staircase, which is about 41 cm high (Fig. 3a), is composed of 3 levels, each one composed of 2 stairways (Fig. 3c). Additional features were integrated such as pins to help centering and relative positioning. The print of each level took about 70 h.

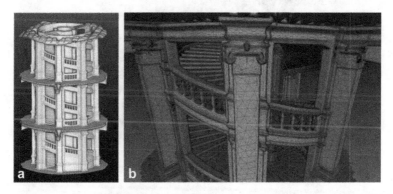

Fig. 2. (a) Dense point clouds of the double staircase; (b) Light and manifold solid model of the double staircase

Fig. 3. (a) 3D print of the model; (b) Stairway unscrewed from double staircase; (c) One level composed of two stairways

3.3 Pieces of the Lapidary Deposit

This third application deals with the photogrammetric acquisition of some selected pieces of the lapidary deposit of the Château de Chambord. The lapidary deposit is a place where stones removed during restoration are conserved due to their particular interest. These pieces are therefore precious, always damaged, and sometimes volumi-nous, which prevents their easy handling. In order to make it possible to handle them without touching them, we decided to create digital replicas using photogrammetric acquisition. Here, the challenge was to obtain comprehensive complementary orienta-tions while having sufficient and constant illumination for each point of view. In this case, photogrammetry was used to create high resolution point clouds with high color fidelity (Fig. 4).

Fig. 4. Rendering of 3D textured model of pieces of the lapidary deposit of Chambord, by photogrammetry.

4   Lessons Learned

The main lessons learned concern the solving of technical challenges, and making the interdisciplinary approach effective.

The main technical challenge is due to the fact that we decided to rely exclusively on rigorous *in-situ* acquisitions. That makes the resulting raw data complex, inhomo-geneous, dense, voluminous, and sometimes locally incomplete. Moreover, the combi-nation of laser scanning and photogrammetry, including the accurate projection of pictures oriented using photogrammetry on meshes resulting from laser scanning involved developing a specific code, especially for the implementation of the Fish-eye lens. More globally, the processing and the viewing of our models required up-to-date technological surveillance due to recent evolutions of software such as MeshLab and CloudCompare.

To make the interdisciplinary approach effective, obviously, the key was to create bridges between disciplines. This means that at least some scientists in the consortium have to make a step in the direction of other sciences to create those bridges. This involve-ment requires time, curiosity, and willingness, in order to understand the necessary basics to allow relevant scientific exchange between disciplines. The problem is that this involvement may not result in short term scientific findings in our respective scientific fields, so it may be discouraged due to the emphasis placed on scientific evaluation; it is, however, necessary for such a project to produce added value. The good point is that this interdisciplinary added value is welcomed and appreciated by non-academic partners such as built heritage managers and regional development organizations.

5 Conclusion

The selection of applications presented in this communication makes it possible to assess the potential for tourist development of the VALMOD program. The search for a common ground between architecture, history of built heritage, and 3D acquisition technologies has shown that it is possible to produce original content while maintaining high scientific quality. Whether to illustrate the architecture of the Château de Chambord, physically unscrew the double staircase, or virtually handle stones that are too fragile to be made available to the public, all these initiatives reveal the possibilities opened up by an inter-disciplinary approach. The creation of innovative scenarios for tourist development from these examples is still in progress. The next steps will be to benefit from the contribution to other programs of the "Chantier Chambord Château" to build up interdisciplinary interactions and enrich content, and to find appropriate media for dissemination of the results.

Acknowlegments. The authors acknowledge the teams of the CESR laboratory, the LI laboratory and the Domaine national de Chambord for their involvement in the project. The authors express their gratitude to the French region "Centre Val de Loire" for its financial support. Students from Polytech Orléans deserve to be thanked for their essential contribution to the VALMOD program: BARBERIO Laurianne, BARGOT Quentin, BERNANOSE Alain, BRINON Clémentine, CANAL Christophe, CARLES Laetitia, CAVROIS Valentin, COMPAGNOT Emeline, CORREA Laercio, CORREARD Jérôme, DELORAS Camille, DITTE Lucille, DURAND Fabien, DUPE Karl, FEVRE Frédéric, FRICK Céline, GIUSTA Melissa, GORCE Joris, GROSLIER Alexandre, HOURSON Mathieu, JOBARD Benoit, LAFFITE Marc, LANÇON Arnaud, LEBERT Simon, LEMOUSSU Anne, LEPETIT Valentin, MIDOU Gauthier, PAQUIS Laurianne, RAYMOND Quentin, RODRIGUES Jennifer, UEBERSCHLAG Yann, TAHMI Nadjia, XIA Fan.

References

1. Al-Omari, A., Brunetaud, X., Beck, K., Al-Mukhtar, M.: Preliminary digital health record of limestone walls in Al-Ziggurat, Al-Nimrud city, Iraq. Int. J. Architectural Heritage **16**(5), 737–740 (2015)
2. Brunetaud, X., De Luca, L., Janvier-Badosa, S., Beck, K., Al-Mukhtar, M.: Application of digital techniques in monument preservation. Eur. J. Environ. and Civil Eng. **16**(5), 543–556 (2012)
3. Brunetaud, X., Stefani, C., Janvier Badosa, S., Beck, K., Al-Mukhtar, M.: Comparison between photomodeling and laser scanning applied to realizing 3D model for digital health record. Eur. J. Environ. Civil Eng. Supp. **16**, 48–63 (2012)

4. Janvier-Badosa, S., Beck, K., Brunetaud, X., Al-Mukhtar, M.: A historical study of Chambord castle: A basis for establishing the monument health record. Int. J. Architectural Heritage **7**(3), 247–260 (2013)

5. Janvier-Badosa, S., Beck, K., Brunetaud, X., Al-Mukhtar, M.: The occurrence of gypsum in the scaling of stones at the castle of Chambord (France). J. Environ. Earth Sci. **71**(11), 4751–4759 (2014)

6. Janvier-Badosa, S., Beck, K., Brunetaud, X., Guirimand-Dufour, A., Al-Mukhtar, M.: Gypsum and spalling decay mechanism of Tuffeau limestone. J. Environ. Earth Sci. **74**(3), 2209–2221 (2015)

7. Janvier-Badosa, S., Stefani, C., Brunetaud, X., Beck, De Luca, L., Al-Mukhtar, M.: Documentation and analysis of 3D mappings for monument diagnosis. In: Toniolo, L., Boriani, M., Guidi, G. (eds.) Built Heritage: Monitoring Conservation Management, pp. 347–357. Springer, Heidelberg (2015)

8. Janvier-Badosa, S., Brunetaud, X., Beck, K., Al-Mukhtar, M.: Kinetics of stone degradation of the Castle of Chambord - France. J. Architectural Heritage **10**(1), 96–105 (2016)

9. Stefani, C., Brunetaud, X., Janvier-Badosa, S., Beck, D.L.L., Al-Mukhtar, M.: Developing a toolkit for mapping and display stone alteration on a web-based documentation platform. J. Cult. Heritage **15**(1), 1–9 (2014)

10. Racines, D., et al.: Des Ailes: Rêves de pierre, du domaine de Chambord aux châteaux d'Écosses broadcast on 07/10/2015 - France 3

11. Chambord, le château, le roi et l'architecte. broadcast on 05/12/2015 - Arte – Réalisation: Marc Jampolsky, Coproduction: ARTE, Domaine national de Chambord, INRAP, CNRS Images, Région Centre – Production: GEDEON PROGRAMMES

Novel Approaches to Landscapes in Cultural Heritage

Geological Heritage and Conservation: A Case Study of the Visual Axis Through Digital Terrain Modeling

Pedro Casagrande(✉), Nicole Rocha, Ítalo Sena,
Bráulio Fonseca, and Ana Clara Moura

GIS Laboratory of School of Architecture and Urban Planning School,
Federal University of Minas Gerais, Belo Horizonte, Brazil
{casagrande,nicarocha,italosena,brauliomagalhaes,
anaclara}@ufmg.br

Abstract. The use of GIS tools for monitoring environmental and cultural heritage through digital terrain models and visual axis in order to ensure a local preservation and demonstrate the relevance to conservation. This conservation is to maintain the local as a tourist, cultural and historical place. Since the survey can be done in a digital platform, there is a new possibility to work for the preservation of the cultural and environmental heritage.

Keywords: Geological heritage · Conservation · Visual axis · Digital modeling · Urban planning · Conservation policies

1 Introduction

Until the twentieth century, the discourse of preservation has always been linked to the concepts of cultural or environmental heritage, especially when it came to preserve the memory and the landscape of a place. The policies for the goods of Cultural and Environmental Heritage dates back to the late of the eighteenth century, which sought to ensure the existence and maintenance of monuments intended to invoke the memory and prevent forgetfulness of the past deeds and as the material resources which were used, record the occurrence of endemic species, and reserve genetic information in the areas protected for future use (Zanirato and Ribeiro [1]; UNESCO [2]; Choay [3]).

Following these criteria, a good could be considered a heritage since endowed with historical and artistic value that shows the importance for the development of art or history. The understanding of this about the history and their testimony restricted the ability to assign to other agents and their creations one story sense. Thus the cultural heritage concepts and environmental, underwent some changes over the time, moving towards a conception of heritage that understood as a set of cultural assets, referring to collective identities. Being considered as well, property and intangible, tangible and intangible (Zanirato and Ribeiro [1]; UNESCO [22]; Choay [3]; Filgueiras et al. [4]).

When the matter was directing the assessment of abiotic or its preservation, despite being predict that addressed the subject resented further studies on geology, to preserve

© Springer International Publishing AG 2016
M. Ioannides et al. (Eds.): EuroMed 2016, Part II, LNCS 10059, pp. 63–71, 2016.
DOI: 10.1007/978-3-319-48974-2_8

the memory of a place, the concept of geological heritage occurred from the twentieth century (Brilha [5]; Azevedo [6]; Nascimento [7]).

The concept of goods, which were on natural question concerned the environmental and landscape issues with the focus on "areas that are natural landscapes or transformed by man and delineated areas which constitute urban settlements or non-municipal structures, which have particular value of civilization" (Zanirato and Ribeiro [1]). It is given priority to the goods that have a unique geographical or ecological character and a relevant interest to natural history, or to document the civic transformation of the natural environment by human activities. This definition resulted from the realization that the cultural identity of a people is forged in the environment that they live, and that the most significant human constructions get part of their beauty of the place where they are located (Zanirato and Ribeiro [1]).

Just since the twenty-first century, when it starts working new themes and concepts on the issue of heritage, were included other elements for the preservation, which before was very connected to the biotic, recently expanded to the abiotic (Brilha [5]; Azevedo [6]; Nascimento [8]).

In Brazil, the concept of Geological Heritage began to spread in the 90 s, after the First International Symposium of the Geological Heritage Protection which was held in Digne- les- Bains, France, which marked the beginning of actions to conserve the European geological heritage and also dissemination through the geotourism. Among the consequences of this first symposium, was the mark of appreciation of the geological heritage and UNESCO Geoparks program created in 2004, which had among its objectives to create a territory with boundaries and with the significant presence of geological heritage, ecological, archaeological, historical and cultural (MINEROPAR [9]; CPRM [10]; Ruchkys [11]; Nascimento et al. [8]; Schobbenhaus and Silva [12]).

An important contribution of Geoparks program was the possibility of aggregate the geological heritage to visitors, that is, the geotourism, which planned and directed, is able to contribute to the conservation and protection, seeking to "connect people to the place ", fulfilling the value function and becoming a tourist resort and preservation of great value (Ruchkys [11]; Murta and Goodey, 1995).

In addition, the geotourism enabled tourism coupled with the heritage, work up the concept of geoconservation that in designing a Geopark, consists of strategies related to conservation and tourism and educational use of geodiversity (Ruchkys [11]; Nascimento et al. [8]; Schobbenhaus and Silva [12]).

Seeking help Geological Heritage management associated with tourism, it is possible to use some GIS tools (Geographic Information System), specifially the tools for the terrain analysis, the ability to manipulate systematically a large volume of data. This feature enables documentation, visualization and analysis of the place, facilitating the investigation of spatial relations through representation by maps and charts. Mainly for simulation of possible spatial scenarios to evaluate interventions and make predictions and have a higher realm of the possible outcomes of a project or proposed laws and parameters in order to assist in making more systematic and accurate decisions by the managers.

According to Fisher [13], determining the visible areas of a location in the landscape is the process through which the landscape architects have long handled. With the spread of GIS observed the increase in the application of spatial analysis of visibility in many spheres of human activity, especially for tourism planning, strategies for conservation and preservation of natural landscapes, archaeological studies and management of the urban landscape (Germino *et al.* [14]; Moura [20]; Sevenant e Antrop [15]; Popelka e Vozenilek [16]; Chamberlain e Meitner [17]; Phillips *et al.* [18]).

Thus, this article aims to apply GIS tools to demonstrate the study of the potential target axes to preserve the natural landscape, presenting the case study of the Serra da Calçada, in the Region of the Iron Quadrangle, state of Minas Gerais, Brazil.

2 Case Study

The Serra da Calçada (Fig. 1) is located in the Iron Quadrangle, located in the center-southeastern of the state of Minas Gerais/Brazil, occupying an area, of approximately, 7.000 km^2 with considerable geotouristic potential, for geological and geomorphological peculiarities, and for the tourism. The Iron Quadrangle is an important historical and mineral pole for Brazil.

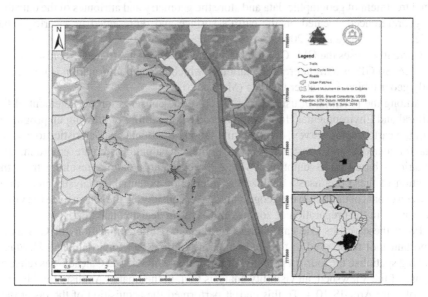

Fig. 1. Location of the Serra da Calçada. Soure: Authors

Throughout the development of the history of Brazil, passing through the colonial and imperial times, the gold mining had a preponderant role in the emergence of what we now have as geological heritage, with its peak during the second half of the eighteenth century. During this period, known as the Gold Cycle, the exploration of gold spread across multiple locations in Brazil, meeting its end in the early nineteenth century. The Serra da Calçada, as well as other formations of the Iron Quadrangle, boasts wide variety of historical trace dating back to the Gold Cycle, significantly integrating the landscape of the place. These cultural elements associated to the privileged geographical location and the great scenic beauty of the place grants to Serra da Calçada a significant potential for geotouristic and geoconservation (Sena *et al.* [19]).

Because of these characteristics is an important area for geosciences and natural sciences, which is often visited for academic purposes, tourist and sports practice (Ruchkys [11]). Justified the choice of this region to be a much visited place, with a great diversity of attractions for all the visitors.

3   Methodology

"(…) Establish a process that will bring progress, one forward walking, in spelling or representation of the earth." Geoprocessing means not only represent, but associate to this act a new look at the space-generating knowledge through of information. Includes digital image processing, digital mapping and geographic information system (GIS). The GIS is a set of methods and techniques for the collection, processing, representation and spatially localized data analysis (Moura [20]).

The GIS's are, according to CÂMARA *et al.* [21], "systems that perform computational treatment of geographic data and store the geometry and attributes of the data that are georeferenced, located on the earth's surface and represented in a cartographic projection" (Câmara *et al.* 2004, p. 27) [21].

Currently it uses the GIS (Geographic Information System) to make representations of space. So GIS is a digital representation in which the map information is not necessarily geographica, but rather the data (Moura [20]).

Among the potential of using GIS to support the conservation management of the Cultural and Environmental Heritage include: The possibility of drawing up prognoses from the cartographic survey; creating simulations - fictional characteristics to a set of data for analysis and construction of hypothetical situations; create environmental scenarios - based on assumptions, which "…represent situations resulting from the adoption of these premises"; analyze the interaction potential - analysis interactions between events or entities in the geographic space, considering the set; analyze the visual axes; assist in the preparation of zoning; and assist in decision making.

From these results one can address different possible applications of GIS as an important tool to be used in the study area of Cultural and Environmental Heritage. Seeking spatialise the tourism potential of the heritage of Serra da Calçada was released the use of the Viewshed, an visibility analysis tool, in the Spatial Analisty toolkit from the software ArcGIS 10.4. To this end, it performed the acquisition of the raster data relating to the altitude, which were obtained in EarthExplorer platform, from the United States Geological Service (USGS). The data are from the mission Shuttle Radar Topographic Mission (SRTM), and were originally acquired with a resolution of 90 m, yet are available with pixels of 30 m, held by digital image processing (Fig. 2).

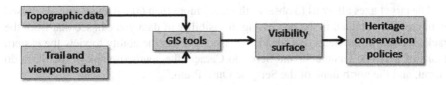

Fig. 2. Methodological framework.

The visibility analysis algorithm works on a matrix structure representing a digital elevation model, each input pixel lifting receives a numerical output value according to the position (x, y, z) of a given observer. That is, a pixel can be viewed from various points, in which each point is given a numerical value larger than a pixel to be viewed from another point with the lowest number of observers. The points without visibility will receive zero (0). The analysis was based on the vector files lines representing tourist tracks, where the vertices are considered the same observers points (Fig. 3).

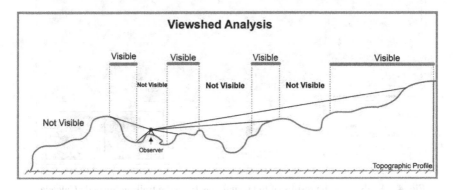

Fig. 3. Representative scheme of visibility analysis according to Moura (2005 [20]).

The representation also hold an visualization in 3D, linking the information lithology of the region, with the help of software ArcScene 10.4.

4   Results and Final Considerations

From the result it is possible to address different applications of GIS as a tool with relevant application in the field of cultural and landscape heritage studies. We can discuss the use of GIS to observe and monitor the change of the elements protected in different time phases, especially with the advent of new measurement technologies and presentation of relief data, such as the LiDAR technology.

In addition, you can discuss how the easy access to information and its virtual availability encourages the establishment of a broad dialogue among the various kind of people involved; government agencies, civil, institutional or individuals and developing heritage registry maps.

The target axes allow us to observe the areas more than 60 km away (Fig. 4). Based on the results obtained in the processing of visibility of data you can see that from the tracks located in the Serra da Calçada the spectator has the ability to view the eastern flanks of Serra do Gandarela and Serra do Caraça, the southern flank of the Serra do Curral, and the north flank of the Serra de Ouro Preto.

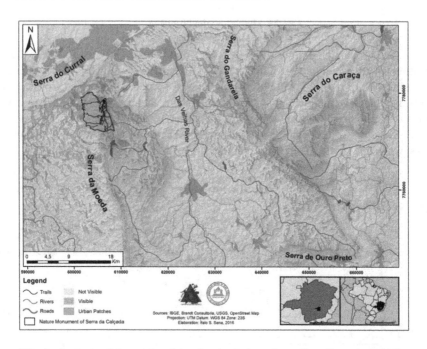

Fig. 4. Analysis of the results of the visual axis from the trails at Serra da Calçada.

In addition, there is an very high importance of the region in the Brazilian tourism scene, and its relevance as the preservation of geological and mining heritage. This mining heritage can happen even in a mining area that still being used until today. This happen because of the functions of the landscape in build a mental map for the people who lives in the region, once the occupation, by people, of this area is linked with mining activities and the landscape view (Moura [23]). Because it is a location close to a major urban center, the Serra da Calçada, attract considerable number of tourists. It stands out among the activities that can be practiced on site for adventure sports (trekking, mountain bike), contemplation of nature (photography, birdwatching).

Thus, it can be seen by Fig. 5(A) and (B), which the data is generated by the tool Viewshed data are consistent with the reality. Once the Fig. 4 you can see that the Serra do Gandarela is visible over the study area, and confirmed by Fig. 5(A), and the track, with the target to the south (Fig. 5B) shows the same principle as evidenced by the visibility map.

Fig. 5. (A) View to the east Axis of Serra da Calçada - With the Serra do Gandarela in the landscape; (B) Trail at Serra da Calçada; (C) View of the historic site of the Brumadinho's Fort; (D) Interior of the historic site of the Brumadinho's Fort; (E) Historical site of Grande Canal. (BORGES *et al.* [25]); (F) Cave with paintings located at Serra da Calçada (BORGES *et al.* [24]).

Figures 5(C) and (D) correspond to the cultural heritage, since they are images of Brumadinho's Fort, place there during the colonial mining period, where worked a British farm, where gold castings were made, and agricultural activities to grown food for the gold exploration employees. In addition to this function on mining, today is a point of tourist visits, well preserved and of great importance in regional history.

Since Fig. 5(E) corresponds to a drainage channel, which was used in the period of gold mining for lead the water to the site where the gold is found and thus make the mining process (Antonil [24], 1711, ed. 1997).

And, by the end, Fig. 5(F) corresponds to cave paintings, also linked to the cultural and heritage due to its location in a cave at the area and its great archaeological importance, being one more place for tourist that visits the area.

Therefore, the application of GIS tools for analyzing the target field shows to be advantageous, mainly because of the availability of free data, and the versatility to be used in regional analysis and it can prove through digital data relevant landscape view, since it is not always possible to have an easy access to a particular location to show the local visual axis. In addition, it assists in the preservation and maintenance of the heritage by the ones who are responsible for that, being easy on handling and processing all the data.

5 Acknoweledgments

With the support of PhD scholarships - CAPES/DS and contribution to the Project "Geodesign and Parametric Modelling of Territorial Occupation: new resources of geo-technologies to landscape management of Pampulha Region, Belo Horizonte", with the support of CNPq – National Council for the Scientific and Technological Development. Call MCTI/CNPQ/MEC/CAPES N° 22/2014, Process: 471089/2014-1, and to the Project "Programa Pesquisador Mineiro – PPM IX", Process TEC – PPM – 00059-15.

References

1. Zanirato, H., Ribeiro, W.C.: Patrimônio cultural: a percepção da natureza como um bem não renovável. Revista Brasileira de História, São Paulo 26(51), 251–262 (2006)
2. UNESCO. Centro del Patrimonio Mundial de la. Carpeta de información sobre el patrimonio mundial, Paris, p. 2 (2005)
3. Choay, F.: A alegoria do patrimônio. Ed. Unesp, São Paulo (2001)
4. Filgueiras, N.L., Jácome, R.C.G., Martins, R.M., Mourão, A.C.: O uso das ferramentas do Sistema de Informações Geográficas (SIG) no apoio ao processo de inventário dos bens do patrimônio cultural. In: Anais XVI Simpósio Brasileiro de Sensoriamento Remoto - SBSR, Foz do Iguaçu, Brasil, INPE (2013)
5. Brilha, J.: Patrimônio Geológico e Geoconservação A conservação da Natureza na sua vertente Geológica. Palimage editores, Lisboa (2005)
6. Ruchkys, A.Ú.: Patrimonio Geologico e Geoconservação no Quadrilátero Ferrifero, Minas Gerais: Potencial para criação de um Geoparque da UNESCO. PhD diss. University of Minas Gerais (2007)
7. Nascimento, M.A.L.: Diferentes ações a favor do Patrimônio Geológico brasileiro. Estudos Geológicos, vol. 20 (2) (2010)
8. Nascimento, M.A.L., Azevedo, U.R., Mantesso neto, V.: Geoturismo: um novo segmento do turismo no Brasil. Revista Global Tourism, vol. 3 (2007)
9. MINEROPAR. Serviço Geológico do Paraná. http://www.mineropar.pr.gov.br/modules/conteudo/conteudo.php?conteudo=134. Accessed 22 Jun 2015
10. CPRM. Serviço Geológico do Brasil. http://www.cprm.gov.br/publique/Gestao-Territorial/Geoparques/Geoparques-1404.html. Accessed on 22 Jun 2015
11. Ruchkys, U.A.: Patrimônio Geológico e Geoconservação no Quadrilátero Ferrífero, Minas Gerais: Potencial para a Criação de um Geoparque da UNESCO. Tese de Doutorado. Universidade Federal de Minas Gerais, Belo Horizonte, Minas Gerais, Brasil, p. 211 (2007)
12. Schobbenhaus, C. Silva, C. R. (Orgs.). propostas do Brasil, Geoparques/CPRM, Rio de Janeiro, p. 750 (2012)
13. Fisher, P.F.: Extending the applicability of viewsheds in landscape planning. Photogram. Eng. Remote Sens. 62(11), 1297–1302 (1996)

14. Germino, M.J., Reiners, W.A., Blasko, B.J., Mcleod, D., Bastian, C.T.: Estimating visual properties of Rocky Mountain landscapes using GIS. Landscape Urban Plan. 53(1), 71–83 (2001)
15. Sevenant, M., Antrop, M.: Settlement models, land use and visibility in rural landscapes: two case studies in Greece. Landscape Urban Plan. 80(4), 362–374 (2007)
16. Popelka, S., Vozenilek, V.: Landscape visibility analysis and their visualisation. ISPRS Arch. 38, 4 (2010)
17. Chamberlain, B.C., Meitner, M.J.: A route-based visibility analysis for landscape management. Landscape Urban Plan. 111, 13–24 (2013)
18. Phillips, N., Ladefoged, T.N., Mcphee, B.W., Asner, G.P.: Location, location, location: a viewshed analysis of heiau spatial and temporal relationships in leeward Kohala, Hawai 'i. J. Pacific Archaeol. 6(2) (2015)
19. Sena, Í.S., Ruchkys, U.A., Lobo, C.F.F.: Potencial Geoturístico do Patrimônio Geocultural da Serra da Calçada, Quadrilátero Ferrífero, Minas Gerais, Brasil. In: XV Encuentro de Geógrafos de América Latina, 2015, Havana. Memorias de lo XV Encuentro de Geógrafos de América Latina. Havana: Editora GEOTECH, vol. 1 (2015)
20. Moura, A.C.M.: Geoprocessamento na gestão e planejamento urbano. 2ª edição. Ed. Da autora, Belo Horizonte (2005)
21. Câmara, G., Carvalho, M., Fucks, S., Monteiro, A.M.: Analise Espacial e Geoprocessamento. In: Fucks, S., Carvalho, M.S., Câmara, G., Monteiro, A.M. (Org.). Analise Espacial de Dados Geograficos, pp. 21–52. Emprapa, Brasilia (2004)
22. UNESCO. "About—UNESCO's role in geopark initiative". Geopark Iskar Panega website. Geopark Iskar Panega (2007)
23. Moura, A.C.M.: La geoelaborazione nella gestione del paesaggio minerario – Confronto di metodologie per l'analisi ed il monitoraggio ambientale delle georisorse. In: Bruno, R., Focaccia, S. (eds.) Formazione avanzata nel settore delle rocce ornamentali e delle geoelaborazioni, pp. 102–152. Editora Asterisco Bologna-Itália (2009)
24. Antonil A.J.: Cultura e opulência do Brasil (1711). Ed. Itatiaia, Belo Horizonte, ed. 1997
25. Borges, G.C. (org.). Patrimônio Cultural da Serra da Calçada: Relatório de Monitoramento. Associação para a Recuperação e Conservação Ambiental em Defesa da Serra da Calçada (ARCA-AMASERRA). Relatório Técnico. Belo Horizonte, Minas Gerais, p. 120 (2008)

A GIS Database of Montenegrin Katuns (Kuči Mountain and Durmitor)

Olga Pelcer–Vujačić[1]([✉]) and Sandra Kovačević[2]

[1] Historical Institute, University of Montenegro,
Podgorica, Montenegro
olgapelcer@gmail.com
[2] University of Montenegro, Podgorica, Montenegro
sandraa@t-com.me

Abstract. A two year ongoing project (2015–2017) Valorizing the Montenegrin Katuns through sustainable development of agriculture and tourism –
KATUN is innovative because of its multidisciplinary and comprehensive
approach of all the aspects of the katuns (temporary centre of traditional summer
livestock rearing lasting for centuries in the Montenegrin society). The main
idea of this project, being implemented by the interdisciplinary research team, is
to create a knowledge base for the multipurpose use of the Montenegrin
mountain resources, by combining the traditional agriculture with boosting
tourism activities and protecting the cultural heritage. Katuns as nuclei of traditional agriculture in mountain areas face many challenges. This uniqueness of
Montenegro has to be preserved and revitalized via new opportunities in tourism
and other complementary activities (handcraft, trade, culture, services). Dealing
with mountain cultural heritage the first step was creating a pertaining database
and mapping and GPS positioning of the katuns, and objects of
cultural-historical importance in research area, inventorying of the katuns,
determining their condition, origin and characteristics and documenting current
condition (photo, video, graphic and textual) of the katuns.

Keywords: Montenegro Katuns · Research Mountain cultural heritage GIS
database

1 Introduction

A two year ongoing project Valorizing the Montenegrin Katuns through sustainable
development of agriculture and tourism – KATUN started in 2015 and an innova-
tiveness of the project lays primarily in its holistic approach (multidisciplinary and
comprehensive treatment of all the aspects of the katuns (temporary center of traditional summer livestock rearing lasting for centuries in the Montenegrin society) in line
with rural society expectations to breathe new life into the katuns by high integration of
the sustainable development of agriculture and agro-tourism) and in the outcomes
(specific forms of knowledge transfer, new dairy products, new types of tourism offer
and for the first time valuable data on cultural-historical heritage).

© Springer International Publishing AG 2016
M. Ioannides et al. (Eds.): EuroMed 2016, Part II, LNCS 10059, pp. 72–80, 2016.
DOI: 10.1007/978-3-319-48974-2_9

The Montenegrin katuns constitute a special example of rural buildings; used as seasonal settlements, they are organized in areas of mountain pastures for summer cattle grazing. Even if in most case they were abandoned during recent years - since people living there moved to more confortable residences within urban settlements - their contemporary potential for preserving traditional cattle-raising procedures and dairy products, rich cultural-historical heritage and perspectives of organized tourism activities, appears a very intriguing task to be approached.

One of the project tasks was creating a pertaining database on mountain cultural heritage on these katuns with the aim to valorize Montenegrin katuns through the implementation of a Geographical Information System. This first step could pave the way for possible future planning of their restoration, within the general framework of a concerted approach aimed at their safeguard and the general sustainability of the areas where they are located, fighting the progressive abandonment of rural land. The exploitation of their unexpressed potential in the sector of tourism usage, together with cultural heritage, rich tradition and old infrastructure, would therefore reveal an efficient way for their valorization. The first steps were mapping and GPS positioning of the katuns, sites and objects of cultural-historical importance in research area, than inventorying of the katuns, determining their condition, origin and characteristics and documenting current condition (photo, video, graphic and textual) of the katuns. Having been the centre of traditional summer livestock rearing for centuries, katuns in Montenegro gathered all the cultural, social and economic tendencies of their inhabitants. Their disposition, number, location and size testify to the historical and social position of their settlers, providing a picture of their place in contemporary coordinate system. Not protecting that heritage leads to losing of a great (even the greatest) part of our picture of the past, and without its precise and comprehensive inventory such protection is impossible. Also, this category is clearly recognized in European policy documents on rural heritage protection [5]. Due to many different factors, there have been very few efforts made in this direction so far, resulting in almost unbelievable lack of relevant information on katuns' positions, size, affiliation and other characteristics. But,"...*to protect such vernacular heritage is important; it is the fundamental expression of the culture of a community, of its relationship with its territory and, at the same time, the expression of the world's cultural diversity. Vernacular building is the traditional and natural way by which communities house themselves.... How these forces can be met is a fundamental problem that must be addressed by communities and also by governments, planners, conservationists and by a multidisciplinary group of specialists...*". [4] Therefore, during this KATUN project special attention will be paid to the local historical and cultural heritage protection, providing a wider framework for agricultural and tourism activities. Articulating their place within the course of modern development of Montenegrin approaching the EU, would be a step towards enriching common European heritage with one of the most recognizable country's traditions.

2 Organization and Data Input

Our main task is to determine and document the real current number, condition and characteristics of the katuns on the Mountains of Kuči and later, on Durmitor. This assignment was to be done through several subtasks:

- Desk researches - archival and library researches on existing data on historical, social and cultural aspects of the area;
- Mapping and GPS positioning of the katuns, sites and objects of cultural-historical importance in research area;
- Inventorying of the katuns, determining their condition, origin and characteristics; Documenting current condition (photo, video, graphic and textual) of the katuns;
- Creation of pertaining data base;

Our internal organization in the project comprises a team of six, three historians, one historian of art and one architect and a GIS consultant overseeing the database. We all administrate the contents of the database. As base-maps we used Google Earth satellite imagery and topographic maps. We used those maps, first for the field work of identifying all locations and afterwards for data input. Initially, we used those maps going to field research. We also made provisional information tables and started locating sites and collecting data. All filed research had to be done during the summer months due to the temporary nature of these settlements. Very valuable information were recorded during the conversations with the people still practicing the traditional summer coming to the mountain pastures with family members, cattle and movable household inventory. The team took photos, made architectural sketches and measures of the existing cottages and visible remains. The tables with additional information were filled for every katun on site and later transferred into data for the database (Fig. 1).

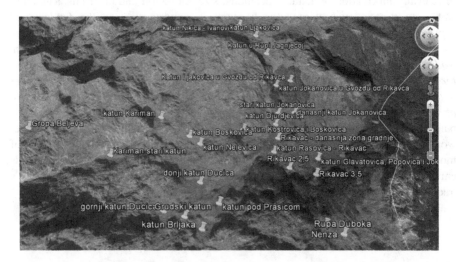

Fig. 1. Part of Kuči katuns labeled in Google Earth

Fig. 2. Katun in Kuči part of Komovi mountain (Photo by Ivan Laković)

This first ever database of Montenegrin katuns was made in QGIS 2.8.3. For time being, our inventory is not online, although we are planning to make available at least some parts as open access. The database listed and mapped not only settlements but building objects as well, namely different types of wooden or stone structure – cottages (local names: glada, koliba, stan). Due to different nature of building materials on Kuči mountains (prevailing stone structures) and Durmitor (mostly wooden structures), we are trying to document every active as well as abandoned katun in Kuči, but only active katuns on Durmitor, as there are no evident visible remains (Fig. 2).

The condition of cottages was further described through auxiliary information in the attribute table. In the attribute table we are entering basic parameters concerning the condition of the object: minor remains, collapsed remains, walled remains, greater roof damage, slight roof damage and completely preserved. Further we are entering data by the types of wall material: stone (drywall, stone with mortar), wooden or new materials and types by roof cover: wooden, tin or new materials. Another significant entry for analysis of cultural heritage is the type of traditional building, by roof style and by front wall construction: without gable - 2 hips, without gable - 4 hips, two gables, two halfgables, one gable, and one half-gable. There is additional information on usage of the object: traditional usage, abandoned or weekend (recreational) cottage. Every entry is accompanied with optional commentary and photos. After one year of the KATUN project, we collected data on 174 katuns and entered 2264 objects (gladas) so far in one vector layer. There are several more mountain sites to visit and collect data by the end of this year (Fig. 3).

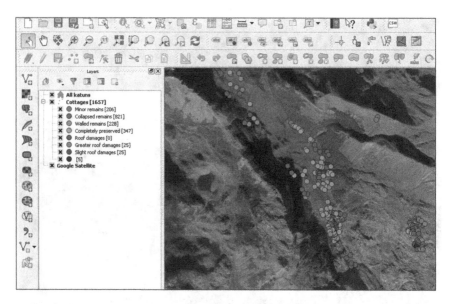

Fig. 3. Overview of some katuns in Kuči in database with Google satelite imagery

3 Possible Outcomes

The traditional audiences for the outcome of similar projects include cultural institutions and/or art historians, historians or archaeologists. The general public, previously considered as a secondary audience, is fast becoming important in the issue of conservation, as attested by the growing number of conservation blogs, websites, and social media platforms being created or used by people interested in conservation and cultural heritage, and growing efforts to expand public appreciation of the importance of the field. The special aspect is the touristic application of this type of heritage databases (Fig. 4).

Geographical Information Systems (GIS) are very powerful tools for developing and implementing tourism programs able to diversify and reinvigorate local economies [3, 7]. In some countries, especially in Europe, tourism development strategies have combined agriculture and tourism to create agro-tourism, developing a GIS based model that maps the spatial distribution of rural buildings [2, 8, 10]. The first step in this research involved the identification of location-based factors that may influence agro-tourism development based on the building valorization. As previously said, this was accomplished through a survey of the literature and associated topics such as general tourism, rural economics, travel research, and geographic information systems. Second, a comprehensive geo-database of agro-tourism operations in the rural area was gradually developed. In recent years, there have been numerous examples of Geographic Information Systems utilized for suitability modeling, which is commonly used to identify the best location for an agricultural enterprise and the surrounding context. Using GIS in the decision making process helps reduce the risk of failure and creates opportunities for efficient marketing and advertising (Fig. 5).

	Code	No of katun	Type	Type of traditional cottage	Conditions	Usage	Walls	Roof
13	5	Dobri Do	traditional	one half-gable	walled remains	abandoned	stone	()
14	6	Dobri Do	traditional	one half-gable	minor remains	abandoned	stone	wooden
15	7	Dobri Do	traditional	one half-gable	minor remains	abandoned	stone	()
17	9	Dobri Do	traditional	one half-gable	walled remains	abandoned	stone	()
18	10	Dobri Do	traditional	one half-gable	collapsed remains	abandoned	stone	()
22	4	Podamar	traditional	one half-gable	collapsed remains	abandoned	stone	no roof
25	7	Podamar	traditional	one half-gable	collapsed remains	abandoned	stone	no roof
26	8	Podamar	traditional	one half-gable	collapsed remains	abandoned	stone	no roof
27	9	Podamar	traditional	one half-gable	minor remains	abandoned	stone	no roof
52	6	Radan	traditional	one half-gable	collapsed remains	abandoned	stone	no roof
59	13	Radan	traditional	one half-gable	collapsed remains	abandoned	stone	no roof
63	17	Radan	traditional	one half-gable	completely prese...	abandoned	stone	tin
91	17	Katun Hum Orah...	traditional	one half-gable	greater roof dam...	abandoned	stone	tin
94	20	Katun Hum Orah...	traditional	one half-gable	walled remains	abandoned	stone	no roof
96	22	Katun Hum Orah...	traditional	one half-gable	collapsed remains	abandoned	stone	no roof
283	7	Gladišta	traditional	one half-gable	walled remains	abandoned	stone	no roof
311	4	Momonjevo gornj...	traditional	one half-gable	collapsed remains	abandoned	stone	no roof
328	11	Momonjevo donji...	traditional	one half-gable	completely prese...	abandoned	stone	tin
335	18	Momonjevo donji...	traditional	one half-gable	walled remains	abandoned	stone	no roof
347	30	Momonjevo donji...	traditional	one half-gable	walled remains	abandoned	stone	no roof
349	32	Momonjevo donji...	traditional	one half-gable	completely prese...	traditional usage	stone with mortar	tin
492	5	Gropa Mičkova	traditional	one half-gable	completely prese...	traditional usage	stone with mortar	combination of m...
507	7	Katun Mala Rupa	traditional	one half-gable	collapsed remains	abandoned	stone	no roof

Fig. 4. Snapshot of attribute table of Montenegrin katuns database

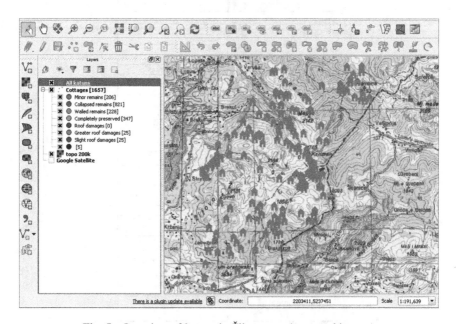

Fig. 5. Overview of katuns in Žijevo area (topographic map)

We will try to make exemplificative maps valuable for describing the territory, with selection of the most stimulating points of interest. The resulting geo-database contains for each building their corresponding location, the relation with infrastructures, land cover, morphology, vegetation, etc. Eventually, this will provide the centralization of all interesting data from different sources, in a unified environment and the visualization of data on maps. As already pointed out [9], maps and information on natural and cultural heritage connected to tourism application are an exceptional contribution to capacity building and awareness-raising of visitors. They are the most natural way to present data and the most user-friendly way to present tourist information. We expect that in time more layers will be added and all layers can be interconnected and integrated with non-geographical information such as: opening hours of museums and other attractions; hotels and restaurants rates and costs; events calendar; historic data, intangible heritage, flora and fauna; perhaps some information concerning society and economy. An interesting feature would also be studying toponyms and vocabularies demonstrating how landscapes are conceptualized and presented [6]. In the future, we could perhaps try to merge a trend of finding a better model how humans socialize, share information, and form social groups within the complex geographic landscape [1]. This would enable us to present a useful (for tourists and academics alike) open access database on our website www.katun.me.

Code	
No of katun	
Type	modified
	new object
	traditional
Type_of_traditional_cottage	without gable - 2 hips
	without gable - 4 hips
	two gables
	two half-gables
	one gable
	one half-gable
Condition	greater roof damage
	slight roof damage
	minor remains
	completely preserved
	collapsed remains
	walled remains
Usage	traditional usage
	abandoned
	weekend cottage
Walls	wooden
	stone with mortar
	stone
	new materials
Roof	wooden
	combination of materials
	tin
	no roof
	new materials
Comment	
Date	
Photo	
Admin	

Fig. 6. Options for the cottages in the attribute table

4 Challenges

The unstructured narrative formats of historic and cultural heritage research is at odds with an online environment that relies on structured data for access and use. Any kind of heritage GIS system always integrates inclusive and very detailed documentation data on physical characteristics of heritage properties and settings through textual reports, drawings and photographs. Most of these systems have a common problem, they only use GIS for recording properties' position without additional data integration through geo-referencing approach. Therefore, although within a same geospatial context, the wealth of heritage information on individual property is always isolated and not open to be analysed through spatial approaches. There is a feeling that there are no data standards for conservation information. As beginners we are facing certain obstacles in determining the limits of the project and aspirations to make something more than academic conservation inventory.

An important aspect of this project and GIS database is identification of the features to be protected, definition of the geographical area to be protected and definition of the degree of legal protection. Most inventories, like this one, have traditionally informed authorities, scholars, and the public of essential information about cultural assets, such as their location and spatial extent, their association with historical periods, cultures, and events, and whether they incorporate particular architectural styles and building technologies. We face all these challenges as well. So far, we concentrate on mountain heritage, namely traditional architecture. As a "spatial toolbox" [11] for archaeological, historical, cultural and social investigation, GIS has become an important technology for cultural heritage conservation in the past two decades. A plan for the identification and cataloguing of katun through the implementation of ICT tools as a GIS and a Decision Support System may reveal a fruitful way for implementing suitable actions aimed to the valorization of rural building heritage all over this area, so contributing to the protection of natural resources and stimulating at the same time the local economies. Therefore, we are aware that our database is not something new in terms of computer graphics and spatial analysis but as previously said, this is the first database of cultural heritage in Montenegro (Fig. 6).

Acknowledgments. This research was supported in the program Higher Education and Research for Innovation and Competitiveness by the Ministry of Science of Montenegro and financing the project Valorizing the Montenegrin Katuns through sustainable development of agriculture and tourism – KATUN (KATUN-INVO HERIC No 01-646). We are thankful to our colleagues Ivan Laković, Tatjana Koprivica, Senka Babović-Raspopović and Aleksandra Kapetanović who helped us collecting the data and provided expertise that greatly assisted the research. All photos and graphic material are made by team members. All the data in this paper are published with consent of the Project Coordinator, prof. Milan Marković.

References

1. Andris, C.: Integrating social network data into GISystems. Int. J. Geogr. Inf. Sci. **30**(10), 2009–2031 (2016)
2. Baskerville, B.G.: Building a GIS Model to Assess Agritourism Potential. University of Nebraska, Lincoln (2013)
3. Beedasy, J., Whyatt, D.: Diverting the tourists: a spatial decision-support system for tourism planning on a developing island. Int. J. Appl. Earth Obs. Geoinf. **1**(3/4), 163–174 (1999)
4. Charter On The Built Vernacular Heritage, Ratified by the International Council on Monuments and Sites' (ICOMOS) 12th General Assembly, Mexico, October 1999. http://www.icomos.org/en/get-involved/work-and-volunteer-for-icomos/icomos-wg-projects/179-articles-en-francais/ressources/charters-and-standards/164-charter-of-the-built-vernacular-heritage
5. European Rural Heritage Observation Guide – CEMAT (CEMAT-CHF 80 (2003) 19). http://www.coe.int/t/dgap/localdemocracy/cemat/VersionGuide/Default_en.asp
6. Klippel, A., Mark, D., Wallgrün, J.O., Stea, D.: Conceptualizing landscapes. In: Fabrikant, S.I., Raubal, M., Bertolotto, M., Davies, C., Freundschuh, S., Bell, S. (eds.) COSIT 2015. LNCS, vol. 9368, pp. 268–288. Springer, Heidelberg (2015). doi:10.1007/978-3-319-23374-1_13
7. Parolo, G., Ferrarini, A., Rossi, G.: Optimization of tourism impacts within protected areas by means of genetic algorithms. Ecol. Model. **220**, 1138–1147 (2009)
8. Romano, G., Dal Sasso, P., Trisorio-Liuzzi, G., Gentile, F.: Multi-criteria decision analysis for land suitability mapping in a rural area of Southern Italy. Land Use Policy **48**(11), 131–143 (2015)
9. Ruoss E., Alfarè L.: Sustainable Tourism as Driving Force For Cultural Heritage Sites Development. Planning, Managing and Monitoring Cultural Heritage Sites in South East Europe, April 2013. http://www.cherplan.eu/sites/default/files/public_files/Sustainable%20tourism%20in%20SEE.pdf
10. Statuto, D., Gatto A.G., Tortora A., Picuno P.: The use of a Geographical Information System to identify and valorize some pathways along the "Herculia Way". In: Bambi G., Barbari M. (eds.) Proceeding of International Conference: "The european pilgrimage routes for promoting sustainable and quality tourism in rural areas", 4–6 December 2014, Firenze (Italy), pp. 637–648. Firenze University Press (2014)
11. Wheatley, D., Gillings, M.: Spatial Technology and Archaeology: The Archaeological Applications of GIS. CRC Press, New York (2002)

Future Development Plans for Conservation Areas in Taiwan

Tung-Ming Lee[✉] and Alex Yaning Yen

China University of Technology, 56 S. 3 ShingLong Road,
Taipei 116, Taiwan
{tmlee,alexyen}@cute.edu.tw

Abstract. The protection of cultural heritage assets by the United Nations Educational, Scientific, and Cultural Organization (UNESCO) focuses mostly on the authenticity and integrity of such asset in the twenty-first century, the concept of cultural heritage protection focuses on an integrity conservation approach, in which the authenticity and integrity of a conservation area should be examined. This approach should be the key to developing theories on conservation area development in the twenty-first century.

Keywords: Conservation area · Integrity · Authenticity · Monuments · 21st Century · Landscape

1 Origin of the Research

The protection of cultural heritage assets by the UNESCO focuses mostly on the authenticity and integrity of such assets. In addition to buildings being adequately preserved, proximal environments should be protected to the same level, and attention should be paid to the historical and cultural pathways and spaces to maintain the integrity and authenticity of monuments or historical buildings.

Although Articles 33–36 of the Cultural Heritage Conservation Act stipulate the definition of a conservation area and regulate its development, the topic of conservation areas is complicated, and thus current legal regulations continue not to satisfy the demands of conservation areas. Therefore, relevant examples of conservation areas are scant, and no concrete achievements serve as a reference for communities in Taiwan society. Neither are there legal regulations that can be followed in developing a conservation area, thereby creating a predicament where the management of conservation areas focuses on tangible but not intangible assets (Fig. 1).

© Springer International Publishing AG 2016
M. Ioannides et al. (Eds.): EuroMed 2016, Part II, LNCS 10059, pp. 81–88, 2016.
DOI: 10.1007/978-3-319-48974-2_10

Fig. 1.   (a) Taketomi Island of Okinawa, Japan (b) Hukou old street in Hsinchu, Taiwan

2   Current Situation and Problems of Taiwan Conservation Areas

The aforementioned problems can be divided into five major issues:

A. Unclear Concept of Integrity Conservation
   From legally to nationally designate monuments, most sites are not managed according to integrity conservation, and initiatives for designating conservation areas are often neglected.
B. Legal Regulations on Tangible Asset Conservation
   Currently, comprehensive and in-depth actions must be conducted to preserve cultural heritage. Additionally, other tangible and intangible elements such as landscape and culture must be preserved with integrity.
C. Ambiguity in Future Benefits and Relevant Measures
   Moreover, no long-term plan has been formulated to establish specific measures for conducting the operations management, safety, and disaster prevention of a conservation area as well as for sustaining the QOL of nearby residents, all of which are critical topics that must be elaborated.
D. Difficulty of Administrative Coordination between Urban Planning and Cultural Authorities
   Coordinating all these departments and offices is a difficult task, and thus it is not surprising that problems occur when designating conservation areas or integrating related data.
E. Difficulty of Data Integration
   With the data related to conservation areas stored in culture and urban planning departments or scattered between them, problems of overlapping or scattered data may reoccur.

3   Concept of Conservation Area Development in the Twenty-First Century

3.1   Concept of Integrity

In the twenty-first century, the concept of conservation area development must emphasize authenticity and integrity, and a comprehensive and integrated method must be applied to rethinking the development of conservation areas. The designation of a conservation area should first involve considering the integrity of the area to comprehensively account for a list of items in the area that require conservation.

Promoting the concept of integrated revitalization at a conservation area advances the integrity conservation and future development of that area. Preserving a historical site pertains to maintaining the integrity of the tangible and intangible environments related to the site; and the related initiatives must focus on the integrity of nearby residents' lives and well-being (Fig. 2).

Fig. 2. (a) Senado Square in Macau (designated as a World Heritage site in July 2005) (b) Hukou old street in Hsinchu, Taiwan

3.2 Relevant International Discourses

A. Xian Declaration on the Conservation of the Setting of Heritage Structures, Sites, and Areas
  - Acknowledge the contribution of settings to the significance of heritage monuments, sites, and areas.
  - Understand, document, and interpret the settings in diverse contexts.
  - Develop planning tools and practices to conserve and manage the settings.
  - Monitor and manage change that affects the settings.
  - Work with local, interdisciplinary, and international communities for cooperation and awareness in conserving and managing the settings.
B. Quebec Declaration on the Conservation of the Spirit of the Place through the Safeguarding of Tangible and Intangible Heritage
  - Rethinking the Spirit of Place
  - Identifying the Threats to the Spirit of Place
  - Safeguarding the Spirit of Place
  - Transmitting the Spirit of Place

The following commonalities can be observed in the Xian Declaration and the Quebec Declaration:

- Dimension of space: A spatial environment must incorporate tangible and intangible cultural assets, with the content involving the past and present as well as the specific and expanded environments of cultural heritage areas in terms of social dimension and human–nature interaction.

- Integration of different disciplines: Because of the diverse dimensions involved in cultural heritage areas, personnel of different disciplines must mutually assist and communicate with each other to examine, record, and interpret the culture heritage areas. Data can be publicized and updated through a contemporary digital information platform.
- Management and maintenance measures: Local governments must stipulate comprehensive management measures through legislation, planning, and training and cooperate with local or relevant organizations to ensure that cultural heritage sites are sustainable managed.
- Mechanism for training and reeducation: Training, education, and exhibition should be implemented and promoted to increase people's knowledge of heritage site conservation and to enhance their inheritance of the spirit of local culture.

3.3   Three Key Topics in Developing Conservation Areas

The dimensions involved in the future development of conservation areas are extensive. In addition to the advancement of the techniques used for preserving heritage areas, the dimensions of land use, urban planning, construction land use, site conservation, and economic issues are key topics that merit further discussion. The practice of area conservation must also consider topics including operations management, QOL, and safety and disaster prevention. Accordingly, governmental and civil resources should be integrated to propose projects for developing conservation areas in the future. Therefore, the future development of conservation areas must focus on the local residents' lives and on operations management, QOL, and safety and disaster prevention (Fig. 3).

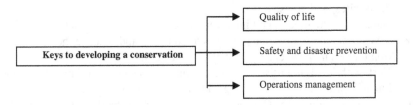

Fig. 3.   Three keys to developing a conservation area

3.4   Topics Entailed in Conservation Areas

Topics associated with developing conservation areas must involve sustainable development. In addition to discussing the historical spaces and cultural heritage sites that require conservation, attention must be focused on residents' rights to their lives and on the research and development of conservation techniques whose implementation in historical and heritage areas can elevate residents' living standards and daily life functions and achieve sustainable development of the conservation areas (Fig. 4):

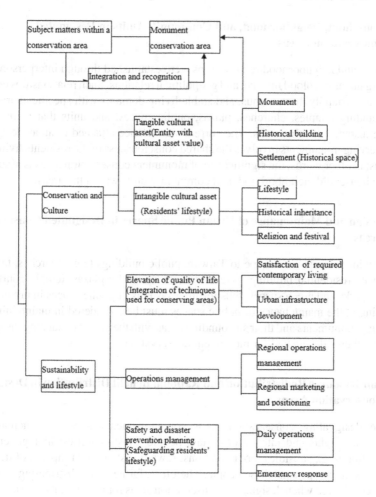

Fig. 4. The future develop concept of reservation area

4 Theory of Conservation Area Development in the Twenty-First Century

Since the twenty-first century, the international concept of preserving monuments has changed considerably. Expanding the concept of conservation areas by incorporating the concepts of landscape quality, the footprint of historical development, and urban fabric has achieved consensus among interest groups. Accordingly, designating monuments as conservation areas should consider these theoretical and practical implications.

4.1 Household, Neighborhood, and Community Units in Designated Conservation Areas

Household and neighborhood relationships were established through interpersonal and social organization, blood lineage, and geopolitical relations. Such relationships enabled establishing friendly, harmonious, and stable living domains with specific characteristics, including temples, churches, plazas, public spaces, and units that were within walking distance of other units. The current significance attached to areas designated for preserving monuments involves the shared consciousness of the residents living near the areas; in other words, the significance of monument conservation areas is associated with the household, neighborhood, and community units within the areas.

4.2 Design and Maintenance of Urban Public Spaces in Designated Conservation Areas

From traditional cities in Europe to Taiwan, public buildings (e.g., churches, temples, and private residential buildings) are often surrounded by plazas, temple courtyards, roads, or parks and green spaces, thus forming systems of public spaces in urban cities. Accordingly, the maintenance of public spaces must be considered in maintaining and preserving monuments and their surrounding areas with the aim of enhancing the quality of environments designated for monument conservation.

4.3 Fair Resource Redistribution and Rational Benefit Distribution in Designated Conservation Areas

Because designating conservation areas for monuments inevitably increases or decreases the rights and interest of certain people, most countries offer government subsidization (e.g., subsidies, tax reductions, reward systems, or transfers of development rights) to compensate these people. Therefore, fairness in redistributing resources must be considered when designating conservation areas for monuments, and the rationality of benefit compensation must be maintained after the resource redistribution.

4.4 Integrated Coordination in Designated Conservation Areas

Designating conservation areas for monuments entails managing and coordinating landscapes and public facilities (e.g., ornamental plants, landmarks, architectural styles, and water and electricity infrastructure) through urban planning and urban design measures. For example, expanding the designation of a conservation area through urban renewal measures must be coordinated with the regulations on the transfer of development rights. Accordingly, conservation areas should be designated according to a set of integrated methods.

4.5 Expansion of Designated Conservation Areas

Designating conservation areas for monuments should include improving undesirable surrounding environments, using resources effectively, and maintaining and enhancing the area's socioeconomic activities. The designation should expand in coordination with overall development projects for cities and towns to ensure that the designated conservation areas are embedded with specific significance.

4.6 Revitalization of Designated Conservation Areas

A lack of management and maintenance at monuments and their surrounding environments can cause these valuable assets to be lost someday. Accordingly, after conservation areas are designated, governments should provide subsidies for the purpose of preserving and maintaining the environments of these areas, thereby improving and revitalizing the QOL of local residents.

5 New Orientations for Conservation Area Development in the Twenty-First Century

Developing conservation areas provides an opportunity for people to preserve and examine the various cultural heritage sites left by their predecessors over the last century as well as to learn about universal values and formulate personal goals.

- Conservation of the Outstanding Universal Value of Monuments: A Central Initiative and Goal of Conservation Area Development
- Both Prominent Monuments and Common Ancient Buildings Must Be Preserved to Realize the Practical Significance of Conservation Area Development
- Monument Conservation Is No Longer Limited to Preserving Monumental Cultural Heritage Sites: Industrial Heritage Is Extensively Emphasized in Recent Years and Is Critical to Conservation Area Development
- Reducing the Impact of Contemporary Construction in Monument Complexes: Crucial to Concretizing and Expanding Conservation Areas, Protecting the Urban Fabric, and Structuring Urban Development Programs
- Conservation of a Cultural Landscape that Emphasizes and Reflects Human Life and Culture and Land Use: A New Direction of and the Key to Successful Conservation Area Development

6 Conclusion

Previously, the conservation and maintenance of monuments neglected the surrounding environments and areas. However, subtle changes in the conservation and maintenance schemes of international cultural heritage areas have occurred in recent decades. The focus of monument conservation and maintenance has expanded to include relevant building complexes (not merely individual historical buildings), the essence or pathways of historical developments in cities and towns, and even the associated intangible values, operations management, and education projects in preserved areas. In recent years, attention has focused on maintaining and protecting heritage areas; hence, more appropriate concepts have been developed to comprehensively preserve the internal and external environments of a heritage. This approach should be the key to developing theories on conservation area development in the twenty-first century.

Topics on developing conservation areas must be analyzed according to the current conditions of conservation areas in Taiwan. After the pertinent problems have been determined and the entry points determined, theoretical analysis can be performed, such as discussions regarding current discourse on conservation area development. Furthermore, current regulations on conservation areas should be examined; for example, integrated analysis can be conducted to investigate the "coopetition" among the Cultural Heritage Conservation Act, the Fire Services Act, the Land Use Act, and the Government Procurement Act.

After the relevant fundamental topics have been discussed, methods for increasing QOL as well as research and development on techniques for managing safety and disaster prevention can be further explored. In addition, discussions on establishing an information-sharing platform that targets conservation area development could be conducted in the future. Only after the fundamental discussions have been conducted can a project for developing the integrity conservation of a heritage area be established.

References

1. Lee, T.-M., Hatano, J.: The history of Arcade (Din-A-Ka) in Di-Hwa Street, Taipei City. In: The 2nd International Symposium on Architectural Interchange in Asia, Biol., vol. 147, pp. 195–197 (1998)
2. Lee, T.-M., Hatano, J.: The design and formative background of town-houses. J. Archit. Plan. (Trans. AIJ) **547**, 237–242 (2001)
3. Lee, T.-M.: Study for generally conservation and sustainable development of traditional town area in Taiwan. Research Project Report of Architecture and Building Research Institute, Ministry of the Interior, Taiwan, R.O.C (2004)
4. Lee, T.-M.: Study of spatial and facade character of town-house in traditional town area, Taiwan. Research Project Report of Architecture and Building Research Institute, Ministry of the Interior, Taiwan, R.O.C (2005)
5. Lee, T.-M., Yen, A.Y.: A preliminary study of historical conservation areas in Taiwan. In: The 10th Session of the Conference on the Science of Conserving and Reusing Cultural Properties (Ancient Remains, Historic Buildings, Settlements, and Cultural Landscapes) (2007)
6. Lee, T.-M., Yen, A.Y.: A study for the future development direction of historical conservation areas in Taiwan. In: The 13th Session of the Conference on the Science of Conserving and Reusing Cultural Properties (Ancient Remains, Historic Buildings, Settlements, and Cultural Landscapes) (2010)

Innovative Methods on Risk Assessment, Monitoring and Protection of Cultural Heritage

The Protection of Cultural Heritage Sites from Geo-Hazards: The PROTHEGO Project

Kyriacos Themistocleous[1(✉)], Branka Cuca[1], Athos Agapiou[1], Vasiliki Lysandrou[1],
Marios Tzouvaras[1], Diofantos G. Hadjimitsis[1], Phaedon Kyriakides[1],
Demetris Kouhartsiouk[1], Claudio Margottini[2], Daniele Spizzichino[2], Francesca Cigna[3],
Giovanni Crosta[4], Paolo Frattini[4], and José Antonio Fernandez Merodo[5]

[1] Remote Sensing and Geo-Environment Laboratory,
Department of Civil Engineering and Geomatics, Cyprus University of Technology,
Saripolou Str. 2-8, 3036 Limassol, Cyprus
k.themistocleous@cut.ac.cy
[2] ISPRA-Istituto Superiore Per La Protezione E Ricerca Ambientale,
Via Brancati, 48, 00144 Rome, Italy
[3] Natural Environment Research Council, Polaris House, North Star Avenue,
Swindon SN2 1EU, UK
[4] University of Milano, Piazza Dell'Ateneo Nuovo, 1,
20126 Milan, Italy
[5] Instituto Geológico Y Minero de España, Rios Rosas, 23,
28003 Madrid, Spain

Abstract. Examining natural hazards responsible for cultural heritage damages all over Europe, especially over large or remote areas is extremely difficult, expensive and time consuming. There is a need identify and respond to natural hazards before they create irreparable damage to cultural heritage sites. The PROTHEGO project uses radar interferometry to monitor surface deformation with mm precision to analyze the impact of geo-hazards in cultural heritage sites in Europe. The project applies novel InSAR techniques to monitor monuments and sites that are potentially unstable due to landslides, sinkholes, settlement, subsidence, active tectonics as well as structural deformation, all of which could be affected of climate change and human interaction. To magnify the impact of the project, the approach will be implemented in more than 400 sites on the UNESCO World Heritage List (WHL) in geographical Europe. After the remote sensing investigation, detailed geological interpretation, hazard analysis, local-scale monitoring, advanced modelling and field surveying for the most critical sites will be carried out to discover the cause and extent of the observed motions. PROTHEGO (PROTection of European Cultural HEritage from GeO-hazards) is a collaborative research project funded in the framework of the Joint Programming Initiative on Cultural Heritage and Global Change (JPICH) – Heritage Plus in 2015–2018.

Keywords: Cultural heritage · Geo-harzards · InSAR · UNESCO

© Springer International Publishing AG 2016
M. Ioannides et al. (Eds.): EuroMed 2016, Part II, LNCS 10059, pp. 91–98, 2016.
DOI: 10.1007/978-3-319-48974-2_11

1 Introduction

Cultural heritage sites are continuously impacted by several environmental and anthropogenic factors, including climate change, precipitation, natural hazards, wars, etc. [1–4]. However, there is limited data available regarding the effects of geo-hazards on cultural heritage sites. This paper presents the PROTHEGO project, which uses radar interferometry to monitor surface deformation with mm precision to analyze the impact of geo-hazards in cultural heritage sites in Europe. PROTHEGO uses novel space technology based on radar interferometry (InSAR) to retrieve information on ground stability and motion in the 400 + UNESCO's World Heritage List monuments and sites of Europe as shown in Fig. 1 [3, 4]. PROTHEGO provides a new, low-cost methodological approach for the safe management of cultural heritage monuments and sites located in Europe. The project will apply InSAR techniques to monitor monuments and sites that are potentially unstable due to landslides, sinkholes, settlement, subsidence, active tectonics as well as structural deformation, all of which can be effected of climate change and human interaction. The research methodology is focused on long-term low-impact monitoring systems as well as indirect analysis of environmental contexts to investigate changes and decay of structure, material and landscape.

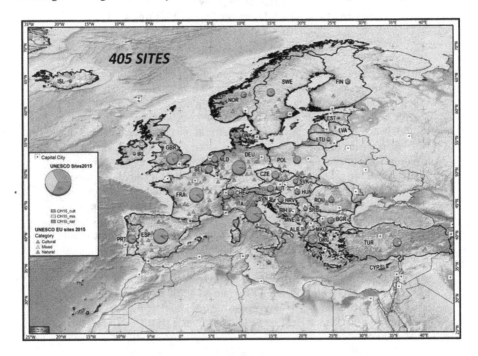

Fig. 1. UNESCO world heritage sites in Europe

In the past decades, it was widely recognized that cultural heritage can be highly vulnerable to geological disasters induced by earthquakes, volcanoes, floods and catastrophic landslides. As well, cultural heritage is vulnerable to other non-catastrophic slow-onset geohazards that can slowly affect the integrity and accessibility of the heritage, such as slow-moving landslides, sinkholes, ground settlement and active tectonics. Even if these phenomena can be responsible for large damages, they are largely neglected in the literature [5–7]. The long-term vulnerability of Cultural Heritage is commonly focused on the heritage itself (i.e., degradation and corrosion of building materials) in response to environmental risks [8, 9], without fully considering or understanding the entire geological-geotechnical context.

The innovation of the PROTHEGO project lies in the explicit focus on the context that controls slow-onset hazards responsible for cultural heritage damages. Since natural hazards, differently from catastrophic events, can be identified in advance, monitored and efficiently mitigated, the outcome of the project could be extremely useful for the protection of Cultural Heritage. Historically, surveying and monitoring of Cultural Heritage has been done through ground-based techniques, such as photogrammetry, laser scanning, and topographic surveying [10]. However, these on site techniques frequently fail in the recognition of the wider geological context. Currently, satellite technology can assist cultural heritage scientists to enhance their understanding of land deformation processes and geological hazards. By examining vast regions of interest from 800 km above the Earth's surface, Synthetic Aperture Radar (SAR) imaging satellites, Interferometric SAR (InSAR) and Persistent Scatterers (PS) processing techniques [11–13] are capable of estimating, with up to millimetre precision, subtle and non-catastrophic, long-term and seasonal land processes that are triggered by a variety of natural and anthropogenic causes and drivers that can cause damage to the tangible heritage. Once vulnerable sites are identified by InSar, detailed geological interpretation, hazard analysis, local-scale monitoring, advanced modeling and field surveying for the most critical sites will be carried out to discover cause and extent of the observed motions.

2   Research Design and Methodology

The PROTHEGO research design and its interdisciplinary approach for the protection and conservation of cultural heritage includes the following key aspects:

(1) The multi-scale methodology proposed in PROTHEGO will integrate (a) continent-scale satellite radar interferometry analysis of ground deformation, (b) GIS analysis of existing European geo-hazard datasets, (c) local-scale monitoring, (d) site-specific numerical modelling of geological and geotechnical hazards associated to cultural heritage sites.

(2) Radar interferometry is capable of monitoring surface deformation with mm precision. Time motion history of selected ground based persistent scatters (PS) will be analysed and systematically interpreted (up to hundreds of PS for each site), and applied to the more than 450 UNESCO world heritage sites in geographical Europe, in order to test the methodology and then to be transferred into national operational level. This will allow the recognition of cultural heritage sites affected by ground motions, which could possibly endanger the heritage.

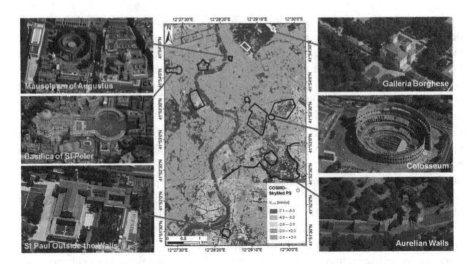

Fig. 2. Historic centre of Rome Italy

(3) The radar interferometry results will be interpreted with the support of existing geo-hazard datasets (landslides, floods, active faults, etc.) in order to reach a first under-standing of possible causes and to classify the heritage sites according to the typology of vulnerability to geo-hazards. For this, a multicriteria analysis will be developed, together with a new taxonomy of heritage vulnerability. As a result, the most critical heritage sites will be identified, classified and ranked in terms of vulnerability.

(4) Several demonstration sites across Europe in the countries of the PL and PIs, including the Historic Centre of Rome in Italy (Fig. 2), Alhambra in Spain (Fig. 3), Derwent Valley Mills in the UK (Fig. 4) and Choirokoitia in Cyprus (Fig. 5) will be selected to test the integration of methodologies. Respective key Stakeholders and practitioners in the heritage preservation and conservation sectors, as well as academia have also been invited to join the Demonstration Sites Stakeholder group, to provide support in the interpretation of the data, calibration of the methodology, and definition of requirements and standards.

(5) Detailed field surveys and geo-hazard investigations will be implemented for several different critical sites underlined from continent-scale analysis, at least one in each involved Country, to validate the remotely sensed ground/monument defor-mation and to understand the causes and the possible evolution. The sites will be selected to be representative of different vulnerability conditions (i.e., different classes in the vulnerability taxonomy). The local-scale monitoring will focus on non-invasive techniques in order to limit aesthetic and functional impacts on the heritage site.

(6) The local-scale monitoring data will be the base for the development of geological and geotechnical modelling of the investigated sites. This activity will be performed by using advanced numerical modelling tools (e.g. finite element analysis), which will provide evolution models for the deformation processes affecting the heritage

Fig. 3. Alhambra, Granada Spain

Fig. 4. Derwent Valley Mills, UK

Fig. 5. Choirokoitia, Cyprus

sites in order to recognize the best mitigation strategies and to evaluate the effectiveness of these strategies under different future scenarios, also including the effect of Climate Change. Particular attention will be devoted to non-invasive and low-impact mitigation techniques.

The PROTHEGO project is divided into 6 separate work packages (WP) to analyze the impact of geo-hazards in cultural heritage sites in Europe, as summarized in Fig. 6.

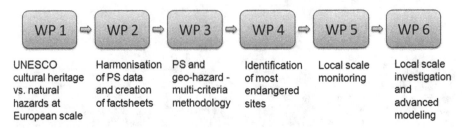

| WP 1 | ⇨ | WP 2 | ⇨ | WP 3 | ⇨ | WP 4 | ⇨ | WP 5 | ⇨ | WP 6 |

UNESCO cultural heritage vs. natural hazards at European scale

Harmonisation of PS data and creation of factsheets

PS and geo-hazard - multi-criteria methodology

Identification of most endangered sites

Local scale monitoring

Local scale investigation and advanced modeling

Fig. 6. PROTHEGO work packages

The methodology of the PROTHEGO project is to analyse the state of the art concerning UNESCO World Heritage List (WHL) sites and geo-hazards at European scale. All European UNESCO WHL sites are analysed in terms of potential causative factors and triggering mechanisms for natural hazards, acting in the surrounding of each cultural heritage site. From this analysis, a geo-database is created of European UNESCO Heritage at risk. Once the geo-database is created, all available InSAR and PS datasets for the European UNESCO WHL sites are collected. The PROTHEGO project then gathers and homogenises the recent information on ground stability from existing satellite InSAR ground motion datasets generated by the over 10 year-long project ESA-GMES-Terrafirma [14–16]. A detailed analysis of available InSAR and PS datasets and derived products is undertaken in order to assess a general and preliminary overview of useful coverage at European scale. The InSAR and PS datasets are analysed in order to create hands-on digital factsheets showing the observed ground motion scenario of each WHL site over the past two decades. In addition, a GIS-based multi-criteria analysis is implemented to identify and, when possible, to rank the most critical UNESCO Cultural Heritage sites at the European scale. The multi-criteria methodology developed is implemented across all UNESCO WHL sites for which both PS data and geo-hazard information are available, and a hazard level map at the European scale will be generated. The demonstration sites of the Historic Centre of Rome in Italy, Alhambra in Spain, Derwent Valley Mills in the UK and Choirokoitia in Cyprus are used to calibrate the methodology.

Based on the results of the demonstration site, the methodology is validated through detailed local-scale analysis of type of Heritage Vs type of natural hazard. As a result, best practices and identification of cultural heritage in critical condition are defined, with particular reference to the interaction between structure vs the geological and geotechnical settings. In-situ observation, as well remote sensing, mainly PS techniques, are used to validate the impact of natural hazards. Topographic surveying (e.g. differential GPS, total station) and InSAR data are used in order to map slow movements, and compared and validated with ground based geotechnical monitoring, to evaluate cultural heritage sites deformation trend and to understand its behaviour over the last two decades. Finally, advanced modelling analysis are conducted that will focus on numerical modelling of geo-physical processes responsible for hazard (e.g. slope deformation, settlements, rock weathering, tectonic deformation, rock-fall); simulation of potential future scenarios of evolution of these processes, including the contribution of climate change; simulation of the response of the site to different mitigation actions and assessment of the effectiveness of these actions for cultural heritage protection.

3 Conclusions

The results of the PROTHEGO project to date include the risk analysis on European WHL sites for natural hazards including earthquakes, volcanoes, tsunamis, changes to ocean waters, storms, floods, drought, desertification, temperature change, other climate change impact, avalanche/landslide, erosion, siltation/deposition and fires (wildfires). A risk vector compared each natural hazard on both 1st level and 2nd level multi-criteria analysis to UNESCO WHL sites.

PROTHEGO provides a new low cost remote sensing tool and a new methodological approach, for the safety management of cultural heritage, covering monuments and sites located in Europe. The outcomes of PROTHEGO support correct planning and rebalancing the contrast between endogenous (structural and materials decay, the societal development, the anthropogenic pressure) and surrounding exogenous forces (natural hazards acting on the heritage) affecting the European cultural heritage. The expected results of the project include an updated European scenario and catalogue of UNESCO CH affected by Geo-hazards, a standardized methodology of geo-hazard Vs CH at European scale and geotechnical advanced model in selected portion and monitoring system implementation.

Acknowledgements. The "PROTection of European Cultural HEritage from GeO - hazards (PROTHEGO)" project HERITAGE PLUS/0314/36 is funded in the framework of the Joint Programming Initiative on Cultural Heritage and Global Change (JPICH) – HERITAGE PLUS under ERA-NET Plus and the Seventh Framework Programme (FP7) of the European Commission and the Cyprus Research Promotion Foundation, contract ΚΟΙΝΑ/ΠΚΠ-HERITAGE PLUS/0314/36.

References

1. Agapiou, A., Lysandrou, V., Themistocleous, K., Hadjimitsis, D.G.: Risk assessment of cultural heritage sites clusters using satellite imagery and GIS: the case study of Paphos District, Cyprus. J. Intl. Soc. Prev. Mit. Nat. Haz. **8**(1), 1–15 (2016). doi:10.1007/s11069-016-2211-6
2. Agapiou, A., Lysandrou, V., Alexakis, D.D., Themistocleous, K., Cuca, B., Sarris, A., Argyrou, N., Hadjimitsis, D.G.: Cultural heritage management and monitoring using remote sensing data and GIS: the case study of Paphos area, Cyprus. CEUS Comp. Env. Urb. Sys. **54**, 230–239 (2015). doi:10.1016/j.compenvurbsys.2015.09.003
3. Margottini, C., Spizzichino, D., Cigna, F., Crosta, G.B., Frattini, P., Themistocleous, K., Fernandez Merodo, J.A.: European UNESCO cultural heritage and geo – hazards: the PROTHEGO project. In: Proceeding of the Fourth International Conference on Remote Sensing and Geo-information of Environment, 4–8 April 2016, Paphos, Cyprus (2016)

4. Themistocleous, K., Cuca, B., Agapiou A., Lysandrou, V., Tzouvaras, M., Michaelides, S., Hadjimitsis, D.G., Margottini, C., Cigna, F., Crosta, G., Fernandez Merodo, J.A.: The protection of cultural heritage sites from geo-hazards. In: Proceeding of the European Geosciences Union General Assembly, 17-22 April 2016, Austria, Vienna (2016)

5. Gutiérrez, F., Cooper, A.H.: Evaporite dissolution subsidence in the historical city of Calatayud, Spain: damage appraisal and prevention. Nat. Haz. **25**(3), 259–288 (2002)

6. Rohn, J., Ehret, D., Moser, M., Czurda, K.: Prehistoric and recent mass movements of the World Cultural Heritage Site Hallstatt. Austria. Env. Geol. **47**(5), 702–714 (2005)

7. Canuti, P., Margottini, C., Fanti, R., Bromhead, E.N.: Cultural heritage and landslides: research for risk prevention and conservation. In: Sassa, K., Canuti, P. (eds.) Landslides–Disaster Risk Reduction, pp. 401–433. Springer, Heidelberg (2009)

8. Brimblecombe, P.: Air pollution and architecture, past, present and future. J Archit Conserv **6**, 30–46 (2000)

9. Fort, R., de Buergo, M.A., Gomez-Heras, M., Vazquez-Calvo, C. (eds.): Heritage, Weathering and Conservation. In: Proceeding International Heritage Weathering *and* Conservation Conference (HWC-2006), 21–24 June 2006, Madrid, Spain. CRC Press (2006)

10. Andrews, D., Mills, J., Bryan, P., Bedford, J., Blake, B., Barber, D.: Metric survey specifications for cultural heritage. English Heritage Archaeological Monographs (2009). ISBN: 9781848021716

11. Rosen, P.A., Hensley, S., Joughin, I.R., Fuk, K.L., Madsen, S.N., Rodriguez, E., et al.: Synthetic aperture radar interferometry. Proc. IEEE **88**, 33–382 (2000)

12. Ferretti, A., Prati, C., Rocca, F.: Permanent scatterers in SAR interferometry. IEEE Trans. Geosc. Rem. Sens. **39**(1), 8–20 (2001)

13. Crosetto, M., Monserrat, O., Iglesias, R., Crippa, B.: Persistent scatterer interferometry: Potential, limits and initial C- and X-band comparison. Photogr. Eng. Rem. Sens. **76**, 1061–1069 (2010)

14. Bianchini, S., Cigna, F., Del Ventisette, C., Moretti, S., Casagli, N.: Monitoring landslide-induced displacements with TerraSAR-X Persistent Scatterer Interferometry (PSI): Gimigliano case study in Calabria Region (Italy). Intl. J. Geosc. **4**(10), 1467–1482 (2013). doi:10.4236/ijg.2013.410144

15. Tapete, D., Cigna, F.: Rapid mapping and deformation analysis over cultural heritage and rural sites based on Persistent Scatterer Interferometry. Intl. J. Geophys., Article ID 618609, p. 19 (2012). doi:10.1155/2012/618609

16. Cigna, F., Lasaponara, R., Masini, N., Milillo, P., Tapete, D.: Persistent scatterer interferometry processing of COSMO-SkyMed StripMap HIMAGE time series to depict deformation of the historic centre of Rome, Italy. Rem.Sens. **6**(12), 12593–12618 (2014). doi:10.3390/rs61212593

Sensing the Risk: New Approaches and Technologies for Protection and Security of Cultural Heritage. The "PRO_CULT" Project

N. Masini, F.T. Gizzi, M. Biscione[(✉)], M. Danese, A. Pecci, M.R. Potenza, M. Scavone, and M. Sileo

Institute of Archaeological and Monumental Heritage,
National Research Council (IBAM CNR), C. da S. Loja, 85050 Potenza, Italy
m.biscione@ibam.cnr.it

Abstract. The PRO_CULT project promotes the development and the use of innovative low cost methodology for both monitoring and protecting cultural heritage and the growth of a cultural identity of local communities. It aims to develop sensing technologies and operating procedures in the field of security and the preservation of artistic, archaeological, architectural and landscape heritage with particular reference to emergency situations and to involve new different end users types. This approach has led to the release of products, technologies and operational methods, low cost and user-friendly paying attention to accessibility, sustainability, and citizen participation [1].

Keywords: Diagnostics · Monitoring · ICT · Cultural heritage protection · Risk

1 Introduction

The evaluation and analysis of risks, natural (seismic, hydrogeological, volcanic, and environmental) and man-made (clandestine excavation, urbanization), which affect the monumental and archaeological heritage is a prioritary and strategic aim of international bodies such as ICCROM (International Centre for the Study of the Preservation and Restoration of Cultural Property), UNESCO (United Nations Educational, Scientific and Cultural Organization), ICOMOS (International Council on Monuments and Sites) and WHC (World Heritage Centre). International guidelines suggest that a true action of contrast to the risks must necessarily include the development of prevention strategies as well as the post-disaster management.

In line with these indications and the objectives of the Regional Operational Programme ERDF 2007/2013 program and the Lisbon Strategy, the Institute of Archaeological and Monumental Heritage of the Italian National Research Council (CNR-IBAM) by means of PRO_CULT Project, financed by Basilicata Region, has sought to build around security innovation, conservation of cultural heritage and ICT a knowledge economy with particular reference to:

© Springer International Publishing AG 2016
M. Ioannides et al. (Eds.): EuroMed 2016, Part II, LNCS 10059, pp. 99–106, 2016.
DOI: 10.1007/978-3-319-48974-2_12

1. monitor the critical conditions and dangers present both in ordinary as well as in post-disaster emergency phase, with particular reference to monuments and works of art (paintings, sculptures);
2. estimate the dynamic properties of buildings and the hazardous static-structural conditions of monuments;
3. monitor by remote control the material decay of historical built heritage.

That being stated, this paper will go through the manifold activities performed in the PRO_CULT framework during 2012–2015, paying also attention to the discussion of the project outcomes.

2   Monitoring the Critical Conditions and Dangers Present Both in Ordinary as Well as in Post-disaster Emergency Phase

2.1   ZbSens: Risk Management and Smart Monitoring System to Protect Artistic Heritage in a Post-disaster Emergency Phase

The number of artworks that are dispersed when they are moved to the safety immediately after emergency occurrences (earthquakes, floods, fires) or those that are stolen (because they are positioned in not-protected places) cannot be quantified; however, the risk to which they are exposed is very high. Therefore, in order to propose methods and tools to protect movable cultural heritage from theft and dispersion, we decided to apply technologies widely used to draw commercial products (i.e. food or transport), integrating them with Location Based Services [2] and Open Sources applications [3]. In particular, a monitoring system for artistic heritage risk management for two main high-risk scenarios (theft and earthquakes) was designed and built. Such system, named ZbSens, includes two different modules: (i) one static, ensuring the identification and the indoor artworks presence or position, (ii) the second one dynamic, which guarantees the artwork identification and signals its outdoor traceability. ZbSens is comprehensive and flexible to the needs of the artwork or context type. In particular it allows to:

- sign each mobile artworks a unique identifier profile;
- draw the box and ensure the transfer, so as to avoid dispersion;
- alert promptly in case of unlawful abduction or displacement;
- facilitate the recovery and subsequent reintegration into the load-from context even after many years.

In addition, great attention was paid to how to apply sensors on artworks. In fact, they are not to be visible to thieves and vandals, non invasive and easily removable [4]. The employed modules use RFID and wireless sensors and, as communication or location protocols, ZigBee, GPS and GPRS and GSM network. The management system for these two different products is low cost and user friendly in order to keep costs down as much as possible and ensure their wide-scale use an Open Source platform, using applications of GFOSS (Geospatial Free and Open Source Software), was developed. It is sufficient to have a browser and be able to surf on the web to check protected cultural heritage: in this way the end user (from the parish priest to the police or the responsible for the movement of artworks) can use it easily and automatically raise the alarm. Furthermore, the addition of sensors to detect temperature or humidity also ensures environmental monitoring. The small size and the low cost of implementation of the sensors make ZbSens a non-invasive system, suitable for environments with high artistic values allowing, at the same time, a quick analysis of the environmental context in case of high-risk of material decay [5].

2.2 Citizens as Actors in Heritage Safeguard: The SAVEHER APP

In recent years there has been a rapid spreading of applications for mobile devices (tablets and smart phones) with use in different fields such as medicine, engineering, economy, biology, etc. In the wide range of uses, the mobile applications can have a significant role for purposes related to the disclosure and dissemination of tourism contents relevant to cultural heritage [6]. The applications allow, in fact, being more performing than traditional information tools (e.g. websites, audio guides, and information brochures) thanks to the services based on the geographical location and image recognitions. The characteristic common to most of these applications is, however, the absence of a primary role of end-user. The user, in fact, is always considered as passive actor that's he/she "undergoes" the information, does not generate it. Reversing the point of view, users/citizens should be asked to perform, through the use of the tools provided by ICT, an important role in the protection of artistic and architectural heritage. As a matter of fact, an essential element for smart interventions on cultural heritage is to count on a widespread network of "sentries" scattered over the territory: this role can be performed well by citizens and tourists by involving them in the "monitoring" of monuments. Another ingredient to make the safeguard actions fast is just the use of New Information Computer Technologies (ICT) that offers new opportunities. With this in mind, we planned and developed *SAVHER* (http://www.appsaveheritage.com), an App that puts at community's disposal an innovative tool that allows citizens/tourists to interact with institutions [7]. Through *SAVHER* mobile application, the institutions can get in real time and free of charge the information sent by users about the problems affecting the heritage. Moreover, the data collected by the mobile application could be useful for everyone who is interested in the field of cultural heritage. The free-of-charge application was developed for mobile devices such as smartphones and/or tablets. To make the application cross-platform we used the *Cordova Phonegap* by *Apache Software Foundation*©. This application works through eight main steps: (1) the users become conscious that the monument they are visiting is affected by a problem; (2) the users take a picture of the affected monument by *SAVEHER*; (3) the mobile application stores the user's location; (4) the users answer a simple questionnaire which consists of questions aimed to identify the problems observed, such as vandalism, damage after extreme weather events, the effects of an earthquake or landslide; (5) all the data (georeferenced photos and the replies to the questionnaire) are sent to a remote server (cloud) that manages the information; (6) the website administrator checks the information quality and reliability; (7) the data (with credits) are published on-line on a dedicate public web page (http://www.appsaveheritage.com/) where a map will indicate both the location of the affected monument and the report on it; (8) the institution in charge of safeguarding the monuments/works art visualizes the report and starts-up proper intervention actions.

3   Estimating the Dynamic Properties of Buildings and the Hazardous Static-Structural Conditions of Monuments

3.1   Building Features and Safeguard of Church Towers

The safeguard of historical heritage is a challenge that engages more and more scientists and stakeholders. To achieve the purpose it is essential to know in-depth the features of the monuments to put into the field proper actions to mitigate the risks. Among these, particular consideration should be paid to monuments located in sites where the seismic hazard is high such as the Mediterranean area and Italy particularly that alone hosts about three-quarters of the worldwide cultural heritage.

With this in mind, we performed a research activity aimed at using non-invasive and non-destructive technique to investigate the features of a special built heritage, the church bell-towers [8]. The research activity has considered two major aspects.

The first aspect looks at the estimation of the fundamental periods of the bell-towers and their comparison with the dynamic features of the foundation soils on which the heritage itself is founded. In this way, potential resonance phenomena that can be responsible of possible building damage increase during future earthquake shaking can be highlighted. The fundamental periods of the bell-towers and the soils are estimated through the measurements of the ambient noise vibrations. The techniques used to get the dynamic values of the towers are both the Horizontal to Horizontal Spectral Ratio (HHSR) and the Horizontal to Vertical Spectral Ratio (HVSR). The latter technique is also adopted to evaluate the main frequency of the soil and, therefore, to detect possible soil-structure resonance (with respect to HVSR technique applications see [9]; with specific regard to cultural heritage see [10].

The second aspect considers the relationship between the fundamental frequency as derived by the experimental analysis and the Finite Element (FE) modeling. Therefore, the Finite Element model has been set up with the aim to reproduce the results of ambient vibration measurements and to identify the elastic modulus of masonry. In order to reach the aim, we have taken into account, through in situ survey, the architectonic-constructive-geometric features of the monuments, such as the height of the towers and number of storeys, the building materials, the dimensions and presence of openings, tie rods, and adjoining buildings.

The final purpose of the research that will go also on in the next months is to setup a typological classification of such special built heritage, so contributing to their knowledge and, there, safeguard. That will be reached once performed the surveys and the computer-aided analyses of a statistically significant number of bell-towers each of them having structural, architectonic and dimensional features different from each other. For this purpose, the area considered for this research is the Basilicata region (Southern Italy), located in an area characterized by a high seismic hazard.

3.2   Innovative Monitoring of Monuments to Detect Hazardous Static-Structural Conditions

Building materials are subjected to ageing or fatigue that can lead to failure phenomena. This is especially suitable when we take into account the monuments and historical buildings that are made up of materials subject to loads (static or dynamic) over a long time. The use of Acoustic Emission (AE) technique can be a useful tool to detect in advance critical problems affecting materials under stress.

In detail, the ultrasonic acoustic technique is an approach based on the detection of acoustic emission produced over the frequency of 15–20 kHz. The technique can be passive or active [11]. The first is based on the detection of the spontaneous wave emission phenomena by materials and it is used to detect fracture events during structural loading; the second, that is used to detect sub-surface flaws, refers to the acoustic wave generation by a transmitter and their recording by a receiver after the waves passed through the sample to be analyzed.

In order to evaluate the potentiality of AE technique to detect potential hazardous static-structural problems, we carried out an AE monitoring in Santa Maria Assunta Cathedral located in Tricarico (Matera, Basilicata region) (Fig. 1). The monitoring was performed in collaboration with SME S.r.l. (Security Materials Environment, Rome). The Tricarico Cathedral dating back to the XI century and it was damaged by several historical earthquakes, among which those of 1694, 1857, 1930 and 1980.

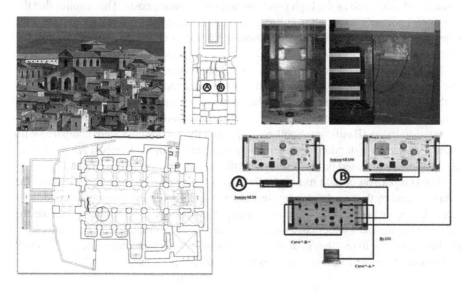

Fig. 1. AE multi-channel system used to monitor the acoustic emission in the pillar of the Cathedral of Santa Maria Assunta (Tricarico, Basilicata)

As a consequence of these natural extreme events, the structure underwent several restorations/interventions. Especially after the 1980 earthquake the pillars and the walls exhibited structural problems with different degree of severity as evidenced by diagnostics investigations based on georadar and seismic investigations [12]. Recently (2013), the vertical structures and the arches were involved in consolidation and rein-forcement works through injections and the vaults were consolidated by the application of a reinforced concrete jacket at the extradoses.

AE monitoring was conducted with the aim of investigating the response of one of the pillars of the Cathedral on which consolidation works were carried. Two sensors of low (15 kHz, LF) and high frequency (150 kHz, HF) were used to detect the acoustic emission. The monitoring was performed from March 2014 to February 2015.

The analysis of AE raw data as well as the use of more sophisticated investigations (e.g.: "hammer effect", [13]) to correlate the acoustic emissions with the possible causes (such as the microclimate thermo-hygrometric parameters, seismic events occurred in the area, static stress change due to the recent consolidation works, etc.) is still ongoing. Preliminary results of HF-AE analysis show as daily temperature range affects the trend and amount of the recorded AE. Further studies will pay particular attention to LF-AE, the frequencies that can be more useful to detect the "state of health" of the cathedral.

4   Monitoring by Remote Control the Material Decay of Historical Built Heritage

The environmental monitoring system apparently appears to be an easy tool, but it hides some drawbacks such as the high purchase and maintenance costs. This implies that the use of technologies to monitor cultural heritage is somewhat limited to analyze sites where the decay conditions are of particular relevance or the importance of cultural heritage assumes special relevance.

Starting from this point of view, a prototype to monitor the indoor microclimate environment of monuments was planned, taking into account the low cost (LC) approach as the basic assumption. In order to evaluate the LC performance, the system was tested in relationship with the decay problems affecting the paintings of the crypt of St. Francis of Assisi in Irsina (Basilicata, Southern Italy) and the survey data were compared with those recorded by a standard commercial product. In detail, the low cost Arduino wire-less platform was based on open source hardware and user friendly software.

The comparison of data has highlighted an almost complete matching between the data collected by the two different systems so as to identify the environmental conditions (e.g.: dew point) critical for suitable heritage conservation [5]. In order to reduce the barriers that prevent a wider large-scale use of microclimate monitoring, the outlook for the future impose to test that system in different indoor monumental contexts. This will be the aim of further research activities that are still in progress.

5   Conclusions

The first stages of PRO_CULT project was devoted to the overview of technologies, methods and approaches for the risk assessing and monitoring of cultural heritage. However, this overview put in evidence some problems which make not possible their full operational use in the field of cultural heritage. The discussion followed was the stimulus for the creation of new tools, techniques and operational protocols that rely on the technological and 'human' sensors to get information about heritage risk. Some of the products realized fulfill a certain type of cultural asset or to a specific requirement (ZbSens system for tracking and protecting movable works of art). As a whole, the project has allowed to develop two prototypes, a patent, protocols, algorithms with a particular attention to costs and friendly use for end users not experts in science and technology. To this aim, before the activities of research and technological development and validation it was important to define *a priori* with end user requirements, needs and application areas. This was, for example, the case of the two monitoring systems of material decay and static-structural conditions.

The choice of pilot projects has played a fundamental role for the validation of prototypes and procedures. The field work have allowed to evaluate their effectiveness of products, making it possible their continuous improvement and sometimes also expanding the possible applications, as in the case of sensors Zgbee, designed as a system for tracking and then also capable to measure environmental parameters.

The relation between Science/Technology and cultural heritage is not only seen as Science/Technology at the service of the cultural heritage. Cultural heritage in its turn is ever more a privileged area-laboratory where experimenting new technologies and methodologies of analysis to be used also for other civil applications.

References

1. Gizzi, F.T., Masini, N. (eds.): Salvaguardia, Conservazione e Sicurezza del Patrimonio Culturale, nuove metodologie e tecnologie operative, a cura di, Zaccara Editore, Lagonegro (PZ), Novembre 2015 (2015). ISBN: 978-88-995-2000-7
2. Labrador, M., Michael, K., Küpper, A.: Advanced location-based services. Comput. Commun. **31**(6), 1053–1054 (2008)
3. Biscione, M., Danese, M., Masini, N.: Un approccio operativo e a basso costo alla protezione del Patrimonio artistico: il sistema ZbSens. In: Gizzi, F.T., Masini, N. (eds.) Salvaguardia, Conservazione e Sicurezza del Patrimonio Culturale. Nuove metodologie e tecnologie operative - Zaccara Editore, Lagonegro (PZ), pp. 225–240 (2015). ISBN: 978-88-995-2000-7
4. Biscione, M., Danese, M., Masini, N., Fachechi, L., Bellusci, D., Lorenzetti, W.: Artworks in high-risk context: integrated and low cost approach to theft and dispersion protection. In: Rogerio-Candelera, M.A. (ed.) TecnoHeritage 2014, Science, Technology and Cultural Heritage. Proceedings of the TechnoHeritage International Congress on Science and Technology for the Conservation of Cultural Heritage II, 24–27 Giugno, Siviglia, Spagna, pp. 397–402. CRC Press (2014)
5. Sileo, M., Gizzi, F.T., Masini, N., Biscione, M., Boccia, M.P.: Approcci low-cost al monitoraggio microclimatico di ambienti confinati: il caso della Cripta di S. Francesco in Irsina (Matera). In: Gizzi, F.T., Masini, N. (eds.) Salvaguardia, Conservazione e Sicurezza del Patrimonio Culturale. Nuove metodologie e tecnologie operative, Zaccara Editore, Lagonegro (PZ), pp. 53–94 (2015). ISBN: 978-88-995-2000-7
6. Dowling, C., Whalen, M.: ARCH-APP: the city as classroom builder. In: Proceedings of INTED 2014 Conference, Valencia, Spain, 10–12 March 2014, pp. 3729–3739 (2014). ISBN: 978-84-616-8412-0, http://www.mimiwhalen.net/wpcontent/uploads/2013/12/Inted-2014-Paper.pdf. Accessed 7 Sept 2015

7. Gizzi, F.T., Biscione, M., Danese, M., Deufemia, V., Masini, M., Murgante, B., Paolino, L., Saulino, N., Sileo, M., Potenza, M.R.: SAVHER - an app for smart and community-shared approaches to the safeguard of cultural heritage. In: Proceedings of the 4th EARSeL Workshop on "Remote Sensing for Cultural Heritage", Matera, Italy, 6–7 June 2013, pp. 251–260 (2013). ISBN: 9788889693254

8. Gizzi, F.T., Liberatore, D., Masini, N., Sileo, M., Zotta, C., Potenza, M.R., Scavone, M., Sorrentino, L., Bruno, M.: Building features and safeguard of church towers in Basilicata (Southern Italy). In: Rogerio-Candelera, M.A. (ed.) TecnoHeritage 2014, Science, Technology and Cultural Heritage. Proceedings of the TechnoHeritage International Congress on Science and Technology for the Conservation of Cultural Heritage II, 24–27 Giugno, Siviglia, Spagna, pp. 369–374. CRC Press (2014)

9. Mucciarelli, M., Gallipoli, M.R.: A critical review of ten years of HVSR technique. Bollettino di Geofisica Teorica e Applicata **42**, 255–266 (2002)

10. Liberatore, D., Mucciarelli, M., Gallipoli, M.R., Masini, N.: Two applications of the HVSR technique to cultural heritage and historical masonry. In: Mucciarelli, M., Herak, M., Cassidy, J. (eds.) Increasing Seismic Safety by Combining Engineering Technologies and Seismological Data, pp. 325–336. Springer, Heidelberg (2008). ISBN: 978-1-4020-9196-4

11. Paparo, G., Gregori, G.P.: L'emissione Acustica come strumento diagnostico di deformazioni di strutture. Giornale delle Prove non Distruttive, n. 4, Dicembre 2001 (2001)

12. Leucci, G., Masini, N., Persico, R., Soldovieri, F.: GPR and sonic tomography for structural restoration: the case of the cathedral of Tricarico. J. Geophys. Eng. **8**(3), 76–92 (2011). doi: 10.1088/1742-2132/8/3/S08

13. Gregori, G.P., Lupieri, M., Paparo, G., Poscolieri, M., Ventrice, G., Zanini, A.: Ultrasound monitoring of applied forcing material ageing, and catastrophic yield of crustal structures. Nat. Hazards Earth Syst. Sci. **7**, 723–731 (2007). http://www.nat-hazards-earth-syst-sci.net/7/723/2007/

Intangible Cultural Heritage
Documentation

The Europeana Sounds Music Information Retrieval Pilot

Alexander Schindler[1]([⊠]), Sergiu Gordea[1], and Harry van Biessum[2]

[1] Digital Insight Lab, Digital Safety and Security Department,
Austrian Institute of Technology, Vienna, Austria
{alexander.schindler,sergiu.gordea}@ait.ac.at
[2] Research and Development, Netherlands Institute for Sound and Vision,
Hilversum, The Netherlands
hvbiessum@beeldengeluid.nl

Abstract. This paper describes the realization of a Music Information Retrieval (MIR) pilot for a huge audio corpora of European cultural sound heritage, which was developed as part of the Europeana Sounds project. The demonstrator aimed at evaluating the applicability of technologies deriving from the MIR domain to content provided by various European digital libraries and audio archives. To approach this aim, a query-by-example functionality was implemented using audio-content based similarity search. The development was preceded by an elaborated evaluation of the Europeana Sounds collection to assess appropriate combinations of music content descriptors that are capable to effectively discriminate the various types of audio-content provided within the dataset. The MIR-pilot was evaluated both by using an automatic and a user based evaluation. The results showed that the quality of the implemented query-by-example algorithm is comparable to state-of-the-art music similarity approaches reported in literature.

1 Introduction

The Europeana Sounds project aims at emphasizing on Europe's cultural audio heritage by aggregating content provided by 20 partner institutions including digital libraries and audio archives. The descriptions of the contributed audio content is made accessible to the public through the Europeana portal. Moreover, the object descriptions and Web Links to the media files are also available through a public API, making these data-sets reusable for 3rd party applications and for research purposes. The aggregated sound content ranges from music to interviews, animal or ambient sounds, broadcasts, news, etc. This high variety of content, the large number of audio items - more than 350.000 items - and the various languages used to describe it (i.e. there are 28 languages used in Europeana) states a problem concerning the retrieve-ability of the provided content. Although the items are rich in descriptive meta-data, these descriptions are often not sufficient to support sophisticated search scenarios or (musicological) research. Simple queries like finding recordings by artist name or a certain year

© Springer International Publishing AG 2016
M. Ioannides et al. (Eds.): EuroMed 2016, Part II, LNCS 10059, pp. 109–117, 2016.
DOI: 10.1007/978-3-319-48974-2_13

are well supported by the prevalent retrieval system. More complex scenarios, like searching for contemporary music that was inspired by a classical composer or music style would certainly be problematic, as this information is not available in the meta-data. Especially in the case of music recordings, it is not feasible to describe in details the quality and the emotions generated by particular tunes. Within this paper we present the Music Information Retrieval (MIR) Pilot developed within the scope of the Europeana Sounds project with the aim to develop alternative search and exploration functionality for the sound content available in Europeana. The content based search algorithms are aiming at helping end users to overcome various barriers like the language, the domain expertise such as knowing in advance the name of specific music genres like *Tarantella*, and the lack of extensive content description. This demonstrator has the goal of evaluating the feasibility of implementing effective audio retrieval services for this large and heterogeneous sound data-set, while the main target is to provide a reliable service powering the content based retrieval in Europeana Music Collection[1]. A preliminary evaluation of the demonstrator was performed to quantify the accuracy of the proposed algorithm. As presented in Sect. 4 the experimental results are comparable with state of the art solutions applied on large music data-sets [6]. Furthermore, an user evaluation was carried out with the goal of measuring the user satisfaction when employing the system for completing special music retrieval tasks.

2   Europeana Sounds Data

For creating the development and evaluation data-set, meta-data descriptions of 400,615 items were collected via the Europeana API[2]. Out of these, 389,120 items included Web URLs pointing to the corresponding audio data. A part of these URLs were outdated, pointed to corrupt audio files, or they couldn't be processable by the audio feature extractors. The final dataset size of 312,096 records makes the relevance of this evaluation comparable to large scale experiments on the Million Song Data-set [6]. The statistical analysis by type of content shows that **Music** is by far the biggest category of the collection varying by style, instrumentation and recording quality. **Spoken Word** in form of interviews, radio news broadcast, public speeches, etc. **Animal Sounds** are field recordings of a wide range of animals. Recordings of **Radio Broadcasts**. These audio items are long mixed-content files. They consist of spoken content, music and radio commercials.

3   Implementation

In order to implement an effective retrieval algorithm, capable of providing a good accuracy over different types of audio content, appropriate feature set have

---

[1] http://europeana.eu/portal/collections/music.
[2] http://labs.europeana.eu/api.

been selected. Effective retrieval of different music styles needs to take in consideration various music properties such as timbre, rhythm and harmony, as well as their progression and variety over the complete performance. Different feature sets are known to work better on certain music genres, but to be inferior when applied on other genres. A further obstacle is the presence of old historic recordings for which, scratches and noise resulting from decaying media distort the feature values. *Spoken word* shows completely different spectral properties than *music* and thus require different audio features to distinguish them from music content. For *animal sounds* it was considered to be sufficient to match animals by the same family. A more detailed discrimination of animal sound was not required for this demonstration.

Fig. 1. User interface of the MIR pilot demonstration developed for Europeana Sounds.

3.1 Audio-Content Descriptors

The following audio-content descriptors were evaluated in preceding experiments:

- **Statistical Spectrum Descriptors (SSD)** subsequently computes seven statistical measures for the 24 critical bands of hearing. Mean, median, variance, skewness, kurtosis, min- and max-values, for different segments of a song are aggregated by calculating the median of the descriptors of all segments. SSDs are part of the *Psycho-acoustic Music Descriptors* as proposed by [5] and are based on a psycho-acoustically modified Sonogram representation that reflects human loudness sensation.
- **Rhythm Patterns (RP)** describe rhythmical characteristics by applying a discrete Fourier transform to the transformed Sonogram, resulting in a (time-invariant) spectrum of loudness amplitude modulation per modulation frequency for each individual critical band which provides a rough interpretation of the rhythmic energy of a song. For feature extraction we employed a Python-based implementation[3].
- **Mel Frequency Cepstral Coefficients (MFCC)** [8] are derived from speech recognition and also apply log-scale transformations to anneal the feature response to the human auditory systems. MFCCs are good descriptors of timbre.
- **Chroma** [8] features project the entire spectrum onto 12 bins representing the 12 distinct semitones of the musical octave. Both MFCC and Chroma were extracted using the well known MARSYAS toolset [8].
- **Root Mean Square (RMSE)** is a way of comparing arbitrary waveforms based upon their equivalent energy. The RMS method takes the square of the instantaneous voltage, before averaging, then takes the square root of the average.
- The **Spectral Centroid (SPEC CENT)** [8] is the frequency-weighted sum of the power spectrum, normalized by its unweighted sum. It determines the frequency area around which most of the signal energy concentrates and gives an indication of how *dark* or *bright* a sound is.
- **Tempo** measured in Beats per Minute (BPM) [2] is calculated from audio events which are detected in the audio signal.
- **TONNETZ** features [3] are able to detect changes in the harmonic content of musical audio signals based on a model for Equal Tempered Pitch Class Space using 12-bin Chroma vectors. Close harmonic relations such as fifths and thirds appear as small Euclidean distances. Peaks in the detection function denote transitions from one harmonically stable region to another.
- **Zero Crossing Rate (ZCR)** [8] measures the noise behavior of an audio-signal.

The summary of these feature sets together with their weighting for similarity computation is presented in Table 1.

---

[3] https://github.com/tuwien-musicir/rp_extract.

Table 1. Overview of the audio-content *descriptors*, their corresponding acoustic *categories*, their assigned feature weight *(f. W.)* as well as the cumulative category weight *(c. W.)*.

Category	Feature	Description	f. W.	c. W.
Timbre	MFCC	Timbre description	23 %	39 %
	SSD	General spectral description	8 %	
	SPEC CENT	Pitch description	8 %	
Rhythm	RP	Rhythmic patterns	18 %	25 %
	BPM	Tempo	7 %	
Harmony	CHROMA	Harmonic Scale	12 %	24 %
	TONNETZ	Traditional harmonic description	12 %	
Loudness	RMSE	Loudness description	9 %	9 %
Noise Behaviour	ZCR	Noisiness description	3 %	3 %

3.2 Composite Feature-Sets

Content based audio and music features attempt to capture certain aspects of music. To provide an ensemble description of a recorded music track it is required to make use of multiple features. The introduced audio features were grouped into the following five music properties which have been chosen to describe music similarity upon:

- **Timbre** is a fundamental property of music and generally reflects the instrumentation used during the performance. Timbre is often a good discriminator for music styles as well as moods expressed by a song.
- **Rhythm** is a similarly strong intrinsic music property.
- **Harmony** describes the tonality of a composition. In terms of an analytic perspective, it analyses how the spectral energy is distributed among a certain (usually western) scale.
- **Loudness** is actually not relevant for music similarity, it was considered referring to recent observations in contemporary music which tends to steadily increase on loudness [7]. By reducing the dynamic range the resulting sound is subjectively more attractive.
- **Noise Behavior** analysis refers to the different recording qualities of audio content. This captures the degradation of the original carriers such as shellac or wax tapes. Adding these features to the stack prefers performance over composition, and thus groups the records with similar sound quality.

3.3 Similarity Calculations

Exhaustive experimentation was applied using the audio features introduced in Sect. 3.1 and a selection of 18 distance measures discussed in [1]. No general pattern could be identified on which distance measure works best for all features. A general observation was that L1 based metrics usually rank high for the presented feature combinations. Among them the Canberra distance [4] includes an implicit normalization step. The Canberra distance was mostly top-ranked and provided stable results with increasing result list length. Thus, it was decided to use this distance measure for the MIR-pilot. A *late fusion* approach was used to combine the different feature-sets. The similarities are calculated for each feature separately and the distinct similarity values for each song are combined arithmetically. *Feature weighting* was applied to reduce overrated influence of distinct audio-descriptors. Feature weight estimation and optimization was approached empirically through a predefined set of similar records. During an iterative process the weights of the different features were adapted. The final feature weights used for the implementation are provided in Table 1.

3.4 User Interface

The user-interface was aligned to the design of the Europeana portal. The MIR pilot supports the following use cases:

- **Term-based queries** accept text-based input to query the meta-data to facilitate elementary means to explore the Europeana Sounds collection, or to search for content based on certain terms such as "blues", "love" or "piano".
- **Query by Example** through supplying an example song the system searches for similar ones based on their acoustic properties.
- **Usage of External Content to Query for Europeana Content**. To demonstrate further possibilities the query by example approach has been extended to accept also content which is not contained in the Europeana Sounds collection. The Soundcloud API[4] was used which facilitates computational access to the Soundcloud music streaming service. By supplying a Soundcloud URL the corresponding audio data is downloaded, processed and its calculated features are analyzed for similarity within the Europeana Sounds data-set.

4 Evaluation

The evaluation of the system was subdivided into a computational part which facilitated the automated evaluation of a large number of queries on a pre-defined ground truth, and a user-questionnaire part which focused on the overall user-perception of the system.

4.1 Automatic Evaluation

For the automatic evaluation the rich meta-data of the data-set has been analyzed to identify a set of semantically descriptive audio categories. The advantage

[4] https://developers.soundcloud.com.

of the data provided by Europeana is that all data items, including their corresponding meta-data, have been curated and edited by domain experts working for national libraries and audiovisual archives. The selected categories provide an overview of various, representative and well known music and sound genres available in the data-set. For each category the corresponding data-set items have been selected. Similar items have been calculated for each of them. The precision was measured by the number of items of the same category at different cut-off points. For very large categories the number of queries was randomly sub-sampled to 1000 items. Results presented in Table 2 describe precision values for queries of the five major categories (Jazz, Classic, Folk, Sounds, Spoken word) at different granularity. Generally it can be observed that spectral homogeneous tracks such as animal sounds and spoken word are better discriminated than polyphonic music. The calculated average precision of 28.7 % for all performed queries (including queries not listed in Table 2 is slightly above the top result of 27.4 % presented in [6] where k-nearest neighbors classification results on data-set only 12.2 % bigger than the Europeana data-set was reported. The results for k = 1 are equivalent to the similarity retrieval result at cut-off 1.

Table 2. Precision values for the computational evaluation at cut-off points 1,2,3,5,10. Abbreviations: #: number of class items; *Classic q.a.m.*: Classic quartet allegro major; *Flamenco Guit*: Flamenco + Guitarra; *A.S. Crickets*: Animal Sounds - Crickets

Query	#	1	2	3	5	10
Jazz	31801	38.0	35.0	31.4	31.7	28.6
Smooth Jazz	2419	49.1	45.9	43.8	25.8	20.8
Ragtime	57	24.6	15.8	12.3	7.3	3.6
Classical	28569	44.3	42.1	40.5	38.3	35.1
Classic G maj	304	17.1	14.8	14.0	12.6	9.3
Classic q.a.m	191	9.4	6.3	7.3	8.1	5.6
Piano Concerto	510	38.6	32.0	28.0	23.9	17.6
Requiem	463	32.6	26.9	22.0	16.2	10.7
Opera	8278	26.8	24.7	22.7	21.1	18.9
Operette	1081	27.7	22.9	20.8	17.3	14.6
Flamenco	1827	40.7	33.0	29.2	24.3	18.2
Flamenco Guit	287	22.3	17.1	15.3	13.5	10.0
Tarantella	152	33.6	28.0	22.4	16.1	8.5
Tango	3716	30.2	24.9	22.3	19.5	16.0
Animal Sounds	1097	89.7	87.0	85.1	82.8	78.7
Animal Sounds Crickets	113	59.3	55.3	56.6	53.0	48.1
Interview	484	77.5	74.3	72.0	68.6	60.8

4.2 User Evaluation

In order to get an end-user perspective on the results of the MIR pilot, an user evaluation was performed. In sessions of 90 min 13 participants provided feedback on their experience with the MIR pilot. A Likert-scale was used to quantify the perception of the calculated music similarity experienced between audio tracks selected from several different categories as well as the overall experience of the provided system. The participants were asked to specify their perception of similarity according the overall similarity of audio tacks as well as their specific music properties *tempo, rhythm, harmony, timbre, instrumentation* and *quality of the recording*. The participants were selected from three different types of users: *music lovers* as regular music listeners; *hobby musicians* which play music themselves and have a certain level knowledge with regard to musical concepts; and *music professionals* for whom performing, and or recording music is part of their regular work. Each participant evaluated nine reference tracks and the top tree results (27 tracks in total) and provided a narrative feedback about the applied concept of music information retrieval as well. After playing the reference track, the users were asked to listen and evaluate the top three result tracks provided by the system. Apart from the nominal scaled ratings the explanations for the experienced similarities and differences were being noted as well during the evaluation. When analyzing the evaluation results no noticeable differences between the user groups were observed. Participants generally agreed upon the similarity of *timbre* related music properties such as *instrumentation* as well as *harmony* of the similar tracks calculated by the MIR pilot (see Fig. 2). *Tempo* and *rhythm*

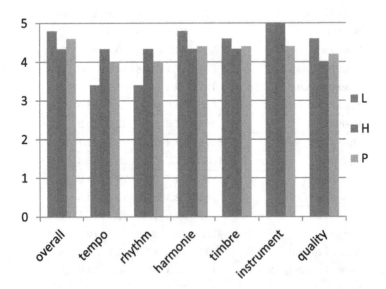

Fig. 2. Quantitative evaluation of the similarity perception over different music properties, tailored by the user groups music lovers (L), hobby musicians (H) and music professionals (P).

earned not as high ratings. From the narrative feedback it was understood that the rhythm dimension was not evaluated in the sense of rhythmic patterns, but as the overall rhythm of the interpretation. Similarly, it was observed very high correlation between the feedback for the *harmony* and *timbre* dimension, which indeed are interdependent musical concepts. The feedback on the *tempo* and *rhythm* dimensions are least correlated with the overall similarity, meaning that their influence on the similarity perception is lower in the case of music content. However, they are good discriminators between music and other types of sound content (i.e. like speech or environmental sounds). While the user evaluation was carried out with a small number of users on a small number of music items, the evaluation results cannot be perceived as an overall evaluation of the systems. However they can be used to validate the weighting of different categories and feature sets in the similarity computation (i.e. which were derived from the experience of the past music information retrieval research and experiments).

5   Conclusion and Future Work

We presented our audio-content similarity estimation based query-by-example implementation on a very large dataset which has been aggregated by the Europeana Sounds project. The presented approach based on weighted combinations of different audio-content descriptors facilitates similarity estimations of the highly heterogeneous data. The evaluation showed that the presented audio descriptor combinations, as well as the evaluated distance measure and feature space fusion methods are appropriate and results are comparable to results reported in literature. Based on these results it was decided to incorporate these results into the core Europeana search system and to extend the audio search functions by audio-content analysis based approaches.

References

1. Cha, S.-H.: Comprehensive survey on distance/similarity measures between probability density functions. City **1**(2), 1 (2007)
2. Dixon, S.: Evaluation of the audio beat tracking system beatroot. Journal of New Music Research (2007)
3. Harte, C., Sandler, M., Gasser, M.: Detecting harmonic change in musical audio. In: Proceeding 1st ACM WS on Audio and Music Computing Multimedia (2006)
4. Jurman, G., Riccadonna, S., Visintainer, R., Furlanello, C.: Canberra distance on ranked lists. In: Proceeding of Advances in Ranking NIPS WS (2009)
5. Lidy, T., Rauber, A.: Evaluation of feature extractors and psycho-acoustic transformations for music genre classification. In: ISMIR (2005)
6. Schindler, A., Mayer, R., Rauber, A.: Facilitating comprehensive benchmarking experiments on the million song dataset. In: ISMIR (2012)
7. Serrà, J., Corral, Á., Boguñá, M., Haro, M., Arcos, J.L.: Measuring the evolution of contemporary western popular music. Scientific reports, vol. 2 (2012)
8. Tzanetakis, G., Cook, P.: Marsyas: a framework for audio analysis. Organised Sound **4**(3), 169–175 (2000)

The Culture of Epigraphy: From Historic Breakthrough to Digital Success

Pantelis Nigdelis[1], Vassilis Bokolas[2], Nikoleta Vouronikou[1(✉)],
and Pavlos Anagnostoudis[1]

[1] Department of History and Archaeology, Aristotle University of Thessaloniki,
Thessaloniki, Greece
{pnigdeli,nvouroni,pavlosta}@hist.auth.gr
[2] HAEF/Xenios Polis, Athens, Greece
vbokolas@haef.gr

Abstract. The aim of the present paper is to direct attention to new perspectives on the role and integration of epigraphy into the digital age. Nowadays, epigraphic and historical studies undergo a period of remarkable vitality, thanks to the finding of new inscriptions that enhance our understanding on past societies. History gives a great example of an interdisciplinary field, drawing not only on epigraphy, but also on numismatics and other related sciences. Despite the various efforts to digitize epigraphic heritage, the existing databases are primarily intended for specialized audiences, academics or researchers. Without overlooking the educational role of epigraphy, this paper examines and proposes new ways in which inscriptions can become more accessible to wider audiences. To this end, digital media can provide the means for more efficient engaging with the public.

Keywords: History · Culture · Epigraphy · Inscriptions · Digital · Education

1 Introduction: Setting the Scene

Concerning the Greek and Roman world one could talk about the culture of epigraphy"
[1] L. Robert
Nowadays, the science of History and applied historical research is undergoing an extremely vigorous, energetic and renewing period [2]. This progress mainly concerns the following three axes:

(a) The broadening of historical themes with "new stories" which emphasize the cultural elements (as compared to the traditional political and military history),
(b) Enrichment of the documents being used as sources to supplement the literary sources with archaeological data (monuments, inscriptions, coins, etc.) and
(c) The introduction of new methods of publicizing historical knowledge which are based on Information and Communication Technology (ICT or "new media").

Specifically the guidelines which have arisen from the movement of "New History" [3] developed nearby the political, social and economic history the cultural history, the

© Springer International Publishing AG 2016
M. Ioannides et al. (Eds.): EuroMed 2016, Part II, LNCS 10059, pp. 118–129, 2016.
DOI: 10.1007/978-3-319-48974-2_14

history of collective consciousness and behavior [4, 5], the history of emotions, daily life stories of women, children and youth, etc. [6–8]. As far as the Ancient Greek History is concerned, the need for new approaches and discussion about methodology is evident [9–13]. Moreover, the idea of proximity or analogy between the ancient times and modern world is currently being put forward more frequently, while experts underline the need of developing an "applied antiquity", which can provide new insight to our experience [14–16].

Studies on ancient Greek and Roman world have been updated with information which is provided by all kinds of inscribed objects. Inscriptions, papyri, and coins are now treated as valuable evidence, which constitute a practically inexhaustible, constantly enriching source of information [17].

Publishing new documents–most importantly inscriptions– is a service that constantly updates historical knowledge with new material and frequently leads to great scientific breakthroughs. According to L. Robert, "*Epigraphy provides ancient history with a constantly renewed freshness. It fights against the unfruitful and endless discussions about the literary documents which are being reviewed for the past four centuries... It is the 'fresh water– νεαρόν ύδωρ' of our studies. It always keeps open the possibility of discovery... Its constant contribution revives the study of Antiquity in the most diverse ways... a true kaleidoscope*" [18].

In recent years, information and communication technologies promoted history and culture and provided them with a privileged position on the internet [19], on television [20], on the silver screen, as well as in digital games etc [21]. The "informal/incidental" learning of history, which was the result of the excessive exposure of historical content in the media [22], creates concerns about information overload [19], but at the same time opens up new opportunities of exploration through dialogue between historical science on the one hand and the so called "public history" on the other [23], which is admittedly based mainly on history taught in organized education and history promoted by digital media.

2 History and Primary Sources the Inscriptions

"*The study of ancient history was a result of the preservation, reproduction and study of classical texts. The great prestige they these texts had received, but also the emphasis given on the study of political history, meant that the margin of interaction between the two disciplines (i.e. history and archaeology) was extremely restricted*" [24].
K. Vlassopoulos

Literary evidence had been the only source for ancient civilizations before the commencing of systematic excavations. Literary sources can be divided as follows: historiography, political theory, philosophy, rhetoric and poetry [25]. However, the works of ancient authorities have not been delivered to us without intermediation. Throughout the centuries the inhered literary tradition has been subjected to falsification and therefore must be critically approached by scholars, whose main task is to emend ancient texts and verify their authenticity and validity [26].

Next to the historical science, archaeology, a field that is closely connected to historical research, has also shown significant progress over the years. Since the last three decades, archaeology –within the post-positivist and post-processualist (interpretative) movement [27]– has been developed into a new field of study, characterized by inter-disciplinary attitude and intense socio-political overtones [28]. Therefore, the efforts for historical interpretation of antiquity combine the literary sources with archaeological evidence. Every antiquary source is capable of providing us with valuable information about the past and can facilitate its reconstruction. Both language and physical objects provide information about past societies. Collecting all available evidence and method-ically arranging it for statistical analysis is a process that can lead scholars to new inter-pretations of the past [29].

A true renewal of classical studies therefore requires the use of archaeological data. For this cause inscriptions are of paramount importance. Inscriptions are written docu-ments engraved on a hard surface (stone, metal, ceramics) that come to us mainly through excavation [30, 31]. They include a large variety of texts which were engraved with the intention to transmit their content to as large audiences as possible. In recent years, the number of inscriptions have been constantly increasing, most of them dating from the Classical period and mainly the Hellenistic and Roman period [32, 33].

Inscriptions offer ample and growing amount of primary sources. This is due to the so-called "epigraphic habit" [34], which affected every aspect of ancient life. Written on walls of main buildings found in the Agora or elsewhere, incised on gravestones, altars and so on, inscriptions provide information about the most important features of civic life in antiquity and capture in the most unique way the pulse of the socio-political space. After all, in Classical and Hellenistic Era the ability to understand public docu-ments was to some extent a prerequisite for successful participation in public life and therefore every citizen must have been expected to have a certain degree of familiarity with epigraphic documents [35]. What inscriptions can teach us is often regarded as a specific "detail"; these details, however, are both exemplary and revealing. What inscriptions tell us that happened once, in reality occurred hundreds of times. Taking this into consideration, inscriptions can no longer be considered as a mean to enrich our knowledge of the past with particular "details", but instead as a guide for the recon-struction of the broader historical context of a given period [36].

Epigraphic evidence is of great importance for five more reasons:

- Inscriptions reach us without intermediary, as opposed to the historical works of antiquity, transmitted by manuscripts copied from one another for centuries [37].
- The inscriptions provide a direct contact with everyday life. Most of the time what stands before us is not merely a document packed with conventional remarks intended to be used for bureaucratic purposes, but instead a genuine and almost always contemporary expression of antiquity itself [38].
- In direct relation to the above, some types of inscriptions –such as the epigram and the issues which addresses– have a more personal tone and present the deepest thoughts of individuals, their beliefs and the "average" person's mentality [39].
- In cases where evidence is scarce, inscriptions often constitute the sole source of information. For example, as noted by P. Gauthier, the study of the institutions of the Greek cities owes much, almost everything, to inscriptions: decrees, laws and regu-lations, conditions and contracts, lists and accounts [40], all are written on stone.

- Finally, what makes the study of inscriptions very "charming" is that new epigraphic evidence is constantly being discovered [41], amounting to over half a million documents [42], a factor that influences scholars to re-evaluate established ideas.

Besides epigraphy, numismatics, the study of coins, is another discipline which significantly contributes to our knowledge about the past. A coin is a piece of money made of metal which conforms to a standard, has a certain weight and bears a design which is related to the issuing authority. Although pieces of metal in various shapes (ingots, rods-spits, discs) were regarded in many cultures around the world as a mean for carrying out transactions long before the invention of money, it was in 7th century Asia Minor that coins were struck in the form that in form that is known today. The vast majority of ancient coins were disk-shaped and were manufactured by striking a blank disk between two engraved dies, the upper (reverse) set in a punch, and the lower (obverse) set in an anvil. Their legends often bear inscriptions, the symbol of the issuing city or authority, a representation of a deity, portraits of king or emperors etc [43].

Although the first coins are known to have been developed in Asia Minor, it is a matter of debate whether the first coins were struck by the Kingdom of Lydia, the Greek cities of the region or wealthy individuals [44, 45]. Even though not much is known about the authorities that were the first to mint coins, it was the Greek cities that spread the use of coinage throughout the Ancient World. The phenomenon of colonization contributed much to that effect. The reason that made coins so popular is that they facilitated trade, providing everyone with a standardized medium of exchange. Soon after the first documented use of standardized money in Ephesus, the cities of mainland Greece followed suit. In the middle of the 6th century Aegina was the first city that struck coins. Soon after Aegina, other cities such as Athens and Corinth adopted the use of coinage around the second half of the 6th century. Although the first coins were made out of electrum, silver became the metal upon which Greece coinage system was based [46].

Coins are among the most important items that can be found on an excavation site, since they can facilitate the dating of other findings. Even though coins found separately on a site can provide archaeologists with valuable information, it is the treasures that are of paramount importance for the study of monetary circulation [45].

3   Collecting Inscriptions from Epigraphic Corpora to Databases

The use of inscriptions as historical source material dates back to the fifth century B.C. Historians, like Herodotus and Thucydides, recognized their value, but it was not until the 19th century that scholars from all around the world began to systematically collect all available evidence in epigraphic corpora. According to P. Herrmann, *"the purpose of the corpus consists in the reliable collection and presentation of the total accessible epigraphic legacy of a geographical area and so to enable the use of this material by the whole spectrum of research into the ancient world. To a great degree it is thankless hard labour but it is held to a particularly high standard of reliability, as it is the task of the corpus to bring together all the scattered material and to set it in order bibliographically"* [47].

The comprehensive collections of ancient inscriptions are the Inscriptiones Graecae (IG) and the Corpus Inscriptionum Latinarum (CIL). The Inscriptiones Graecae are the oldest long-term project of the Berlin Academy of Sciences and as such are directly connected to the beginnings of the Academy itself. The project's founding document is the proposal of the 24th March 1815 by the Philological-Historical Class of the Academy. The Corpus Inscriptionum Graecarum (CIG) which began in this way appeared in four large folio volumes from 1828 to 1859 and included around 10.000 inscriptions. The editor, A. Boeckh, thus became the founder of modern epigraphy and its method. For the first and only time all regions of the ancient world were covered. Even today the CIG is in some parts not superseded by more recent collections. In 1847 a committee was created in Berlin with the aim of publishing an organized collection of Latin inscriptions, which had previously been described and published by hundreds of scholars over the preceding centuries. That led to the creation of Corpus Inscriptionum Latinarum (CIL). The leading figure of this project was T. Mommsen, who also wrote several volumes of this series covering Italy [48].

Boeckh's successor as director of the Greek inscription corpus, A. Kirchhoff had himself brought the CIG to completion. In the meantime, however, the number of known stones had multiplied. Thanks to L. Ross and other scholars, a large number of very high quality transcriptions had been brought to Berlin from Greece. The increase in quantity became a problem for the design of the corpus. That led U. von Wilamowitz-Moellendorff to reorganize and re-energise the project into what is today known as Inscriptiones Graecae. Like CIG, IG were planned on the geographical system; its first volumes dealt with Attica, and those which followed covered the remainder of Greece, Italy, and the western provinces of the Roman Empire [48]. But not all the volumes projected have been completed. Gaps remain, some of them so adequately filled by other publications that there is now no need in these areas to complete the original plans. Despite the difficulties of modern conditions, and the interruptions caused by World War II, work on the great undertaking continues up until the present.

The volumes of Inscriptiones Graecae, however, extend only to Europe. For Asia Minor, the Levant, Egypt and North Africa the situation is much more complex and the material much less easily to be located. No such unified publication exists, although a beginning has been made, under Austrian leadership, of a series entitled Tituli Asiae Minoris, so far confined to the inscriptions of Lycia and Bithynia, but ultimately of wider scope. Otherwise it remains necessary to cite material from the old Boeckh Corpus, from MAMA or other topographical studies. Apart from TAM and MAMA, a new series known as *Inschriften griechischer Städte aus Kleinasien* was initiated in 1972 by R. Merkelbach of the Koln University. Since then, over 60 volumes with inscriptions of various cities of Asia Minor have been published. Other important series and corpora include IGBulg, IGLS, IPE, IC, OGIS, IvO, FD, CID etc [49].

Apart from full-scale corpora, there are hundreds of periodicals and occasional publications concerned with epigraphic studies, with an annual output of considerable proportions. Periodicals such as Supplementum Epigraphicum Graecum (SEG), Bulletin épigraphique and L'année épigraphique provide annual digest of what has been published in a given year for new or re-edited inscriptions. SEG appears annually and reprints the entire texts of newly published material unless the new publication is itself a Corpus or a work of the same character. By listing its material with a volume and reference number in the same way as does the Corpus itself, SEG can serve, as its name suggests, as a running supplement to the volumes of the Corpus. While none of these works can presume to include all epigraphic material from whatever source, since much depends on the availability of the publications and the general co-operation of the scholarly world, it may on the whole be claimed that the researcher who has consulted all of them may rest assured that he has done what he can to discover the information that he needs. Guide de l'épigraphiste provide a useful guide not only to epigraphists, but also to other researchers who wish to become familiar with the keys to the study of the epigraphies of the ancient world [50]. The Guide contains a carefully selected bibliographical apparatus, with brief comments on individual works, a methodological introduction and a rich series of indices.

Corpora and Supplementa are not the only tools which researches have at their disposal. The Packard Humanities Institute, in conjunction with Cornell University and The Ohio State University are making available online an extensive corpus of Greek inscriptions. The database created by the Packard Humanities Institute (PHI) is continuously updated with the goal of providing a complete collection of all edited Greek inscriptions [51]. It does not provide a critical text or commentary. Older, inaccurate publications of inscriptions have not been corrected against the subsequent, more accurate edition of the text, and search options are limited to simple queries. As it was possible to reach an agreement with the publisher de Gruyter through which the Greek text of the newest IG volumes can be included in the database, this permits electronic access to the corpora, but it by no means replaces them.

In Greece, where most inscriptions are found, there is no organized system of recording, classification and presentation of epigraphic data and their publications. The epigraphic science is completely absent in the primary and secondary education, while in higher education there is no systematic teaching in the Departments Philology and History and Archaeology. The Epigraphic Museum in Athens [52] and the small Epigraphic Museum in Rhodes are the only museums in Greece which exclusively exhibit inscriptions and inscribed objects [53]. The center for Greek Language is the first Greek institute who has attempted to digitize a small collection of inscriptions. The aim is to showcase aspects of the public and private life of the ancient Greeks, initiating users into *"the wonderful world of inscriptions"* [54].

4 Epigraphy in the Digital Age Actuality, Possibilities and Prerequisites

At an international level, there are many ongoing projects whose main task is to collect epigraphic and numismatic evidence and to systematically entry it into reachable databases. Besides PHI, which was mentioned earlier, particularly useful for scientific research are the Epigraphic Database Heidelberg, the Epigraphik Datenbank Clauss-Slaby, Wild Winds and many more. Although most databases assure free access to everyone, their content is primarily intended for a specialized audience. This is mainly because they incorporate texts written in ancient Greek or Latin, whose mastering requires excessive amount of time and effort, rendering data-browsing impossible without sufficient language proficiency.

Nowadays, however, database developers try to overcome the difficulties presented above and to think of new ways to manage digital material, especially in cases where important academic or educational value resides. To this end the concepts of participation, interactivity and interchangeability are of pivotal importance. Efforts are being made to make digital content more accessible and more appealing to a wider age range. With the aim of developing and sharing e-learning courses, digital content is designed to fulfil both educational and recreational purposes (edutainment) [55].

Thus far, there have been many attempts to incorporate some of the features presented above in the study and promotion of epigraphy and numismatics. At the University of Florida a multidisciplinary team has created the Digital Epigraphy Toolbox, an online library of digitized inscriptions which utilizes three-dimensional technology [56, 57]. In Italy, the EAGLE (The Europeana Network of Ancient Greek and Latin Epigraphy) [58] funded by the European Union and in collaboration with Europeana [59] organized an online platform for ancient Greek and Latin inscriptions combining primary research, digitization and presentation of inscriptions in a way that is intended for both specialized and non-specialized audiences. In Greece, the Numismatic Collection of Alpha Bank, which is considered one of the most important collections worldwide, attempts to assume a more educational role as it is evident by its publishing activities, its educational programs for students and schools and the development of digital games for educational purposes [60].

Popularizing epigraphy or numismatics is not an easy task, but the progress made during the last years is encouraging. Digitizing epigraphic evidence for educational purposes seems to be a promising field and we are hereby listing some of the basic prerequisites for such a venture:

- Interdisciplinary research combining disciplines like history, archaeology, pedagogics and technology, as well as multinational cooperation.
- Constant process evaluation, investigation of attitudes of the audience towards the content presented to them, evaluation during the project's implementation with the aim of improving the project's design, as well as final evaluation to better evaluate the appeal of the product to the members of a target group.
- Adoption of educational principles and selection of teaching and learning resources that take into consideration the particular needs of each age group.
- Implementation of modern teaching methodology in shaping the content of the material.
- Use of digital tools such as digital photos and maps, educational videos, digital games, internet browsing etc.
- Making content available through the official website, but also developing software applications for mobile devices (smartphones, tablets).

An integrated digital display system of inscriptions and/or coins capable to fulfil educational purposes is expected to address the following objectives:

- Presentation of the history of the inscription or of the coin (where was it found, by who etc.).

- Study of the broader historical context within which it was created.
- Translation of ancient sources into a sufficient number of languages, presented with basic commentary and highlighting of the engraved text.
- Enabling users to further investigate topics of interest.
- Development of better understanding of the arts and science related to each object.
- Awareness of issues concerning preservation of cultural heritage.
- Awareness of issues about interaction between cultures.
- Connecting objects with the location where they were found or the city/museum where are being displayed with the aim to present them as "tourist attractions."

Technological progress can provide us with the means to render epigraphic testimony more appealing to wider audience. Digital imagery, animation, digital video and audio, e-books and video games have a significant impact on the daily life of the majority of people. Digital media have evolved to powerful tools [61, 62] transforming the very nature of their users (digital generation/digital natives). Subsequently, current learning theories support the use of the internet and particularly of digital games [63–68]. It is evident that the content of an epigraphic of numismatic database can become more accessible and appealing by successfully integrating into the digital age.

Archaeologists become increasingly more aware of the potential within digital technology for more efficient engaging with the public. Digital media is not regarded merely as a means for more realistic visualization of ancient monuments through 3D-reconstruction. Nowadays the importance of electronic tools at the "archaeology teaching process" [69] is also realized. Putting educational content, such as historical events, monuments and museum exhibits into engaging formats for learners emerges as an educational necessity [70]. Moreover, studies have shown the positive effect of digital video in the learning process and the satisfaction it brings to the trainee/learner [71–73]. Studies also point out that the use of video can direct students and teachers to invest more willingly in their personal development [74].

The use of video in teaching presupposes specific conditions:

- Information should be presented in simple and accessible language, avoiding diversion and encouraging active learning.
- Video for historical narration must closely and creatively combine image, sound and words [75].

As far as digital gaming is concerned, researchers converge to the conclusion that video games have the potential to reinforce intrinsically motivated behaviour to both adults and children [76, 77]. The utilization of games in learning is also related to the change of current learner's profile. Specifically, Prensky [78] has written about the clear distinction between the students of the "games generation" or "digital natives", who have grown up with computer games, television and other media and which they use instinctively, and the other students, whose interaction with the technology has been through conscious effort and their learning approaches more traditional learning strategies [79].

5   Epilogue

The development of a program about digitizing and publicizing epigraphic and numismatic evidence for scientific and educational use will set high standards for the management of cultural heritage. It requires international and interdisciplinary cooperation, while at the same time makes clear the need for interaction and engagement with the public. Moreover, such an attempt has to incorporate new technology in order to create digital learning environments that offer both synchronous and asynchronous activities, creating new opportunities for e-learning (groups and communities) [80, 81]. In any case it is a new and promising domain.

References

1. Robert, L.: Επιγραφική. In: Ιστορία και οι Μέθοδοί της, Encyclopedie de la Pleiade, vol 2, 18. M.I.E.T., Athens (1981). (Epigraphie, In: L'Histoire et ses méthodes)
2. Cannadine, D.: Εισαγωγή. In: Cannadine, D. (ed.) Τι είναι ιστορία σήμερα, 9–21, Nesos, Athens (2007). (What is history now?)
3. Black, J., MacRaild, D.: Studying History. Macmillan Press, London (2000)
4. Λε Γκοφ, Ζ.: Ιστορία και μνήμη, Nefeli, Athens (1998). (Le Goff, Z.: History and Memory)
5. Dosse, F.: Η Ιστορία σε ψίχουλα. Από τα Annales στη « Νέα Ιστορία ». Crete University Press, Heraklio (1998). (L'histoire en miettes)
6. Noiriel, G.: Τι είναι η σύγχρονη ιστορία, Gutenberg, Athens (2005). (Qu' est-ce que l'histoire contemporaine?)
7. Ίγκερς, Γ.: Η ιστοριογραφία στον 20ο αιώνα, Nefeli, Athens (1999). (Iggers, G.G.: historiography in the twentieth century)
8. Ferro, M.: Η ιστορία υπό επιτήρηση. Επιστήμη και συνείδηση της ιστορίας, Nesides, Athens (1999). (L' historie sous surveillance)
9. Harris, W.V. (ed.): Rethinking the Mediterranean. Oxford University Press, New York (2005)
10. Hansen, M.H.: Polis: An Introduction to the Ancient Greek City-State. Oxford University Press, Oxford (2006)
11. Clarke, K.: Making Time for the Past. Local History and the Polis. Oxford University Press, Oxford (2008)
12. Ober, J.: Democracy and Knowledge. Innovation and Learning in Classical Athens. Princeton University Press, Princeton (2008)
13. Chaniotis, A.: The social and cultural construction of emotions. In: European Research Council (2008–2013)
14. Chaniotis, A., Kuhn, A., Kuhn, C. (eds.): Applied Classics: Constructs, Comparisons, Controversies. Steiner, Stuttgart (2009)
15. Morley, N.: Antiquity and Modernity. Wiley, Oxford (2009)
16. Chaniotis, A.: The illusion of democracy in the Hellenistic World. In: Athens Dialogues, Athens. Onassis Foundation, 26 November 2010. http://athensdialogues.chs.harvard.edu/cgi-bin/WebObjects/athensdialogues.woa/wa/dist?dis=43
17. Hallof, K.: Inscriptiones Graecae, Berlin-Brandenburgische, Akademie der Wissenschaften, 11–12, Berlin (2009)
18. Robert, L.: Επιγραφική. In: Ιστορία και οι Μέθοδοί της, Encyclopedie de la Pleiade, vol 2, 30. M.I.E.T., Athens (1981). (Epigraphie, In: L'Histoire et ses méthodes)

19. Λιάκος, Α.: Πώς το παρελθόν γίνεται ιστορία, Πόλις, Αθήνα (2007). (Liakos, A.: How the Past becomes History)
20. Cannadine, D.: Εισαγωγή. In: Cannadine, D. (ed.) Τι είναι ιστορία σήμερα, 9–21, Νήσος, Αθήνα (2007). (What is history now?)
21. Bokolas, V.: History and Video Games: Forming Pedagogical Criteria for the Evaluation and Development of Digital Games Aristotle University of Thessaloniki (postdoctoral research in process) (2016)
22. Cannadine, D. (ed.): History and the Media. Palgrave Macmillan, Basingstoke, Hampshire, New York (2004)
23. Φλάισερ, Χ.: Οι πόλεμοι της μνήμης. Ο Β' Παγκόσμιος Πόλεμος στη Δημόσια Ιστορία, Nefeli, Athens (2008). (Fleischer, H.: The wars of memory. The second world war in public history)
24. Βλασόπουλος, Κ.: Αρχαιολογικές μαρτυρίες και ιστορικά πορίσματα: προβλήματα μεθόδου και ερμηνείας, Τα Ιστορικά, 33, 381 (2000). (Archeological testimonies and historical outcomes: methodological problems and interpretation)
25. Schuller, W.: Ιστορία της αρχαίας Ελλάδας, 101–104. M.I.E.T., Athens (1999). (Griechische Geschichte)
26. Klaffenbach, G.: Ελληνική Επιγραφική, 19–22. Papazisi, Athens (1989). (Griechische Epigraphik)
27. Schnapp, A.: Η Αρχαιολογία. In: Le Goff, J., Nora, P. (eds.) Το Έργο της Ιστορίας, vol. 2, 74–79. Ράππα, Αθήνα (1983). (Archaeology. In: Faire de l' histoire)
28. Μελάς, Μ.: Η Αρχαιολογία Σήμερα, Κοινωνική-Πολιτισμική Θεωρία, Ανθρωπολογία και Αρχαιολογική Ερμηνεία, 16–17, Καρδαμίτσα, Αθήνα (2003). (Archaeology today. Social-cultural theory, anthropology and archaeological interpretation)
29. Schnapp, A.: Η Αρχαιολογία. In: Le Goff, J., Nora, P. (eds) Το Έργο της Ιστορίας, vol. 2, 74–79, Ράππα, Αθήνα (1983). (Archaeology. In: Faire de l' histoire)
30. Mosse, C., Schnapp-Gourbeillon, A.: Επίτομη Ιστορία της Αρχαίας Ελλάδας (2000-31 π.Χ.), 25–26, Παπαδήμα, Αθήνα (1996). (Precis d' Histoire Grecque)
31. Schuller, W.: Ιστορία της αρχαίας Ελλάδας, 104–106. M.I.E.T., Athens (1999). (Griechische Geschichte)
32. Millar, F.: Epigraphy. In: Crawford, M. (ed.) Sources for Ancient History, pp. 80–136. Cambridge University Press, Cambridge (1983)
33. Pleket, H.: Epigraphy, Greek, pp. 539–543, OCD[3] (1996)
34. Billows, R.: Cities. In: Erskine, A. (ed.) A Companion to the Hellenistic World, pp. 209–214. Blackwell, Oxford (2003)
35. McLean, B.H.: An Introduction to Greek Epigraphy of the Hellenistic and Roman Periods from Alexander the Great down to the Reign of Constantine (323 B.C.–A.D. 337), 2. The University of Michigan Press, Ann Arbor (2002)
36. Robert, L.: Επιγραφική. In: Ιστορία και οι Μέθοδοί της, Encyclopedie de la Pleiade, vol 2, 21–23, 32–33. M.I.E.T., Athens (1981). (Epigraphie, In: L'Histoire et ses méthodes)
37. McLean, B. H.: An Introduction to Greek Epigraphy of the Hellenistic and Roman Periods from Alexander the Great down to the Reign of Constantine (323 B.C.–A.D. 337), 1. The University of Michigan Press, Ann Arbor (2002)
38. Robert, L.: Επιγραφική. In: Ιστορία και οι Μέθοδοί της, Encyclopedie de la Pleiade, vol 2, 27. M.I.E.T., Athens (1981). (Epigraphie, In: L'Histoire et ses méthodes)
39. Gutzwiller, K.: Poetic Garlands: Hellenistic Epigrams in Context. University of California Press, Berkeley, Los Angeles, London (1998)

40. Gauthier, P.: Les Cites Hellénistiques: Epigraphie et Histoire des Institutions et des Régimes Politiques. In: Acts of the Eighth International Conference on Greek and Latin Epigraphy, Athens, 3–9 October 1982, vol. A, 82, Ministry of Culture and Sciences, Athens (1984)
41. Robert, L.: Επιγραφική. In: Ιστορία και οι Μέθοδοί της, Encyclopedie de la Pleiade, vol 2, 30. M.I.E.T., Athens (1981). (Epigraphie, In: L'Histoire et ses méthodes)
42. Crawford, M.: Sources for Ancient History, p. 80. Cambridge University Press, Cambridge (1983)
43. Kraay, C.M.: Archaic and Classical Greek Coins, pp. 2–8. Methuen, London (1976)
44. Les, Rider G.: La naissance de la monnaie. Pratiques monétaires de l' Orient ancien, Paris (2001)
45. Πίκουλας, Γ. Α.: Εισαγωγή στην Αρχαία Ελληνική Ιστορία και Αρχαιογνωσία. 101, Καρδαμίτσα, Αθήνα (2006). (Introduction to Ancient Greek History and Knowledge)
46. Howgego, C.: Ancient History from Coins. Routledge, London, New York (1995)
47. Herrmann, P.: Inscriptiones Graecae. ZRG 116, Bohlau, Wien, pp. 701–703 (1999)
48. Guarducci, M.: Η ελληνική επιγραφική. Από τις απαρχές ως την ύστερη ρωμαϊκή αυτοκρατορική περίοδο, pp. 523–529. M.I.E.T., Αθήνα (2008). (L' Epigrafia Greca dale Origini al Tardo Impero)
49. Woodhead, A.G.: Η μελέτη των ελληνικών επιγραφών, 182–196, Καρδαμίτσα, Αθήνα (2009). (The study of Greek Inscriptions)
50. Berard, F., Feissel, D., Laubry, N., Pettmengin, P., Rousset, D., Sève, M.: Guide de l'épigraphiste: bibliographie choisie des épigraphies antiques et médiévales, Paris (2010). http://www.antiquite.ens.fr/ressources/publications-aux-p-e-n-s/guide-de-l-epigraphiste/
51. Searchable Greek Inscriptions. The Packard Humanities Institute, Los Altos. http://epigraphy.packhum.org/
52. Numismatic Museum, Athens. http://www.enma.gr/mus_gen.htm
53. Οικονομάκη, Ν.–Τζιφόπουλος, Γ. Ζ.: Εισαγωγή στην ελληνική επιγραφική. Από τον 8ο αιώνα π.Χ. ως την ύστερη αρχαιότητα. 76, Κέντρο Ελληνικής Γλώσσας, Θεσσαλονίκη (2015). (Introduction to Greek Epigraphy). http://ancdialects.greeklanguage.gr/sites/default/files/studies/eisagogi_sthn_ellhnikh_epigrafikh.pdf
54. Center of the Greek Language. Anthology of Ancient Greek Inscriptions. http://www.greek-language.gr/Resources/ancient_greek/anthology/inscriptions/index.html
55. Ioannides, M., Bokolas, V., Chatzigrigoriou, P., Nikolakopoulou, V., Athanasiou, V.: Education use of 3D models and photogrammetry content; the Europeana Space project for Cypriot UNESCO Monuments. In: Proceedings of Fourth International Conference on Remote Sensing and Geoinformation of Environment, Cyprus, April 2016 (under publication)
56. Digital epigraphy toolbox. http://www.digitalepigraphy.org/toolbox/
57. Barmpoutis, A., Bozia, E., Wagman, R.S.: A novel framework for 3D reconstruction and analysis of ancient inscriptions. J. Mach. Vis. Appl. 21(6), 989–998 (2010)
58. EAGLE (The Europeana network of Ancient Greek and Latin Epigraphy). http://www.eagle-network.eu/
59. Europeana. http://www.europeana.eu/portal/
60. Alpha Bank. Numismatic Collection. http://www.alphanumismatics.gr/
61. Baker, F.W.: Media Literacy in the K-12 Classroom. International Society for Technology in Education, United States of America (2012)
62. Barrance, T.: Film Education Training. Feasibility study. Media Education Wales, Wales (2010)
63. Prensky, M.: Digital Game-Based Learning. McGraw Hill, New York (2001)
64. Palloff, R.M., Pratt, K.: The Virtual Student: A Profile and Guide to Working with Online Learner. Jossey-Bass, San Francisco (2003)

65. Gee, J.P.: What Video Games Have to Teach Us about Learning and Literacy. Palgrave MacMillan, New York (2003)
66. Ducheneaut, N., Moore, R.J.: More than just 'XP': learning social skills in massively multiplayer online games. Interact. Technol. Smart Educ. **2**, 89–100 (2005)
67. Kiili, K.: Digital game-based learning: towards an experiential gaming model. Internet Higher Educ. **8**, 13–24 (2005)
68. de Freitas, S.I.: Using games and simulations for supporting learning. Learn. Media Technol. **31**(4), 343–358 (2006)
69. Clarke, C.: The politics of storytelling: electronic media in archaeological interpretation and education. World Archaeol. **36**(2), 275–286 (2004)
70. Humphries, S.: Unseen stories: video history in Museums. Oral Hist. **31**(2), 75–84 (2003)
71. Armstrong, A.W., Idriss, N.Z., Kim, R.H.: Effects of video-based, online education on behavioral and knowledge outcomes in sunscreen use: a randomized controlled trial. Patient Educ. Couns. **83**(2), 273–277 (2011)
72. Eric, L., Dey, H.E.: Bringing the classroom to the web: effects of using new technologies to capture and deliver lectures. Res. High. Educ. **50**, 377–393 (2009)
73. Zhanga, D., Zhoua, L., Briggs, R.O., Nunamaker Jr., J.F.: Instructional video in e-learning: Assessing the impact of interactive video on learning effectiveness. Inf. Manag. **43**(1), 15–27 (2006)
74. Masats, D., Dooly, M.: Rethinking the use of video in teacher education: a holistic approach. Teach. Teach. Educ. **27**(7), 1151–1162 (2011)
75. Fulwiler, M., Middleton, K.: After digital storytelling: video composing in the new media age. Comput. Compos. **29**(1), 39–50 (2012)
76. Alessi, S.M., Trollip, S.R.: Multimedia for Learning. Allyn and Bacon, Boston (2001)
77. Oblinger, D.: The next generation of educational engagement. J. Interact. Media Educ. **8** (2004). Special Issue on the Educational Semantic Web. http://www-jime.open.ac.uk/article/2004-8-oblinger/199
78. Prensky, M.: Digital Game-Based Learning. McGraw Hill, New York (2001)
79. Bokolas, V.: History and Video Games: Forming Pedagogical Criteria for the Evaluation and Development of Digital Games Aristotle University of Thessaloniki (postdoctoral research in process) (2016)
80. Palloff, R.M., Pratt, K.: Collaborating Online: Learning Together in Community. Jossey-Bass, San Francisco (2005)
81. McConnell, D.: E-learning Groups and Communities. Open University Press, Milton Keynes (2006)

Exploiting Agriculture as an Intangible Cultural Heritage: The Case of the *Farfalla* Project

Alessandro Pozzebon[1(✉)] and Andrea Ciacci[2]

[1] Department of Information Engineering and Mathematical Sciences,
University of Siena, Via Roma 56, 53100 Siena, Italy
alessandro.pozzebon@unisi.it
[2] Department of History and Cultural Heritage, University of Siena,
Palazzo San Galgano, Via Roma, 47, 53100 Siena, Italy
andrea.ciacci@unisi.it
http://www.diism.unisi.it, http://www.dssbc.unisi.it

Abstract. This paper describes the methodological background and the first results of the "Farfalla" project, a research project financed by the Tuscany Region, Italy, focusing on the promotion of historical agricultural production through an holistic approach bringing together different disciplines, from archaeology and genetics to information engineering. The "Farfalla" project aims at rediscovering historical agricultural techniques and productions through the study of historical testimonies and archaeological sites, combined with genetic and botanic analyses, to exploit them through modern agronomic techniques, and to promote them with new generation ICT technologies focusing on their high value in terms of biodiversity and cultural significance.

Keywords: Agriculture · Intangible Cultural Heritage · Mobile applications

1 Introduction

In the last years the concept of Intangible Cultural Heritage (ICH) has seen a vast diffusion and has drawn the attention of the most significant global institutions. The realization of the UNESCO Convention for the Safeguarding of the Intangible Cultural Heritage [1] is probably the most significant point towards the definition of the concept of ICH together with the need for its safeguarding. Regarding the definition, UNESCO identifies 5 domains in which the ICHs manifested:

- oral traditions and expressions, including language as a vehicle of the intangible cultural heritage;
- performing arts;
- social practices, rituals and festive events;
- knowledge and practices concerning nature and the universe;
- traditional craftsmanship.

M. Ioannides et al. (Eds.): EuroMed 2016, Part II, LNCS 10059, pp. 130–137, 2016.
DOI: 10.1007/978-3-319-48974-2_15

According to this list, agriculture and gastronomy can be at all effects considered ICH. This consideration has been confirmed in the last years by the process of inscription of the sites to the UNESCO Intangible Cultural Heritage List: elements on this list are for example the "Traditional agricultural practice of cultivating the'vite ad alberello' (head-trained bush vines) of the community of Pantelleria" or the "Mediterranean Diet". Agriculture and food are then part of the cultural identity of a territory or a community and need to be safeguarded in the same way of Tangible Heritage [2,3].

The theme of Landscape appears strictly connected with agriculture: the *European Landscape Convention* [4] gives a definition for the term "Landscape" that allows to consider it ICH to all effects. Moreover, European landscape has been slowly modified during the centuries by the hands of farmers and then, safeguarding traditional agricultural productions means at the same time protecting the traditional European landscape. This protection can come only as a valorization of the agricultural and gastronomic heritage through awareness raising campaigns and through the diffusion of the knowledge about this heritage to both citizens and tourists [5], and mobile and Web technologies play a crucial role for the transmission of the information. In this respect, the "Farfalla" project proposes an holistic model for the valorization of traditional agricultural productions addressing to it in a scientific way that involves several different disciplines. The paper is structured as follows: in Sect. 2 the objectives of the project are briefly described. Section 3 is devoted to the presentation of the model proposed by the project, while in Sect. 4 the application of this model to a specific sector is described. In Sect. 5 the mobile application developed for the project is briefly described while in Sect. 6 the final conclusions and future work are presented.

2   The "Farfalla" Project

Tuscany is widely known for its vast cultural, historical and artistic heritage, as well as for its landscape, territory and agricultural productions. In this area, all these factors are strictly interconnected and compose a unique environment where history is merged inside present. Agriculture is one of the most significant components of this peculiar Tuscan identity, tied with history and culture as well as with local economy. This amalgamation has heavily shaped and designed the landscape giving it its peculiar features, colors and identity: this means that the question about the environmental protection strictly intersects with the themes of rural development, quality of life and identity of local communities.

The process of industrialization has lead to the neglect of rural areas and, in many cases, to the marginalization of local productions no longer considered profitable, with the following loss of biodiversity together with tradition farming and processing methods, that can be to all effects considered an Intangible Cultural Heritage at high risk of disappearing.

Nevertheless, in the last years a new model of development, based on sustainability, social innovation and quality of life, is rapidly emerging, together with the request for "typical" agricultural productions and a new model of "slow" tourism. This is leading to the revaluation of "traditional" agriculture as an instrument for social, cultural and economic characterization of several areas in Tuscany, together with a growing awareness about the collective heritage made of agricultural and gastronomic products, of longtime experiences and techniques, that requires to be protected and exploited as a factor of promotion and development for the whole territory.

The "Farfalla" research project (whose Logo is shown in Fig. 1), financed by the Tuscany Region, first of all aims at the development of a pilot initiative for the identification, cataloguing, preservation and valorization of some of the endemic agricultural productions of Tuscany, with a specific focus on those varieties already at a serious risk of disappearance because replaced by other typologies of cultivation.

The "Farfalla" project aims at defining an operating methodology and a model to be applied to each agricultural sector where the rediscovery and the revaluation of specific varieties is required. The proposed approach for the creation of the "added value of a traditional agricultural product" requires the cooperation of different disciplines, ranging from archaeology to genetics, with a special focus on the development of innovative ICT solutions for the promotion of the project results and the on-site fruition of the cultural background associated with each specific agricultural production.

Fig. 1. The "Farfalla" project Logo.

3   Methodological Approach

One of the main outputs of the "Farfalla" project is the definition of a structured methodological approach for the study, protection and valorization of traditional agricultural varieties and farming techniques, bringing together different disciplines. These include history, archaeology, genetics, botany, agronomy, marketing and information engineering. Each of these disciplines has a specific role in the process of creation of the added value of historical and traditional agricultural products. Diagram shown in Fig. 2 describes the overall approach of the "Farfalla" model that can be applied to every agricultural production. For each

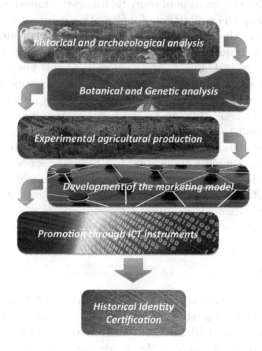

Fig. 2. Schematic diagram of the "Farfalla" methodological approach.

agricultural product, the first phase of the methodology deals with the historical and agricultural analysis. Historical sources are studied to identify the agricultural varieties cultivated along the centuries in the specific territory: ancient maps and archival documents are precious sources of information about the destination that certain areas had centuries ago. Once the historical analysis has identified a set of areas where traditional agricultural varieties could have been preserved, an archaeological analysis of this sites is carried out. Through this analysis, the persistence of a specific type of cultivation is verified.

The second step of the methodological approach concerns the genetic and botanical analysis. In the areas identified in the previous phase, the surviving varieties are sampled and studied. The DNA of these cultivations is analyzed in order to identify the species: when rare or unidentified varieties are detected, additional samples are collected. In this step, together with the study of the varieties, also the agricultural techniques are studied to identify possible fragments of historical landscape to be protected.

Following this phase, the third step sees the planting of the collected varieties in order to create botanical collections that can be used to set up experimental agricultural productions. This phase is crucial for the safeguarding of the varieties at risk of disappearance.

In the fourth step a marketing model has to be developed in order to provide these cultivations with an economic added value that could encourage their cultivation. This includes the creation of touristic itineraries aimed at the promotion of these products and the realization of information campaigns.

The last step sees the development of innovative technological solutions for the promotion of the products together with the diffusion of the knowledge. Two different technological instruments are employed for this purpose: the Internet and the smartphones. An Internet portal has been developed to store all the information collected during the project realization: this portal is addressed to both tourists and citizens and can be used as a simple information source or even as an instrument to plan visits to a territory with a specific focus on traditional agriculture, landscape and gastronomic products. Together with the Internet portal, also a mobile application has been developed, to drive citizens and tourists towards the discovery of the agricultural heritage directly on-site.

The final goal of the methodological approach is to provide a specific product with a sort of "Historical Agricultural Certification" that can be used as an instrument to certify the historical traceability of that specific product.

4   A Use Case

A use case useful to understand the methodology of the "Farfalla" project concerns the identification, protection and valorization of the traditional vineyards still existent within the Medieval City Walls of the city of Siena and in the close neighborhoods. As a result of this study, several century old vine plants have been discovered, belonging to unique grape varieties that cannot be found anywhere.

In this case the process has been applied as follows:

– The historical sources available in the State Archive in Siena have been studied, identifying all the areas where in the past centuries the grapevine was cultivated;
– The identified areas have been visited in order to detect places that could preserve traditional grape varieties. Together with the varieties, also some portions of traditional landscape with ancient traditional cultivation techniques have been identified;
– Through the botanical analysis of the surviving plants, some samples have been collected to be genetically analyzed;
– Genetic analysis on the collected samples has been carried out. Through these analysis several rare grape varieties have been identified, together with a set of varieties still unidentified;

- The collected samples of these varieties have been planted in two sites in the City of Siena (See Fig. 3), in order to preserve them. At the same time, in cooperation with two farms located close to the city, a sub-set of these varieties has been planted in a larger quantity in order to produce a novel typology of wine;
- A study about the promotion of the recovered varieties and the wine produced with them has been carried out;
- A visit route across the city has been designed. A mobile application exploiting innovative storytelling techniques is being developed.

Work is still going on to promote the knowledge about this heritage that is both natural and cultural because while on one side it represents a unique botanical legacy, on the other side it is a sort of time capsule of the medieval farming techniques.

Fig. 3. The "Orto dei Pecci" site, storing the recovered and planted traditional grape varieties

5   The Mobile Application

While mobile applications for tourism are widely diffused [6], the most part of them are simple reproductions of paper guides with few additional features. One of the most interesting concept emerged in this field in the last years is the concept of Storytelling [7].

The mobile application developed for the "Farfalla" project tries to emphasize the concept of Intangible Cultural Heritage by providing a novel storytelling tool based on the recording of the voice of the farmers directly involved in the vineyards cultivation.

The "Farfalla" application is provided with the standard navigation tools (See Fig. 4): through an interactive map the user is able to detect his/her position and to open an information page presenting some data on the specific point of interest. Together with the basic cultural information, additional data on the agricultural production is provided, clearly linking agriculture and products with history and archaeology, thus making available all the research background of the project. Information is also provided on farms cultivating these varieties, and on shops and restaurants that may sell products deriving from these varieties: this comes from the need to create an economic added value for these productions.

The most interesting section of the mobile application is the Storytelling tool. For each point of interest a person linked with this site has been identified: this person is in most cases the farmer still cultivating the specific agricultural variety that can be found in the point of interest. This person has been interviewed asking him/her information about the traditional cultivation techniques. While the whole interviews will be available on the project site, fragments of these

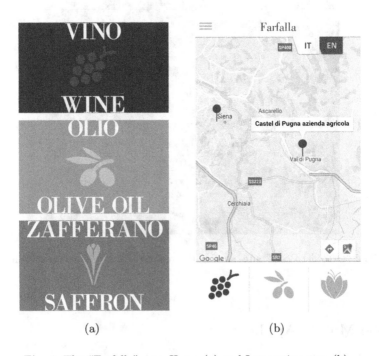

(a)   (b)

Fig. 4. The "Farfalla" app: Home (a) and Interactive map (b).

interviews are integrated on the mobile application and can be heard directly on site, adding an additional Intangible Cultural asset to the visit according to the UNESCO Convention definition of ICH.

6   Conclusion

In this paper the methodological approach of the "Farfalla" project has been presented. This approach tries to exploit traditional agriculture as an Intangible Cultural Heritage, focusing on its importance in conjunction with the history, the culture and the traditions of a specific territory. Of great importance is the support that can came from new technologies for the diffusion of knowledge: in this sense, the realization of a novel mobile application has been presented, trying to involve citizens and tourists in the safeguard of this fragile heritage. While in this paper a single use case focusing on wine and vineyard cultivation has been presented, work is going on to apply this model to the production of olive oil and saffron: these two products, together with the linked tourist itineraries, will be introduced in the developed mobile app, in order to turn it in a sort of guide to all the traditional agricultural productions available in the Tuscan territory. At the same time, the model is expected to be replicated for any other kind of traditional cultivation in Tuscany, to create a wide repository of historical and traditional agriculture.

References

1. World Heritage Committee: Convention for the safeguarding of the intangible cultural heritage (2003)
2. Daugstad, K.: Agriculture's Role as an Upholder of Cultural Heritage. Nordic Council of Ministers (2005)
3. Daugstad, K., Rnningen, K., Skar, B.: Agriculture as an upholder of cultural heritage? Conceptualizations and value judgements. A Norwegian perspective in international context. J. Rural Stud. **22**(1), 67–81 (2006)
4. Europe Council. European Landscape Convention. Report and Convention (2000)
5. Sun, Y., Jansen-Verbeke, M., Min, Q., Cheng, S.: Tourism potential of agricultural heritage systems. Tourism Geographies **13**(1), 112–128 (2011)
6. Ioannidis, Y., Raheb, K., Toli, E., Boile, M., Katifori, A., Mazura, M.: One Object Many Stories: introducing ICT in museums and collections through digital storytelling. In: Digital Heritage International Congress (DigitalHeritage), vol. 1, pp. 421–424, 28 October–1 November 2013
7. Nordmark, S., Milrad, M.: Mobile digital storytelling for promoting creative collaborative learning. In: IEEE Seventh International Conference on Wireless, Mobile and Ubiquitous Technology in Education (WMUTE), pp. 9–16. IEEE, March 2012

Digital Applications for Materials' Preservation and Conservation in Cultural Heritage

Application of Digital Technologies in the Restoration of Historic Buildings and Heritage Objects

A Selection of Practical Examples

Yves Vanhellemont[1]([✉]), Michael de Bouw[1], Liesbeth Dekeyser[1], Samuel Dubois[1], Simon Vermeir[2], Peter Van Damme[3], and Joeri-Aleksander Van der Have[3]

[1] Belgian Building Research Institute (BBRI), Lombardstraat 42, 1000 Brussels, Belgium
{Yves.vanhellemont,Michael.de.bouw,Liesbeth.dekeyser, Samuel.dubois}@bbri.be

[2] SIRRIS, Celestijnenlaan 300C, 3001 Leuven, Belgium
Simon.vermeir@sirris.be

[3] Flemish Construction Confederation, Lombardstraat 34-42, 1000 Brussels, Belgium
{Peter.vandamme,JoeriAleksander.vanderhave}@vcb.be
https://www.bbri.be, https://www.sirris.be,
https://www.vcb.be/international

Abstract. Three institutes have been aiming to stimulate the application of digital technologies for the restoration of historic buildings. This project was not aiming to develop techniques, but merely to point out to building professionals how such techniques might help in optimizing the restoration process, including the actual manufacturing of elements to be employed while restoring a building. The application of scanning technologies is already quite well known for the purpose of documentation and preparation of architectural work. In this project we wanted to go further, to explore how techniques such as additive manufacturing (3d-printing) and CNC (Computer Numerical Control) might help to produce elements that can directly be used in the restoration of buildings, particularly the more complex, sculptural parts of buildings. Applications are possible in the field of natural stone (as well as its replacements with artificial stone), metals (bronze, brass and cast iron) and ceramics. In this paper represents a state of the art as it exists in Flanders: an overview of several techniques and their possibilities, and future prospects.

Keywords: Restoration · Reconstruction · Additive manufacturing · Artificial stone · Metal · Ceramics

1 Introduction

Historic buildings are characterized by a large variety in (often complex) shapes and materials. In this project, we aimed at the positive profiling of craftsmanship, thereby placing it into a trajectory path towards the future. The project is definitely not aiming at the replacement of craftsmanship. It is merely pointing towards the future, where

© Springer International Publishing AG 2016
M. Ioannides et al. (Eds.): EuroMed 2016, Part II, LNCS 10059, pp. 141–150, 2016.
DOI: 10.1007/978-3-319-48974-2_16

certain activities in the process of shaping materials might be replaced by easier steps, thereby creating a mix between tradition and technology. The technical aim of this project is the accelerated introduction of 3D-shaping and registration techniques, in order for the efficient modelling of architectural elements, preferentially based on intact or damaged, but still existing, models.

Evidently there are many deontological discussion points in this field, especially when it comes to the reconstruction or replacement of building parts. We do realize that we balance on the thin edge between conservation and new construction. We will not go into details of this (very relevant) discussion here, it is the subject of the design process as accompanied by the designer, contractors and other parties (such as the heritage administrations).

2   The Digital Model

The making of a digital model is the start of the entire process. Scanning techniques (becoming more and more used in the heritage field) such as laser scanning or photogrammetry, or Computer Aided Design (CAD), or a combination of both, serve as the basic techniques. Numerous publications exist in this field, but a good overview is given by [1].

The advantage of such models is, evidently, their flexibility. Digital operations such as deforming or scaling the model, producing a mirror image, ... enables to produce (digitally) missing parts of buildings. The possibility of scaling images is a large advantage if one needs to make 'copies' of existing metal or ceramic objects, because of the shrinkage of the materials during their production (for instance large parts of cast iron constructions, such as columns or balconies).

When it comes to the precise restauration of valuable artefacts, the application of digital models, together with digital operations such as adding, distraction, ... might lead to a digital model than, when 'materialized', can fit precisely into the damaged object, without having to remove authentic material. This is very fit for art objects, even though we see it less applicable in the construction sector.

When applying digital techniques for registration and creating restoration elements, one can easily deal with irregularities, asymmetrical shapes etc., which are so common in historic buildings. The placement of newly restores stained glass windows in a gothic building (with windows that are mostly visually regular, but very often not so regular at all) is greatly facilitated by using 3D scans of the windows, on which the glass is modelled in the workshop.

The fact that no physical contact is necessary between the scanning devices and the object, may be of major interest: especially when the object is fragile, or when the object is (for instance) polychromed or gilded, the 'classical' way of making a mold may be even totally out of the question. In that case, scanning is the ideal way to copy/duplicate/measure objects (Fig. 1).

Fig. 1. Scanning of objects allows to 'measure' the object with great precision (fractions of millimeters) enabling the restorer to precisely adjust the dimensions of his restoration material to the exisiting situation. A (for the naked eye) regular shape like a gothic window is usually not as regular as it looks. A precise scan allows the glass restorer to adjust exactly the size and shape of new stained glass to the actual size of the window (© Visuaxis)

3   The Actual Realization of the Element to Be Used During the Restoration

Based on a 'ready-to-use' digital model, one can proceed by producing the object that will be placed into the building that is being restored. There are quite some innovative techniques being used in this field. Rather than giving an exhaustive list of technical possibilities, we give some examples that have been realized in Flanders or the Brussels Region (Fig. 2).

3.1   Automated Stone Cutting Based on a Digital Model – The Our Lady Church in Laken (Brussels Region)

The deterioration of natural stone, caused by acid rain and frost, made the restoration of this 19th century neogothic church necessary. It is the church in which Belgian monarchs are entombed, making it an important national symbol.

A large quantity of pinnacles needed replacement, as they were heavily damaged, beyond restoration in a durable manner. They were re-designed, based on the remains of the remains of the original pinnacles. CAD-techniques were combined with scanned models to produce a final model, which was then automatically carved in stone. The fact that large quantities of this object were necessary, it paid off to program an automatic

Fig. 2. Balustrade for the St Martin's basilica in Halle (Flanders, Belgium), which has been cut out of stone, using a digital model created by CAD (© Visuaxis)

Fig. 3. Left: two stages in the automatic modelling of neogothic pinnacles, to replace weathered (original) pinnacles in the Our Lady Church of Laken (Brussels, Belgium) (© Denys). On the right a single statue, cut out of Belgian Blue Stone. The digital model was based on an existing sculpture, the 'copy' had to be created, but 10 % larger than the original (© Renier) (Color figure online)

stonecutting machine to produce the pinnacles. This programming can be quite a challenge, so it quite often only pays of if larger quantities of the object are required.

The technique is, however, sometimes used to produce unique objects. It needs to be stressed that this technique is controversial, as it replaces quite a lot of the activities of traditional stonecutters. On the other hand, the technique might facilitate highly the work of such stonecutters, as it is quite possible (and this is done a lot) to use the device to prepare the stone block (make an approximation of the final model) after which the stonecutter finishes the model. Anyhow, a manual intervention is always necessary, since completely automatically carved objects are usually considered to be somewhat 'dead' (caused for instance by a too flat and perfect surface) (Fig. 3).

3.2 Elements in So-Called 'Artificial (Natural) Stone'

With 'artificial natural stone' (further we'll just refer to this as artificial stone) we mean a type of materials that is supposed to have the look (colour, texture) of natural stone, and which can be used as such (to construct facades, arches, vaults, …). Not to be confused with more 'normal' versions of artificial stone, such as bricks and concrete blocks (that are not supposed to resemble natural stone).

The application of natural stone is not recent. In Belgium there was already, since the 19th century, a blossoming industry of such artificial stone, for decorative purposes (such as vases, balustrades, …) but also constructive purposes: blocks for 'normal' masonry, corniches, arcs, columns, … In some cases we could even see sculptors working on such blocks. Later on, these materials were also applied in situ, not so much as a constructive material, but as a render that would imitate natural stone (to make the illusion complete, false joints were often used in these renders) [2] (Fig. 4)

Fig. 4. An example of historic architecture (Leuven, Flanders) that turns out to be constructed entirely of 'artificial' natural stone, during the reconstruction period after the First World War (around 1920), illustrating the fact that application of artificial stone in itself is not new at all. With the naked eye, this 'concrete' is hardly distinguishable from actual natural stone.

An impressive Belgian example of a recent application of artificial stone we can find in the Antwerp Central Station [3]. Its monumental clock (actually a pavilion composed out of turrets, domes, galleries and sculpture work, 21 m × 17 m × 5 m) was demolished some decades ago, after serious incidents with falling stones. At the time, the building was not listed, so most of the pieces got lost, and no serious documentation of the demolished construction was carried out.

The reason for the security problems was the Vinalmont stone, a Belgian natural stone used largely in the building. It is a stone that may crack in unforeseen ways, therefore causing falling stones, finally resulting in the demolishment of the top pavilion of the station.

In the meantime the station is listed, and has been restored. It was decided to reconstruct the clock, but in artificial stone (for financial reasons, but also because of the unpredicatability of the original natural stone).

Based on old plans and iconographic material, a 3D-model has been developed using CAD. The sculptural parts (a decorative shield, guirlandes) were on a scale 1:1 created in clay, and included in the model (Fig. 5).

Fig. 5. Different stages in the reconstruction of the clock-pavilion of the Antwerp Central Station. From left to right: part of the digital model of the clock-pavilion (© Verstraete&Vanhecke), the EPS-mold and the cast model (©Twinplast), the completed clock-pavilion.

Subsequently this model has been used to create large molds in EPS, by automatic cutting (for instance with a filament). The firm that did this can also create molds in other materials, every one having its characteristic advantages and creating a typical surface texture. These molds were then used to create concrete elements, by filling it with a concrete mixture (with additions, such as pigments to match the stone, fibers to compensate for tensions caused by shrinkage, ...). Each mold is, evidently, only useable once, as it has to be destroyed to get the concrete object out of the mold.

The application of artificial stone in heritage buildings is not unusual, but evidently a bit controversial. But it continues to be applied, because of financial reasons, reasons of security and/or durability, or in cases when the original material is not available anymore.

3.3   Additive Manufacturing

The term 'additive manufacturing' is better known as 3D-printing, and it offers a powerful instrument as a production process for complex shapes. The objects are produced by adding a thin layer of material on top of the already shaped object. It is a process that allows to rapidly produce prototypes, and is being used as such. This field of technology is in full development, but a recent overview of its possibilities can be found in [4].

When it comes to the restoration of buildings, it is principally possible to print directly objects that may be used as a restoration element. But because of several reasons (technical disadvantages when printing certain materials, cost), we usually see additive manufacturing as a tool for creating objects that are used in an intermediate stage of the fabrication process of the final object.

We especially noted useful applications in the field of restoration of metal objects, especially cast iron, bronze or brass. Some of these metals may be printed directly, but this is quite an expensive technique. Following applications are already useable and have been demonstrated:

- **Rapidly forming a prototype** (usually in a polymer) that can be used as a model for the further creation process (model for the production of a sandbed for casting iron). Such polymer models are fairly easy and cheap to produce, and offer a special advantage when one wants to make copies of an original object, in a material that is subject to shrinkage (metals, ceramics). The method is as follows: one 'simply' prints the polymer prototype at a size that is slightly bigger. Using this model, one produces (in a classical way) the mold. Subsequently the final object is being produced I a traditional manner, using the mold. The result is a traditionally produced object, with exactly the good dimensions. Such techniques may be used on a wide variety of metal objects, such as metal doorhandles, decorations on fences or other, as well as on other materials submitted to shrinkage during production (such as ceramics).
- We already mentioned sandbeds, as an intermediate phase to case iron or bronze. **Such sandbeds can be printed directly**, on the basis of a 3d-model (produced using scanning, CAD or a combination of both). The results is a block of 'sand' (actually sand with a binder with high thermal resistance), containing a cavity with all necessary canals (to remove air and to let the molten metal get in). Especially in the case of complex forms, this method offers an important advantage compared to the classical production of sand molds, and skips the step of making a physical model based on which a classical sand mold has to be produced. The molds are very stable, and can be transported over large distances. Another advantage is that one can 'print' the mold slightly larger than the original modal, in order to compensate for the shrinkage while casting the metal. In the restoration sector, this technique proves to be interesting for the production of larger metal objects, such as cast iron columns, balconies, fences, … and maybe even objects such as highly elaborated and richly detailed stoves or radiators in cast iron. This technique has also been used for the creation of concrete molds, even though not for the purpose of restoration of buildings.
- Metal objects are also manufactured using lost-wax casting. In this technique, a wax model of the object (including canals for removal of gases and application of molten

metal) is bedded in a material that, after heating, transforms in a ceramic material. The wax itself burns away. Subsequently, this ceramic hollow object is filled with molten metal. After the metal cools down, the ceramic material is being removed, and the metal object remains (ready for the final finishing touch). **Contemporary applications allow to print the wax model** (including the canals) directly from a digital model, again skipping the step where a physical model has to be formed before the mold is produced. Ongoing developments in the polymer chemistry allows to produce lost-wax models with lesser residue after burning away the polymer, and to produce more stable lost-wax models, that can easily be transported. Such techniques are suitable for highly crafted and detailed metal objects, such as door handles and other metal objects with a (partial) decorative purposes (Fig. 6).

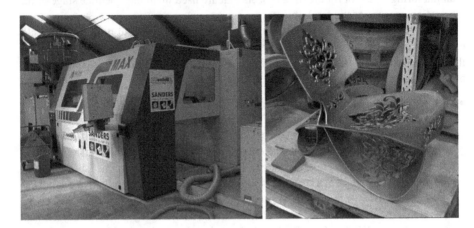

Fig. 6. Large 3D-print installation for the production of massive sand-molds, for cast iron. On the right an example of a complex object, made in one piece, using a single sand mold (installation of the Dutch firm 3dealise)

3.4   Future Prospects – Future Work

Future developments will improve the existing processes. The development of powerful software and image-analysis techniques will stimulate the application of scanning techniques, also for the individual building companies.

Speed, precision and cost may be drastically decreased by new developments in both the CNC- and 3d-printing domain. Also the development of new materials for 3d-printing may increase the possibilities for application in the restoration field. Examples may be the development of deformable polymers to produce molds. In our project, the emphasis lied on the restoration of metals and natural stone-like materials. But other applications should be readily available, such as

- the production of molds for certain decorative plaster applications. Especially when the objects are rather flat ('self-loosening'), printed polymer molds can be produced to produce large series of plaster objects, for instance for ceiling decoration. For more complex shapes, the development of 3d-printing of 'deformable' might be useful.

- the production of molds for several types of wall tiles (see Fig. 7 for some illustrations).

Fig. 7. Different types of ceramic tiles that may benefit from developments in the 3d-printing technology. Quite often one tries to find such tiles in antiques shops (which quite often works out well). In some cases such tiles need to be reproduced. For the two tiles on the left (a flat floor tile, and a tile with a surface relief) the technology is readily available to 3d-print the mold (several materials are available, and one can print the mold taking into account the shrinkage of the clay while cooking). This is not yet the case for the type of tiles in the right image, further research is necessary.

However, even more elaborated techniques could prove to be useful in the restoration sector:

- 3d-printing of complex concrete molds, including the printing of concrete reinforcements. No steel but polymer reinforcements, causing evidently further research on durability of such materials under more extreme circumstances (such as high alkalinity, temperatures, humidity, …).
- 3d-printing of 'lost molds' (i.e. molds that are not removed after filling the mold with, for instance, concrete) in different materials, for instance ceramics. Several examples from the early 20th century exist, and may perhaps even be transformed to a 21st century equivalent.
- There are many potential innovation possibilities in the field of artificial stone. Many stones that are hardly available anymore in good qualities could benefit from an 'artificial' counterpart. The development and application of techniques for producing concrete molds may increase development of new materials to imitate natural stone, next to the revival of 'old' artificial stone 'recipies'.

4   Conclusion

By using digital techniques, including CNC-methods or additive manufacturing, it is possible to facilitate the creation of objects that can readily be used in the restoration of buildings. In most of these processes, the technique forms an addition to, or facilitation of, the existing craftsmanship, and is by no means a replacement of the traditional techniques.

By examining the current state of the art in Flanders, through research and interviews amongst different stakeholders (such as architects, building contractors, the heritage administrations, …) several applications of these techniques have been illustrated, as well as possible new applications of such techniques.

Without any doubt there are useful applications in the field of restoration of other materials, such as ceramic materials, or even glass. Particular interest may be given to the optimization of the production of detailed ceramic wall tiles, where the 3d-printing of the mold may be of particular interest.

We emphasize the fact that such techniques may contribute to a better conservation of buildings and art objects. Precise scanning- and modelling techniques allow to create exactly matching pieces, that can be attached to the existing building or art object, without having to alter the latter (no removal of original material) and (when choosing the right adhesion materials) in a reversible manner.

Acknowledgment. The authors of this contribution gratefully acknowledge the kind support of Flanders Innovation and Entrepreneurship (*Agentschap Innoveren en Ondernemen*, www.vlaio. be/english) for giving them the possibility to research the existing market on potential innovative techniques to be employed in the field of restoration, and to be able to identify new possible applications of such techniques.

References

1. Remondino, F.: Heritage Recording and 3D modeling with Photogrammetry and 3D scanning. Remote Sens. **3**(6), 1104–1138 (2011)
2. Govaerts, Y.: Restoration strategies for stone imitating renders: Guidelines for characterisation, cleaning and composing repair mortars. PhD-research, Faculty of Engineering, Department of Architectural Engineering, Vrije Universiteit Brussel (2016, in press)
3. Peters, S.: Gebruik van kunststeen voor de restauratie van het Antwerps Stationsgebouw (*The application of artificial stone for the restoration of the Antwerp Central Station*). In: Proceedings of the WTA-Conference 'Natuursteen? Natuurlijk!', Aarschot (Belgium), 9 November 2012
4. Gibson, I., Rosen, D., Stucker, B.: Additive Manufacturing Technologies. Springer (2015)

Conservation and Valorization of Heritage Ethnographic Textiles

A. Ispas[1(✉)], C. Popescu[1], G. Roşu[1], H.C. Rădulescu[2], H. Fischer[3], P. Roedel[4],
M. Dinu[5], and R. Radvan[5]

[1] National Museum of the Romanian Peasant, Bucharest, Romania
andraispas@gmail.com
[2] National Research and Development Institute for Textile and Leather, Bucharest, Romania
[3] Faserinstitut Bremen, Bremen, Germany
[4] Institut für Pflanzenkultur e.K, Schnega, Germany
[5] National Institute for Research and Development in Optoelectronics – INOE 2000,
Bucharest, Romania

Abstract. The textiles make up a fragile heritage, continuously exposed to erosion through the natural aging of the fibres, environmental conditions and human actions. The aim of the MYTHOS project is the development of textiles from natural fibers (flax and hemp) which are biologically and technologically similar to the textiles found in heritage collections. A multidisciplinary research, involving specialists in ethnography, physics, molecular biology, chemistry and textile industry started with the analysis of the ethnographic textiles found in the National Museum of the Romanian Peasant's collection and a study of the traditional methods of cultivation and processing of flax and hemp. The textiles obtained as a result, similar to the heritage textiles, will be tested in restoration work, the results of this project seeking to benefit all the cultural organizations which hold collections of bast fibre textiles.

Keywords: Cultural heritage · Historical textiles · Bast fibres · Traditional techniques · Enzymatical ageing · Microbial diversity

1 Introduction

Heritage textiles are an important part of many collections throughout Europe, the conservation and valorization of this delicate heritage being an ongoing concern of specialists from various national and international organizations. Most of these heritage textiles, whether everyday clothes or festive garments, whether interior decoration textiles or those used in food transporting and conservation, are made from natural fibres like hemp, flax, cotton, silk and wool.

Regardless of their previous function, when reaching the museum, these objects already show signs of prolonged use, plus further signs of the way in which they were conserved and later displayed. The conservation state of the museum's textiles is therefore the result of these objects' previous existence, plus the conditions of use, storage/ exposure, as well as the conservation and restoration work undertaken over a period [1].

© Springer International Publishing AG 2016
M. Ioannides et al. (Eds.): EuroMed 2016, Part II, LNCS 10059, pp. 151–159, 2016.
DOI: 10.1007/978-3-319-48974-2_17

Thus, many of these heritage items require urgent conservation and restoration. These processes serve a major role in ensuring the European cultural heritage continuity, which must be undertaken in accordance with common European guidelines. These guidelines ensure that any intervention upon heritage objects should be undertaken with appropriate techniques and by respecting their physical integrity and maintaining their aesthetical significance, historical and social background.

In addition, all materials used in the conservation-restoration processes should not adversely affect these heritage items as well as not present risks to humans and environment. It is preferable to use materials similar to the originals, and when not possible, the substitutes must be compatible with the materials found in the heritage items [2]. Following this compatibility principle, the multidisciplinary research conducted within the MYTHOS project (Development of advanced compatible materials and techniques and their application for the protection, conservation and restoration of cultural heritage assets), which involved collaborations of experts in ethnography, physics, textile industry, molecular biology, chemistry, aims to obtain fibres, yarns and fabrics which will serve as reference materials. They will be greatly similar, biologically and technologically, to the fabrics used in the heritage textiles containing bast fibres. In this way, all restoration and conservation work will be safely carried out, while respecting the cultural and historical value of these heritage objects.

2   Ethnographic Textiles

Across Europe, for centuries, the bast fibres represented, together with wool, an important raw material for the production of clothing, decorative fabrics and household textiles.

In Romania, hemp and flax were cultivated on vast rural areas, ensuring each family's needs of fabrics, the surplus being sold in markets, either as fabrics or as yarns.

The essential component of the traditional Romanian garment, male and female shirts, was made of hemp or flax, wool and cotton being used for their decoration. Within the peasant household, the textile fibres were obtained by numerous and extremely scrupulous operations, requiring great skill and patience, their final quality depending on the final quality of the fibres, their strength, colour and smoothness [3].

The processing of flax and hemp were identical, both crops sharing characteristics of bast plants. Mature plants were harvested, dried and bound in sheafs; these were then retted into water, later removed, rewashed and dried until the fibres could be extracted from the stems. The fibres thus obtained were then combed and separated by length and thickness. The spinning of the hemp also represented a difficult endeavor due to the roughness and thickness of the fibre, hemp being spun by twisting in one direction only, Z, while the thread pulled from the shaft needed to be constantly moistened [4].

Since bast fibres are characterized by stiffness and natural beige-grey colour, to acquire white colour and softness, two further operations were necessary: boiling the fibres in lye (a mixture of warm water and plum or beech ash) and, after weaving, bleaching the cloth by exposure to sunlight and constant watering.

As industrial textiles became more available and more affordable, traditional pieces of clothing and textiles used within the house were gradually replaced by those made of industrial fabrics.

3 Materials and Methods

3.1 The Reference Collection

The Museum's collection is arranged by the material of which the objects are made and the textile pieces are grouped into three collections, by typology: Folk costumes, Textiles and Rugs. Through a dedicated study of the heritage textiles, the reference collection was established, this containing reference pieces to be researched in the MYTHOS project. 3.322 pieces composed of flax and hemp fibers were selected and three criteria analysis were established: the typological criteria, the geographical criteria and the compositional criteria (the mix of fibers used in the objects). Twenty items were selected as a representative sample, some well preserved and some showing various types and degrees of damage. For them, there was complete information regarding their origin, dating, materials and manufacturing techniques used. Non-invasive tests were performed on these pieces.

For structural and genetic analyses samples of raw fibres and yarn were used, as well as samples of spun fibres of varying quality and thicknesses, all originating from traditionally processed hemp from the first half of the twentieth century.

3.2 Morphological and Microbiological Investigation

The surface morphology was investigated using a Scanning Electron Microscope Quanta 200 (FEI) coupled with EDS detector.

For the microbiological analysis sampling was done using dry and wet swab technique, and using small adhesive tapes, without affecting the structure of the textile fibres and yarns. The swabs and adhesive tape were directly inoculated on Petri dishes with sterilised medium. As a culture medium it was used Sabouraud Dextrose Agar Medium (Biomeriuex). The Petri dishes were then incubated at 28 ^{0}C for 14 days. The identification of the fungal species was done by classical and molecular methods.

3.3 Enzymatical Artificial Ageing Protocol

Enzymatic flax fabric treatments were performed as described in [5] using two fabric pieces of 200×200 mm^2, yielding each 10 test specimen of 20×200 mm^2 in warp and weft direction. The flax fabric used as reference (175 g/m^2, #00 1818 00) was obtained from Leineweberei Hoffmann, Neukirch/Lausitz, DE. Treatments were performed using Texazym® AB & APN, 200 mL of reaction solution, using up to 1 g Texazym® AB or 1 mL Texazym® APN (both cellulases) with variation of enzyme concentration and reaction time.

All Enzymes were purchased from INOTEX s.r.o., Dvůr Králové n.L., CZ. The pH was adjusted by adding soda solution. The experiments were carried out at 30°C and 50°C for 20 min (exceptions mentioned in the text). Finally the fabrics were dried for 1 h at 105°C. After re-conditioning in standard climate at 20°C and 65 % relative humidity according to DIN EN ISO 1397 for at least 16 h, the tensile testing was performed according to DIN EN ISO 13934-1 (strip test) with reduced specimen size: specimen width 20 mm (instead of 50 mm) and clamping length 100 mm (instead of 200 mm).

3.4 Hemp Variety Collection Cultivation

Conservation of landraces is problematic as the allowed THC content by EU law is very low and is exceeded by historic landraces. Modern varieties are bred to minuscule THC contents. [6] Therefore historic landraces cannot be preserved by on-farm conservation, but only in genebanks. [7] A collection of historic landraces and modern varieties of hemp (*Cannabis sativa*) was established at the Institut für Pflanzenkultur. Database searches of the landraces and varieties at the German genebank IPK Gatersleben, the Russian genebank Vavilov Institute of Plant Industry and the Romanian Suceava genebank were performed (Table 1).

Table 1. The IFP germplasm as used for the experimental field cultivation

Regional provenance	Variety name	Source of supply	Accession number	Number at IFP
Slovakia, CSSR collecting tour 1977	Landrace	IPK Gatersleben	CAN 16	1
Hungary, bot. gard. Budapest	Landrace	IPK Gatersleben	CAN 17	2
Romania, bot. gard. Iasi, Alexandru Ioan Cuza University	Landrace	IPK Gatersleben	CAN 21	3
China, bot. gard. Beijing	Landrace	IPK Gatersleben	CAN 39	4
Romania	Lovrin 110	IPK Gatersleben	CAN 66	5
Hungary	Kompolti	IPK Gatersleben	CAN 70	6
Romania	Lovrin 200	INF&MP Poznan		7
Poland	Zenit	INF&MP Poznan		8
France	Santhica 27	Faserhanf Uckermark		9

3.5 Hemp Traditional Processing

One of the principle of the conservation-restoration of textile heritage materials is the compatibility of the materials used, to the heritage materials that need to be restored and conserved. For this reason in the Mythos project traditional spinning and weaving techniques were employed to obtain a yarn and a woven with a greater technological ressemblance to the etnographical textiles from the National Museum of the Romanian Peasant.

4 Results and Discussion

4.1 Microbiological and Structural Characterisation

Many of the heritage textiles entered into the Museum Collection after they have been used and stored in families` households. Some of them still present stains or traces of dirt difficult to clean using normal conservation procedures (Fig. 1). The microbiological assessment aimed to determine the presence of microorganisms on the surface of materials to estimate a potential further damage to them. Identification of the fungal species by colony morphology (Fig. 2 left, right) indicated the presence mostly of species capable of degrading cellulose, belonging to the genera *Aspergillus* and *Paecilomyces*.

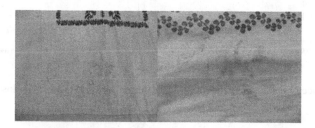

Fig. 1. (left and right) Zones of microbiological sampling were stains were present

Fig. 2. Left: sampling of microbial contamination; Right: Filamentous fungal species isolated from heritage textiles surface

Bast fibres that compose hemp and flax etnographical textiles are made of cellulose, thus they retain the potential of being degraded or just colonised by fungi with celulolitic activity. Further identification of the fungal communities using molecular methods are now under development.

The micrographs from the historical fibres showed the presence of the celullose chaines with presence of impurities due to the storage and transportation.

4.2 Enzymatical Ageing Protocol

The effect of enzyme application in increasing concentrations is displayed in Fig. 3 for Texazym® AB (left) and APN (right), both for warp and weft direction. It is easy to observe, that the influence of both enzymes is different in warp and weft, and that the uncertainty of the values is comparably large.

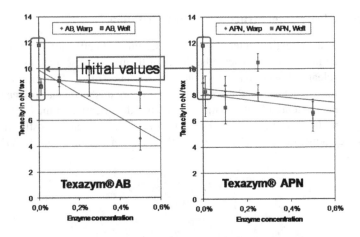

Fig. 3. Influence of cellulose treatment on fabric tenacity (EN ISO 13934-1, Instron universal tester)

The large uncertainty is due to the reduced specimen size (total 800 cm² instead of 3000 cm²). The small width of the specimen causes a variation of the result, even if there is only one thread more or less in the specimen. Using standard specimen size would improve the statistical safety, but would require four times more material and can thus not be recommended for historic samples.

The same considerations are valid for the results of the variation of reaction time, displayed in Fig. 4: again for Texazym® AB (left) a different behaviour in warp and weft direction can be observed, whereas the behaviour in warp and weft direction is the same for Texazym® APN (right). This points to the occurrence of diffusion effects. Although the fibre material is the same in warp and weft, the yarn twist is normally different in both directions, and the warp threads are processed under higher tension in weaving. Consequently the size of the intermediate spaces between the fibre bundles is not the same.

As result the warp threads are easily percolated by Texazym® AB, indicated by the complete reaction after 20 min., whereas in weft direction the reaction is complete after 120 min. From these results can be concluded, that the reduction of fabric tenacity is possible by enzymatic treatment, but the intensity depends on type of enzyme, concentration and processing time, different properties in warp- and weft direction have to be considered due to diffusion effects, the adaption of the process parameters for each fabric type is essential in order to achieve reproducible results.

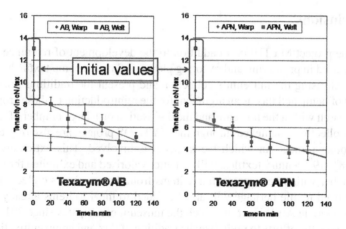

Fig. 4. Influence of treatment time on fabric tenacity (EN ISO 13934-1, Instron universal tester)

Summed up it can be concluded, that the technical fibres used as modern reference material [8] are much better suitable for artificial ageing than fabrics, because they only need a weak treatment to adapt the properties of the historic materials. The fabrics tested here would need a much more intensive treatment to break down their tenacity, and it would be impossible to make them as coarse as the historic originals are. Thus we recommend performing the artificial ageing on raw fibres [8] rather than in later process steps.

4.3 Hemp Variety Cultivation

The cultivation of a collection of hemp modern varieties followed a laborious analysis of historical DNA from the heritage bast samples [9]. The hemp variety collection can be used to compare the physical properties of the fibres to the fibres in the historic textiles. Such an analysis was not performed by now, even analyses for modern varieties as by Baltina and co-workers are very scarce [10]. After growth the flowering and seed-setting hemp was harvested. Harvest was done by manual cutting of the stalks 15 cm above ground to dispose the lignified lower part of the stalk. The stalks were bundled and put on water permeable woven synthetic fabric.

4.4 Hemp Traditional Processing

The hemp fibres designed for producing reference materials for restoration were trans-formed into yarn and woven using traditional techniques. Traditional preliminary oper-ations for spinning the bast yarns are intended to break the bast stalks using "meliţa" and combing the bulk of fibres. After obtaining bast fibres on classes of finesse, the finest ones are chosen for the woven of the clothing, mainly women and man shirts. After spinning the fibres into yarns, these are used to obtain the warp, which is then put on the horizontal loom, traditionally constructed on wood.

5   Conclusions

Through the project MYTHOS, in addition to the development of reference materials that will be used in preserving and restoring pieces of flax and hemp textile heritage, we set out to valorising the museum's collection and present the traditions related to the cultivation of hemp and flax as an argument for the reintroduction of these crops in rural zones. Research within the museum and the digitisation on a large number of items from the textile collections, achieved through the MYTHOS project, are also of great importance for other projects in which the museum is involved. This extremely valuable heritage, 18th–19th century textiles, will be better valorised and exhibited through Europeana, together with other representative items from the museum's collections. A part of this digitised textile heritage will also be added to the 150 items already available through the Google Art Project, in which the museum participates since 2014 [11].

In Romania, the efforts to revitalize the tradition of flax and hemp cultivation follow two directions: an industrial one, focused mainly on the export of seeds and a traditional one, targeting rural households. At this stage of the project, with a view of developing the second direction, we have involved a small producer of traditional fibres. A unique project, "Manual weaving", undertaken and coordinated by Mr. Andrei Sas, is involved in the marketing of fabrics made from natural fibres: hemp, cotton, wool. Through this activity, it has become a keeper of local traditional weaving techniques, prooving that artisans can contribute through their products to their own wellfare and that of the region, thus supplementing their income.

The results obtained until now are a proof that the conservation-restoration it's no longer a single profession activity, it involves the expertize and the synergic action of museum specialists, researchers from many scientific fields and target social communities.

Acknowledgments. Financial support by the Romanian Ministry of Education, Executive Unit for Financing Higher Education Research Development and Innovation, Project PN-II-PT-PCCA-2011-3.1-0408. The authors wish to thank to Mr Andrei Sas from the REST˙ART – Intreprindere Individuala Bertoti Otto (Arad, România) for the traditional spinning and weaving of hemp fibres and to Ms S. Sostman, FIBRE, for carrying out the artificial ageing protocol.

References

1. Zaharia, F.: Principiile conservarii patrimoniului textil romanesc. In: Ion, N.D., Stefanescu, R. (eds.) In Honorem Ioan Opris: Patrimoniu, pp. 409–429. Monumente Istorice, Muzeografie (2014)
2. European Recommendation for the Conservation and Restauration of Cultural Heritage (2013)
3. Marinescu, M.: Arta populară românească. Ţesături decorative. Dacia, Cluj-Napoca (1975)
4. Zaharia, F.: Textilele tradiţionale din Transilvania: tehnologie şi estetică. Accent Print, Suceava (2008)
5. Fischer, H., Müssig, J., Bluhm, C., Marek, J., Antonov, V.: Enzymatic modification of hemp fibres for sustainable production of high quality materials: comparing different commercial enzymes. In: Team of Authors (eds.) 11th International Conference STRUTEX (Proceedings), pp. 301–308. Technical University of Liberec, Liberec (2004)

6. Holoborodko, P., Virovets, V., Laiko, I., Bertucelli, S., Beherec, O., Fournier, G.: Results of Efforts by French and Ukranian Breeders to Reduce Cannabinoid Levels in Industrial Hemp (Cannabis sativa L.) (2014). http://www.interchanvre.com/docs/article-Laiko.pdf

7. Veteläinen, M., Negri, V., Maxted, N. (eds): European landraces: on-farm conservation, management and use. In: Bioversity International, Bioversity Technical Bulletin no. 15, Rome (2009)

8. Fischer, H., Wiese, H., Radulescu, C., Rödel, P.: Development of advanced compatible materials for the restoration of cultural heritage assets (Mythos): Artificial ageing of bast fibres. Vlakna a textil (Fibres and Textiles) 1, 13–16 (2015)

9. Rödel, P., Radulescu, C., Fischer, H.: Development of advanced compatible materials for the restoration of cultural heritage assets (Mythos): Fibre DNA analysis. In: Proceedings of the International Conferrence TexTeh VII Creating the future of textiles, Bucharest, Romania, vol. 7, pp. 229–235 (2015)

10. Baltiņa, I., Zamuška, Z., Stramkale, V., Strazds, G.: Physical Properties of Latvian Hemp Fibres. In: Environment. Technology. Resources, Proceedings of the 8th International Scientific and Practical Conference, vol. 1, pp. 237–243 (2015)

11. Google Arts & Culture. https://www.google.com/culturalinstitute/beta/partner/national-museum-of-the-romanian-peasant

Preservation and Valorisation of Morocco's Ancient Heritage: Volubilis

Muzahim Al-Mukhtar[1]([✉]), Ali Chaaba[2], Mustapha Atki[3], Rachida Mahjoubi[4],
Remi Deleplancque[5], Kévin Beck[1], Xavier Brunetaud[1], Romain Janvier[1],
Khalid Cherkaoui[2], Issam Aalil[1,2], Dalal Badreddine[1,2], and Ayda Sakali[4]

[1] University of Orléans, PRISME - EA4229, 8 rue Léonard de Vinci, 45072 Orléans, France
muzahim.al-mukhtar@univ-orleans.fr
[2] Ecole Nationale Supérieure d'Arts et Métiers (ENSAM), Meknès, Morocco
[3] Conservation of the Archaeological Site of Volubilis, Meknès, Morocco
[4] Moulay Ismail University, Marjane II, B.P. 4024 Meknès, Morocco
[5] Mission Val de Loire, 81 Rue Colbert, 37043 Tours, France

Abstract. The Volubilis project has created an opportunity for the transfer and sharing of knowledge in the field of heritage conservation between teams from both shores of the Mediterranean. The ambition of this project, supported by the region Centre-Val-de-Loire (France), is to develop a set of tools to preserve and develop the archaeological site of Volubilis. This Moroccan and global iconic ancient heritage is exposed to damage that endangers its durability.

The project started in September 2015 and has two main goals. The first one is to carry out a historic inventory of the materials used for the construction of the site and their environment in order to understand the origin of the damage and propose sustainable solutions for remediation that meet the requirements of the ICOMOS Charter, in particular concerning the choice of compatible materials for restoration (mortar and stone). The second one is to promote the site towards local, national and international tourists via historical, scientific and technical media to highlight the cultural importance of this heritage. This project brings together two French partners, the Multidisciplinary Institute of Engineering Research Systems, Mechanics and Energetics (PRISME - University of Orléans) and the Mission Val de Loire, and three Moroccan partners, the Ecole Nationale Supérieure d'Arts et Métiers (ENSAM-Meknes), Moulay Ismail University and the conservation authorities of the archaeological site, Volubilis Conservation.

Keywords: Volubilis · Preservation of built heritage · 3D modelling · Diagnosis of alterations

1 Introduction

Multidisciplinary collaboration has led to major advances in the 3D modelling of buildings and in the diagnosis of alterations and means of restoration. However, this progress is still largely reserved for the monuments of rich countries and the transfer of knowledge, means and technology to preserve built heritage world-wide is still low.

© Springer International Publishing AG 2016
M. Ioannides et al. (Eds.): EuroMed 2016, Part II, LNCS 10059, pp. 160–167, 2016.
DOI: 10.1007/978-3-319-48974-2_18

The archaeological site of Volubilis includes various monuments within the city walls: monumental buildings, houses, temples, statues, inscriptions and mosaics. Unfortunately, the site has been subjected to processes of degradation over time. Due to natural and anthropogenic factors, many monuments have lost their historical, aesthetic and structural integrity. The restoration of monuments on the site is a complex task because of the variety of materials used, the implementation techniques and intervention constraints that are necessary to respect the authenticity and originality of the various monuments.

To ensure the success of the project, Franco-Moroccan multidisciplinary partners have combined their expertise to develop and implement systematic approaches to the restoration of the monuments respecting the requirements of the ICOMOS Charter. To enhance the socio-economic impact and tourist interest of Volubilis and the region of Fez-Meknes in Morocco, initiatives to promote and develop the site are also planned.

2   Presentation of the Volubilis Site

Volubilis has been registered on the UNESCO World Heritage list since December 1997 and it expresses the symbiosis of two types of ancient habitat: Punic-Mauritanian and Roman. The site is 380 m above sea level, 40 km from the city of Fez, and 150 km from the Mediterranean Sea. The climate is Mediterranean with a continental and semi-arid trend characterized by daily changes in temperature of up to 20°C. The site covers about 40 hectares but the excavation work so far has concerned only 23 hectares. The first excavations of the site began in 1887 under the direction of De la Martiniere [1]. The main excavations and restoration work took place during 1930–1967. Recently, some walls were consolidated and the Idrissid bath in the lower quarter was restored as part of the Anglo-Moroccan Volubilis Project (2001–2005). Nonetheless, preservation interventions are more necessary than ever especially in the northeast district [2]. This is a particularly vulnerable area [3] and contains many houses with precious mosaics such as the House of Venus, the most sumptuous house on the site [4] (Fig. 1).

Fig. 1. Central part of the archaeological site of Volubilis.

3 Presentation the Volubilis Project

The Volubilis project involves various tasks to develop the scientific and technical approach as well as initiatives regarding cultural enhancement, tourism and development of the site.

The first task is to carry out a state of the art survey of Volubilis to make an archaeological, historical, and geological inventory of the site and its materials. The second task is to build a 3D model of Volubilis. Historical data from the first task will be used to offer historical interpretations of the house of Venus in order to propose a 3D virtual tour of the house. The project intends to characterize the different materials used (stones and mortars) in the construction of the monuments on the site. A restoration mortar that is compatible with local stones and the climatic environment will be developed. Then, a pilot "experimental wall" will be restored and instrumented on the site and will be used to test several solutions validated beforehand in the laboratory. This should allow the development of specifications, rules of art and standards for the restoration of the site.

Tools for cultural and tourist development (flyers, tourist guidebooks, website, etc.) will be implemented to promote tourism, enriching the historical documentation of the site. The entrance to the site will be arranged to promote cultural exhibitions and trade events including local associations and cooperatives. The site can be a vector to boost tourism and the local economy (restaurants, accommodation, arts and crafts, shops, etc.) as well as sociocultural activities (festivals, events on the site), bringing socioeconomic benefits on the local, regional and national levels.

4 Actions in Progress and Preliminary Results

4.1 Historical Site

Volubilis was a Mauritanian capital founded in the 3rd century B.C. and became an important outpost of the Roman Empire in 40 AD [5]. The town was abandoned by the Romans in 284–285 AD, but continued to be occupied by its residents until the 11th–12th centuries. During the second and third century AD, the city was fortified to reach its maximum extension of about 40 hectares, surrounded by a wall with eight monumental gates. The city expanded westward beyond the enclosure during the Idrissid dynasty [3]. After the death of Idris I in 791, the city was progressively abandoned until the Almoravid period (11th–12th centuries). The destruction of the site is likely related to the earthquake in 1755 [6]. The house of Venus was built in several phases: the first house dates from the second half of the first century while most of the mosaics and baths were added in the second century [3]. It was excavated by R. Thouvenot during 1940–1950 [4]. The house contains columns measuring 0.36 m and 0.46 m in diameter and at least 2.10 m and 2.60 m in height [4]. These historical and architectural data will be complemented by a comparison with other Roman sites to make a 3D model with a virtual reconstruction of the house of Venus.

4.2 Inventory of Materials: Stones and Mortars

The monuments were built with several types of stones. The main stones are a yellowish-beige calcarenite limestone and a compact grey limestone. The calcarenite was used as rubble masonry and for sculptural elements such as columns and capitals. The grey limestone is present as large blocks constituting the corners, the foundations and the gantries. These two stones represent approximately 60 % and 31 % of total building stones on the site [7]. In addition, the site contains decorative stones such as marble and coloured stones and small fragments of tiles can be observed in walls and floors. Various kinds of mortars are found, composed of soil, lime and cement, and sometimes contain fragments of broken brick or tiles (Fig. 2).

Fig. 2. Wall in the House of Venus: Calcarenite stone and large blocks of grey limestone restored with mud-based mortar. (Color figure online)

4.3 Inventory of Degradation of the Monuments

The stones of the site are affected by several degradations, mainly sanding, alveolization and scaling. These alterations are observed primarily on the East side, which is subjected to dry winds, at the level of stone in contact with the ground or adjacent to mortar joints from previous interventions. In addition, the calcarenite stone is affected by reddening and biological colonization by lichen and moss. These appear mostly on the shaded northwest side. On the grey limestone, the main alterations are micro cracking and scaling.

The state of mortar conservation is variable. Some mortars crumble easily or show cracks and no longer adhere to stones, while others appear to be in good condition, without any alteration and with good adhesion to stones. Samples of deteriorated calcarenite stone were analysed by ion chromatography (IC). The test showed that they have high sulphate and chloride contents. X Ray Diffraction analysis (XRD) and Thermal Gravimetric Analysis (TGA) revealed that these samples contain gypsum and halite (Fig. 3). Analysis of the grey limestone samples is still on-going.

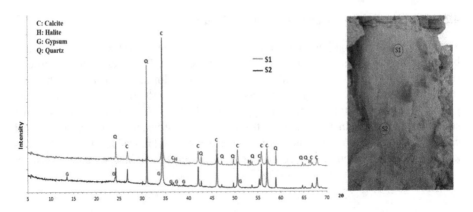

Fig. 3. XRD patterns of two samples from a deteriorated calcarenite.

4.4 Inventory of Previous Restorations Performed on the Site

After starting the first excavations in 1887-1892, which were then resumed in 1915 [1], maintenance and restoration work was undertaken in 1916 by straightening the north portal of the basilica. The Triumphal arch was reconstructed in 1930–1934 but a preliminary study was not carried out, not all the blocks were replaced and cement was used to fill gaps [7]. Partial restorations based on anastylosis were undertaken in the 1960 s by Luquet, enabling the monumental centre and other Volubilis buildings to be restored: the Capitol and the Forum in 1962–1964, the basilica in 1965–1967, the Gate of Tangier in 1967, the temples in 1968 and the house of the Nereids in 1972 [1, 7]. During the 1990 s, the site's conservation service restored a Roman oil mill. Recently in 2000–2007, as part of an Anglo-Moroccan project, some Idrissid baths were restored and a collapsed wall in the house of Venus was restored [3].

Other interventions were certainly performed without being archived as witnessed by the presence of recent mortars and information provided by the site's conservation service. The analysis of some mortars used during the previous interventions by XRD,

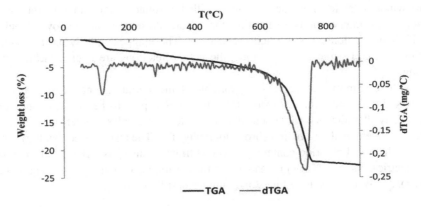

Fig. 4. Thermogravimetric curves of mortar used during a previous intervention

TGA and IC showed that they are likely the origins of the halite and gypsum detected in the deteriorated stones. As an example, Fig. 4 shows a weight loss around 120 °C related to gypsum decomposition. It could be due to the use of large quantities of Portland cement as an additive to lime mortar during recent unplanned interventions between 2004 -2006, to waterproof the top of the walls.

4.5 Development of Mortar Compatible with In-situ Stones

This study is still in progress: the first phase was to determine the hydro-thermo-mechanical properties of the predominant calcarenite stone used in the site. Locally available materials (sand, lime and pozzolan additions) were also characterized. The second phase is devoted to the in-situ characterization of mortars in good condition to determine their constituents. Subsequently, restoration mortars will be formulated and dosage will be optimized to achieve sustainable mortars that are compatible with calcarenite stone and the other main stones in terms of hydro-thermo-mechanical properties. The mortars chosen will be used to carry out an experiment on one wall in order to study the behaviour of the stone-mortar assembly. A wall will also be completed and instrumented (strain gauges, temperature sensors, humidity sensors, capillary pressure sensor) on site to monitor its behaviour under environmental site conditions.

4.6 Visitor Survey

To develop tourism, a survey of visitors is on-going. At least 1,200 people will be surveyed before the end of June 2016 and the data will be processed and analysed. The aim of the survey is to identify visitors' expectations and needs, sketch their profiles and understand their behaviour in order to develop consistent actions matched to the needs assessment. In addition, promotional flyers of the history and flagship monuments of the site have been produced, and will be distributed in Morocco and via travel agencies to develop the attractiveness of the site. A plan is being finalized to guide tourists inside the site with signposts and tourist guides.

4.7 3D Reconstruction of the Archaeological Site

A 3D survey of the whole archaeological site is planned. The purpose of this survey is threefold. The first aim is to ensure conservation and archiving of the vestiges. Secondly, this 3D survey will be used as the support for annotation and mapping in a Geographical Information System (GIS) as well as in a more complete Conservation Information System [8, 9]. Thirdly, the 3D model is expected to lay the metric foundations for a 3D restitution of past structures and a virtual tour of the current site.

In view of the area covered by the site (50 ha) it would be difficult to digitize the whole ancient city with an active method such as Terrestrial Laser Scanning (TLS) in the time allowed by the project. Thanks to improvements in algorithms and the increasing power of computers in recent decades [10, 11], it is now technically possible to accomplish digitization with Structure from Motion (SfM). However, such a large scale SfM study relies on community photo collections and the acquisition of a city scale corpus remains an issue. To tackle that, we plan to perform multiple scale acquisitions. First, an aerial survey will be performed thanks to a DSLR mounted on a UAV. We expect to be able to record photographs of about 1 cm Ground Surface Distance (GSD). This should allow us to compute a high-accuracy Digital Elevation Model (DEM) and generate an orthomosaic for mapping purposes. Then, for areas of greater interest such as high elevation structures or mosaics, we plan to take pictures from the ground so as to obtain detailed 3D models for these critical parts. Lastly, we plan to complete the survey with oblique imagery using a DSLR mounted on a pole. The whole model will be geo-registered thanks to the integration of data from Ground Control Points (GCP), the Global Positioning System (GPS) and an Inertial Measurement Unit (IMU) in the computation.

To date, a feasibility study has already been done: 1620 photos of the House of Venus have been taken and already processed by both some well-established SfM software in the CH domain [12] and some more state of the art approaches [13], leading to promising results. A high density 3D model (Fig. 5) has already been extracted along with ortho-photos of the elevation.

Fig. 5. Dense colored 3D mesh of the House of Venus (Color figure online)

However, a large number of challenges still have to be tackled such as the handling of high radiometric heterogeneities in multi-temporal acquisition and more specifically local colour changes due to projected shadows. Moreover the co-registration of aerial imagery and the terrestrial survey could be an issue as well as the fusion of different acquisition scales. Computer Vision has been quite active in this field during the past few years and we expect to be able to take advantage of this research.

5   Conclusion

The preservation and valorisation of built heritage is a factor of economic growth as it boosts tourism. The various actions of the Volubilis project are designed to share and transfer knowledge and skills between teams from both shores of the Mediterranean. Two PhD theses are currently being carried out under joint international supervision (France – Morocco) on the physicochemical characterization and the development of materials and means for the restoration of monuments on the Volubilis site. Many Moroccan and French students are also involved through Masters courses and training periods in scientific and technical activities, and valorisation tasks.

Finally, the results obtained will be made available to site managers and will, where appropriate, be included in a future UNESCO heritage management plan.

Acknowledgements. The authors would like to thank the authorities of "Région Centre-Val de Loire (France)" for funding this project.

References

1. Kingdom of Morocco: UNESCO World Heritage Centre. Site archéologique de Volubilis. http://whc.unesco.org/uploads/nominations/836bis.pdf
2. Rizzi, G.: UNESCO World Heritage Centre. Site de Volubilis, Morocco. http://whc.unesco.org/archive/2005/mis836-2005.pdf
3. Fentress, E., Palumbo, G., Limane, H.: Reports of Volubilis project: UCL and INSAP (2004)
4. Thouvenot, R.: Maisons de Volubilis: le palais dit de Gordien et la maison à la mosaïque de Vénus. Service des antiquités du Maroc (1958)
5. Panetier, J., Liman, H.: Volubilis: une cité du Maroc antique. Maisonneuve & Larose (2002)
6. Moratti, G., Piccardi, L., Vannucci, G., Belardinelli, M.: The 1755 "Meknes" earthquake (Morocco): field data and geodynamic implications. J. Geodyn. **36**, 305–322 (2003)
7. Dessandier, D., Antonelli, F., Bouzidi, R., El Rhoddani, M., Kamel, S., Lazzarini, L., Leroux, L., Varti-Matarangas, M.: Atlas of the ornamental and building stones of Volubilis ancient site (Morocco). Final report BRGM/RP-55539-FR (2008)
8. Stefani, C., Brunetaud, X., Janvier-Badosa, S.: Developing a toolkit for mapping and displaying stone alteration on a web-based documentation platform. J. Cult. Heritage **15**, 1–9 (2014)
9. Messaoudi, T., Manuel, A., Gattet, E., Luca, L., Véron, P.: Laying the foundations for an information system dedicated to heritage building degradation monitoring based on the 2D/3D semantic annotation of photographs (2014)
10. Wu, C.: Towards linear-time incremental structure from motion. In: 2013 International Conference on 3D Vision-3DV 2013 (2013)
11. Agarwal, S., Snavely, N., Simon, I.: Building Rome in a day. In: Computer Vision (2009)
12. Pierrot-Deseilligny, M., Paparoditis, N.: A multiresolution and optimization-based image matching approach: An application to surface reconstruction from SPOT5-HRS stereo imagery. Arch. Photogramm. (2006)
13. Moulon, P., Monasse, P., Marlet, R.: Adaptive structure from motion with a contrario model estimation. In: Asia Conference on Computer Vision (2012)

Visualisation, VR and AR Methods and Applications

Experiencing Cultural Heritage Sites Using 3D Modeling for the Visually Impaired

Kyriacos Themistocleous[✉], Athos Agapiou, and Diofantos G. Hadjimitsis

Department of Civil Engineering and Geomatics, Cyprus University of Technology,
3036 Lemesos, Cyprus
{k.themistocleous,athos.agapiou,d.hadjimitsis}@cut.ac.cy

Abstract. There is a need to make cultural heritage sites accessible to all individuals, including those who are visually impaired. 3D printing technology provides the capability to print models of cultural heritage structure as teaching tools for the visually impaired. As well, Unmanned Aerial Vehicles (UAVs) have undergone significant advances in equipment capabilities and now have the ability to obtain high resolution images in a cost effective and efficient manner in order to create 3D models for 3D printing. This paper explores the use of UAVs to acquire high resolution images to generate 3D models that are printed using low-cost 3D printers intended to serve as a teaching aid for the visually impaired. A case study is presented for the Curium archaeological site.

Keywords: Cultural heritage · UAV · 3D images · 3D models · 3D printing

1 Introduction

Tactile educational materials are necessary to teach the blind and visually impaired, especially regarding archaeology and cultural heritage sites. Touch tours have become increasingly common in enhancing the museum experience for the blind or visually impaired (artmuseumteaching.com). In many countries, museums and cultural heritage sites provide architectural models that make masterpieces accessible to people who are blind or visually impaired (artbeyondisght.org). Exact architectural structures reproduced as small-scale tactile models offer opportunities to explore the exterior and interior of a building. Art and cultural heritage museums sometimes use three-dimensional props, and replicas of the objects depicted in a work of art to make it accessible to visitors who are blind or visually impaired (artmuseumteaching.com). Three-dimensional interpretations can recreate not only basic composition and color but also translate stylistic properties such as texture and brushwork into a touchable experience. In this study, the Curium archaeological amphitheatre was created as a 3D printed model to serve as a tactile educational tool for visitors to the site who are blind or visually impaired.

3D printers are increasingly being used to document archaeological sites and artefacts with precise 3D models. As well, 3D models can be printed on low cost 3D printers in order to be used as teaching aides, especially for individuals who require tactile materials, such as the visually impaired [1]. To generate a printable 3D model that can

© Springer International Publishing AG 2016
M. Ioannides et al. (Eds.): EuroMed 2016, Part II, LNCS 10059, pp. 171–177, 2016.
DOI: 10.1007/978-3-319-48974-2_19

be used to teach the visually impaired about ancient Curium amphitheatre, Unmanned Aerial Vehicle (UAV) images were taken over the amphitheatre. UAVs have undergone significant advances in equipment capabilities and now have the capacity to acquire high resolution imagery from many angles in a cost effective, efficient manner. Photogrammetry software can be used to determine characteristics such as distances, angles, areas, volumes, elevations, object sizes, and object shape within overlapping images [2, 3]. Aerial imagery from UAVs can also allow the rapid generation of 3D digital models [4–7], unlike data from laser scanners or other methods, which are expensive and take months to acquire and process. This integrated method of using UAV and 3D printing is a fast and affordable means that can be easily used at all archaeological sites.

2   Case Study

The study took place in the south-west of Cyprus in the archaeological site of Curium, which is situated outside the modern city of Limassol (Fig. 1). The mount of Curium, on which the ancient city-kingdom developed, occupies a dominant position on the coast 4 km southwest of the village of Episkopi in the Lemesos district. The city has passed through different phases including the Hellenistic, Roman, and Christian periods. The area is particularly noted for its magnificent Greco - Roman theatre. The theatre was initially constructed on a smaller scale in the late-second century BC.

Fig. 1. Curium archaeological site.

3 Methodology

The overall methodology is presented in Fig. 2. The site of Curium amphitheatre was selected and Ground Control Points (GCPs) were positioned around the site. The UAV was flown over the site at a height of 125 meters. The images were processed to create a 3D model, which was then printed using a 3D printer.

Site selection   UAV flight   Post-processing   3D model   3D printing
and preparation

Fig. 2. Methodology

Prior to the flight, GCPs were positioned and measured over the entire area in order to make the necessary corrections during the post-processing of the images (Fig. 3). These corrections are required to ensure the correct scale of the model, that is necessary to accurately print the model in scale. The GCPs points were recorded using a double frequency GNSS system with estimated accuracy of less than 2 cm. The flight planning software with the UAV provided a pre-determined flight path to be followed, thus ensuring significant image coverage and overlap for generation of stereo-pairs of images. The UAV camera took images with a 60 % overlay within each image. In this way, single images were automatically built into a large detailed map, to correct distortions and create a 3-D model.

Fig. 3. GCP at the Curium site

A total of 331 images were taken and were post-processed using Agisoft PhotoScan software (Fig. 4). Agisoft PhotoScan is an advanced image-based 3D modelling solution aimed at creating professional quality 3D content from still images. The first step in the program's procedure is called Structure from Motion (SFM) [8–10]. At this stage the software analyses the dataset, detecting geometrical patterns in order to reconstruct the virtual positions of the cameras that were used. The second step involves using a multi-viewpoint stereo algorithms to build a dense point cloud. At this stage the dataset of images are employed to produce a high-resolution geometry of the surface. Following, surfacing algorithms employed the dense cloud's 3D point positions and the look angles from the photos to the matched points to build the geometrical mesh. The GCPs were then applied to scale the model in order to scale the model to the correct dimensions. The 3D model was exported in order to clean up, fix, edit, optimize and prepare the generated mesh for 3D printing and a STereoLithography (.stl) file.

Also, a 3D model of the theatre was generated for visualization purposes (Fig. 5).

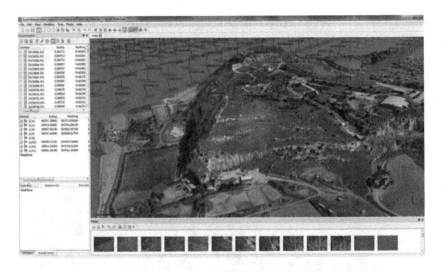

Fig. 4. Image processing

In order to print the 3d model, the 3D model needs to be prepared for slicing by dividing the 3D model into hundreds or thousands of horizontal layers using slicing software. When the 3D model is sliced, the file is uploaded in the 3D printer and the object is ready to be 3D printed layer by layer. The 3D printer reads every slice (2D image) and creates a 3-dimensional object by using a material extrusion process called Fused deposition modeling (FDM) [11–13]. The FDM technology works using a plastic filament which is unwound from a coil and supplying material to an extrusion nozzle which can turn the flow on and off. The nozzle is heated to melt the material and can be moved in both horizontal and vertical directions by a numerically controlled mechanism, directly controlled by a computer-aided manufacturing (CAM) software package. The object is produced by extruding melted material to form layers as the material hardens immediately after extrusion from the nozzle. This technology is most widely used with

Fig. 5. 3D model of the Curium amphitheatre

two plastic filament material types: ABS (Acrylonitrile Butadiene Styrene) and PLA (Polylactic acid) but many other materials are available ranging in properties from wood filed, conductive, flexible etc.

In this study, the Makerbot 3D printer was used to print a 3D model of the Curium amphitheatre (Fig. 6) using Polylactic acid (PLA) material, which is biodegradable thermoplastic aliphatic polyester. The model is now on display with Braille annotations and descriptions in the lobby of the visitor's center at the Curium site, enabling those with visual impairments to interactively experience the history of Curium.

Fig. 6. 3D model of the theatre located at the Curium site

4   Conclusions

The methodology described in this paper provides a fast and affordable means of creating tactile aids for blind and visually impaired that can be easily used at all archaeological sites. The Curium study highlighted the ability of UAVs to acquire high resolution imagery of an archaeological site using a non-invasive technology in a cost effective, efficient manner. The methodology described in this paper discussed how images from UAVs can be used to create a 3D scaled model of an archaeological site, which can be printed on a 3D printer. In addition, this methodology can be used by museums, archaeological sites and cultural heritage sites to document outdoor structures as teaching aids for blind and visually impaired individuals.

Acknowledgements.   The authors wish to thank the Department of Antiquities of Cyprus for their permission to carry out the measurements. We also wish to thank the Cyprus University of Technology and the Cyprus Remote Sensing Society for the use of their equipment. Special thanks to QuestUAV for their assistance in this study. As well, the authors wish to acknowledge the Cyprus Aviation Authority (CAA) and the Sovereign Bases Area Administration (SBAA) for their assistance in providing flight permission.

References

1. Sandberg, R.: 3D printing for blind people: The future potential of a cutting edge technology (2016). http://www.incobs.de/articles/items/3d.html
2. Siebert, S., Teizer, J.: Mobile 3D mapping for surveying earthwork projects using an Unmanned Aerial Vehicle (UAV) system. In: Proceedings 30th International Symposium on Automation and Robotics in Construction and Mining, Held in Conjunction with the 23rd World Mining Congress, ISARC 2013 (2013)
3. Adams, S., Friedland, C., Levitan, M.: Unmanned aerial vehicle data acqui- sition for damage assessment in hurricane events. In: Proceedings of the 8th International Workshop on Remote Sensing for Disaster Response (2010)
4. Themistocleous, K., Agapiou, A., King, Helen, M., King, N., Hadjimitsis, D.G.: More than a flight: the extensive contributions of UAV flights to archaeological research – the case study of curium site in cyprus. In: Ioannides, M., Magnenat-Thalmann, N., Fink, E., Žarnić, R., Yen, A.-Y., Quak, E. (eds.) EuroMed 2014. LNCS, vol. 8740, pp. 396–409. Springer, Heidelberg (2014). doi:10.1007/978-3-319-13695-0_38
5. Fiorillo, F., Jimenez, B., Remondino, F., Barba, S.: 3D surveying and modeling of the archaeological area of Paestum. Italy. Virt. Archaeo. Rev. **4**, 55–60 (2012)
6. Verhoeven, G.: Taking computer vision aloft: archaeological three-dimensional reconstructions from aerial photographs with PhotoScan. Arch. Prosp. **18**, 67–73 (2011)
7. Remondino, F., Barazzetti, L., Nex, F., Scaioni, M. Sarazi, D.: UAV photo grammetry for mapping and 3D modelling-current status and future perspetives. In: Proceedings of the ISPRS - The International Archives of the Photogram metry, Remote Sensing and Spatial Information Sciences, vol. XXXVIII-1/C22, ISPRS Zurich 2011 Workshop, 14–16 September 2011, Zurich, Switzerland, 25–31 (2011)
8. Scopigno, R., Cignoni, P., Pietroni N., Callieri, M., Dellepiane M.: Digital fab rication technologies for cultural heritage (STAR). In: EUROGRAPHICS Work Shops on Graphics and Cultural Heritage (2014)

9. Ingwer, P., Gassen, F., Püst, S., Duhn, M., Schälicke, M., Müller, K., Ruhm, H., Rettig, J., Hasche, E., Fischer, A., Creutzburg, R.: Practical usefulness of struc ture from motion (SfM) point clouds obtained from different consumer cameras. In: Proceedings SPIE 9411, Mobile Devices and Multimedia: Enabling Technologies, Al gorithms, and Applications 2015, 941102, March 11, 2015. doi:10.1117/12.2074892
10. Giuliano, M.G.: Cultural Heritage: An example of graphical documentation with automated photogrammetric systems. Intl Arch. of Photogr., Rem. Sens. and Sp. Inf. Sc. XL.5: 251–255. Gottingen: Copernicus GmbH. (2014)
11. Mikułowski, D., Brzostek-Pawłowska, J.: Problems encountered in technical education of the blind, and related aids: Virtual cubarythms and 3D drawings. IEEE Global Engineering Education Conference (EDUCON), Istanbul (2014). doi:10.1109/EDUCON.2014.6826223
12. Götzelmann, T., Pavkovic, A.: Towards automatically generated tactile detail maps by 3D printers for blind persons. In: Miesenberger, K., Fels, D., Archambault, D., Peňáz, P., Zagler, W. (eds.) ICCHP 2014. LNCS, vol. 8548, pp. 1–7. Springer, Heidelberg (2014). doi: 10.1007/978-3-319-08599-9_1
13. Paolini, P., Forti, G., Catalani G., Lucchetti, S., Menghini A., Mirandola, A., Pistacchio S., Porzia, U.: Roberti M. From "Sapienza" to "Sapienza, state ar chives in Rome". A looping effect bringing back to the original source communi cation and culture by innovative and low cost 3D surveying, imaging systems and GIS applications. Intl Arch. of Photogr., Rem. Sens. and Sp. Inf. Sc., Vol ume XL-5/W8, LowCost3D (LC3D), Sensors, Algorithms, Applications, 1–2 December 2015, Berlin, Germany (2016)

Multimedia Interactive Map for CH Presentation

Nicola Maiellaro[(⊠)] and Antonietta Varasano

Construction Technologies Institute, National Research Council of Italy,
Via Lembo 38 B, 70124 Bari, Italy
{maiellaro,varasano}@itc.cnr.it

Abstract. This article describes a novel Internet-based cultural heritage (CH) application, a multimedia interactive map with various user-friendly functions that allow users to find results according to their needs. Usually, the user selects a Point of Interest (PoI) to navigate a map, selecting it from a list or through a search function, as illustrated in the four cases studied here. The developed application allows the user to select a PoI and also view the previews of its multimedia contents (using the 'Folder', 'Tile' and 'Table' functions). Moreover, filtering functions—such as century (using the time slider), period, physical accessibility level and multimedia type (using the filter panel)— improve the system usability. Finally, PoIs are visualised on the map with multi-shape markers using a set of colours unambiguous to both colour-blind and non-colour-blind people. The interface is illustrated using data acquired from the Municipality of Cetinje (Montenegro). The software components are also illustrated, which contain useful information to other developers.

Keywords: Webgis · Multimedia · Interface · Colour blind · Accessibility

1 Introduction[1]

The use of geographical information systems (GIS) in cultural heritage (CH) sites, which is well documented in [1], is now available on the Web through applications such as WebGIS [2], which are accessible from anywhere using a common web browser. There is a wide variety of approaches for locating a Point of Interest (PoI) as in the four case studies of interactive maps reviewed here (Table 1), chosen for some feature:

- Selecting an interface language[2] (Fig. 1).
- Sending an email with the PoI's location and a message to a friend (using the 'Share' function) or a comment to the map developer (using the 'Report' function) (Fig. 2).

---

[1] Paragraphs 1, 2 and 4 of this paper were written by N. Maiellaro, whereas paragraph 3 was written by A. Varasano.
[2] Unfortunately, the categories and types are often shown in the English language; moreover, not all PoIs are displayed in a different language (for example, only four PoIs are visualised for 'Place of Interest' in the Italian language).

© Springer International Publishing AG 2016
M. Ioannides et al. (Eds.): EuroMed 2016, Part II, LNCS 10059, pp. 178–190, 2016.
DOI: 10.1007/978-3-319-48974-2_20

Table 1. Comparison of the features of the interactive maps used in the case studies (not working and/or incomplete content functions are considered absent)

Features	Malta	Cyprus	Lake Havasu	Oswego
Starting map with markers turned on			√	
PoI classified in the categories and types	√		√	√
Markers with icons		√	√	√
Clustering marker		√		√
Callout with additional information		√	√	
Search function		√	v	
Get-direction function	√	√	√	

Fig. 1. An interactive map of Malta. The legend (with categories and types, without markers) is floating on the right side; clustering not provided; markers without icons [3] (Color figure online)

- Sharing specific content via a social networking site (Fig. 3).
- Building an itinerary (using the 'Add to Trip Planner' function) (Fig. 4).

All the case studies paid little attention to the use of colours and icons in the markers:

Fig. 2. An interactive map of Cyprus. The legend (only categories) is on the left side; clustering is always on, using different colours related to the amount of clustered PoIs [4] (Color figure online)

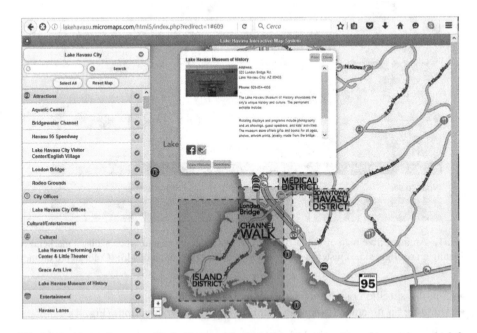

Fig. 3. An interactive map of Lake Havasu. The legend (with categories and types) is on the left side; clustering not provided [5] (Color figure online)

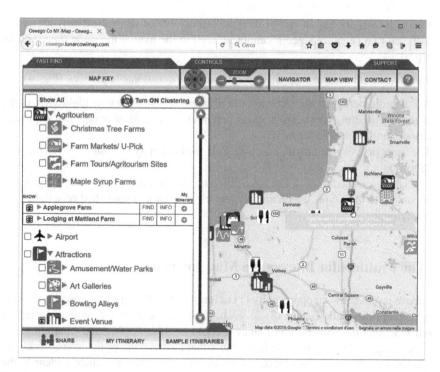

Fig. 4. An interactive map of Oswego. The legend (with categories and types) is on the left side; clustering is off—the default status [6] (Color figure online)

- In the case of the interactive map of Malta, the list of categories and types is only given alphabetically, making it impossible to associate the markers with the types they represent.
- In the case of the interactive map of Lake Havasu, it is difficult to see the presence of categories (such as 'Cultural/Entertainment' in Fig. 3).

Moreover, in all the maps used in the case studies, it is not easy to recognise the categories and types of PoIs because they adopt a unique shape[3], confusing colours and icons as the user could find repeating

- colour in different categories[4] or in different types;
- colour in different types of the same category and in other categories[5]; and

---

[3] An upturned and tilted red drop with a coloured core (Fig. 1); a shield with different background colours and different foreground images (Fig. 2); a circle with different background and perimeter colours and foreground images (Fig. 3); and a square with different background colours and foreground images (Fig. 4).

[4] For example, violet in the 'Historical Sites', 'Landmarks' and 'Museums' categories (Fig. 2); pink in a number of types in the 'Agritourism' and 'Attractions' categories (Fig. 4).

[5] For example, black in the 'Fortification & Towers' and 'Other' types under the 'Places of Interest' category, as well as for the 'Diving Centers' type under the 'Dives Sites' category (Fig. 1).

- icon in a category and in one of its types[6] (moreover, it is not clear why an icon is assigned to a category since it cannot be used in the map at the same time with its types).

Finally, the interactive map of Oswego presents questionable choices (Fig. 4):

- A PoI could belong at the same time to different types; if the user highlights a type in the legend, the map shows markers pertaining also to another type if it is present among the PoI's different types.
- The category 'Agritourism' has two PoIs without a type (listed under the text 'Show').
- The labels attached to each PoI have different colours for the texts and backgrounds according to their type, which are not very clear (such as a white text on a light-grey background).

2 The Multimedia Interactive Map Interface

The above issues show an opportunity (1) to improve the PoI representation on the map using appropriate markers and (2) to go beyond the mere use of navigation and/or search functions in choosing a PoI since it could be time-wasting and frustrating.

Regarding the first point, there is no doubt that the meaning of the icons, which are a visual representation of an object, action, or idea, must be immediately clear to the users to avoid confusion [7]. Unfortunately, there are only a few icons that are universally recognisable to users and there are no standard ones for tourism purposes[7]; however, a custom set of markers available on the Internet for free [9], evidently used in the interactive map of Cyprus, is becoming a 'de facto' standard. In the framework of the '**Mu.S.A.** (**Mu**st **S**ee **A**dvisor) Project[8] [10], an interactive map of Cetinje[9] was developed using some icons available in that set, organizing PoIs only in the categories (Fig. 5a) and in the categories and types (Fig. 5b). Successively, a multi-shape marker was adopted to improve the difference in categories (Fig. 5c), developed with the above-mentioned icons for another project [13]. Now, the interface uses multi-shape markers with a text icon (Fig. 5d), which is a solution less pleasant but more readable.

The rules for a clear recognition of the categories and types are as follows: (1) there should be a unique colour and shape for each category; (2) categories without types should have icons; (3) categories with types should have icons only in each type, and the category marker should be used only in the legend.

---

[6] For example, a farm image in the 'Agritourism' category and in its 'Farm Markets/U-Pick' type; a flag image in the 'Attractions' category and in its 'Bowling Alleys' type (Fig. 4).

[7] A formal standard was developed in other sectors such as the ANSI INCITS 415-2006 standard [8]. The Open Geospatial Consortium (OGC®) started in 2013 a PoI Standards Working Group Charter.

[8] The project aims highlighting less-known sites sharing on the Internet valuable knowledge coming from selected communities through user-friendly tools.

[9] It was developed for the Panel 'Role of information technologies in promotion and valorisation of cultural heritage', held in Cetinje in late 2014.

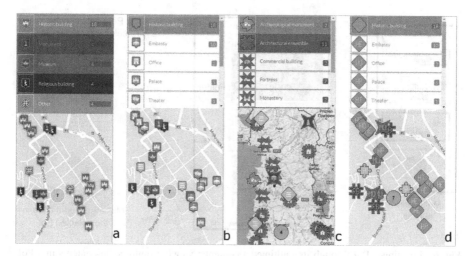

Fig. 5. Legend of the interactive map in different configurations: (a) Categories (no types); unique shape marker [11]. (b) Categories and types; unique shape marker [12]. (c) Categories and types; multi-shape marker [13]. (d) Categories and types; multi-shape marker with a text icon [14].

Regarding the second point, the main innovation is the possibility to choose the PoI through the preview of the multimedia contents belonging to each PoI (Fig. 6).

All the features illustrated in Table 1 are available in the desktop map interface developed through its components (Fig. 7): 'Menu', which has a function that is applied to all PoIs; 'Callout', which has a function that is applied to the selected PoI; and 'Sidebar', which has a multifunction section (legend, search and filter).

The 'Menu' and the 'Callout' components contain the functions 'Folder', 'Tile' and 'Table' for presenting multimedia contents (eventually filtered by type: gallery, sheet, video and 3D), activating the link to their documents and locating[10] the PoI where they belong.

The 'Menu' component has the following functions:

- 'Best site', to locate the most interesting site according to its ranking.
- 'Satellite', to switch the map to/from the earth view.
- 'Slideshow', to switch on/off a moving set of one image/PoI; clicking on one of them locates it on the map, opening its 'Callout' component.
- 'Time slider', to hide/show markers according to the selected century.
- 'Folder', to show in a window (Fig. 8) all multimedia object previews one by one in a sequence (manually/automatically); a toolbar allows filtering items by type.
- 'Table', to list in a window (Fig. 9) all the multimedia objects, alphabetically ordered based on the selected field; a search function is also provided.
- 'Tile', to display in a scrolling window (Fig. 10) all multimedia object previews; a toolbar allows filtering items by type.

---

[10] The locate function is disabled in the 'Callout' component.

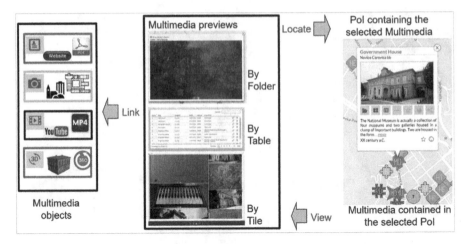

Fig. 6. Locating a PoI through its multimedia contents; viewing multimedia contents in a PoI. A preview of multimedia contents is available through 'Folder', 'Table' and 'Tile' functions.

Fig. 7. The interface components: 'Menu' (on the left side), Callout (in the centre) and 'Sidebar' (on the right). The 'Time slider' and the 'Slideshow' functions have been activated. In the 'Callout' the functions 'Folder', 'Table' and 'Tile' (available also in the 'Menu') have been highlighted. Mono-shape interface [12]

The Callout component, which can be opened by clicking on a PoI box in the sidebar or on a marker in the map, shows the PoI name, address and thumbnail; function icons; PoI description; building period; and status icons.

The function icons here are 'Folder', 'Tile' and 'Table' as in the 'Menu' component; in this case, however, they apply only to the multimedia content belonging to the PoI under examination (the locate function is disabled).

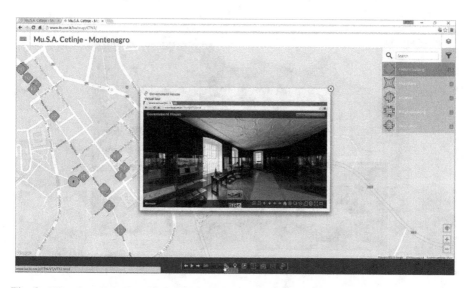

Fig. 8. Virtual tour preview in the 'Folder' window activated by a menu ('Link' and 'Locate' functions are available); in the 'Sidebar' (on the right side), only the category 'Historic Building' is turned on. Multi-shape interface [13]

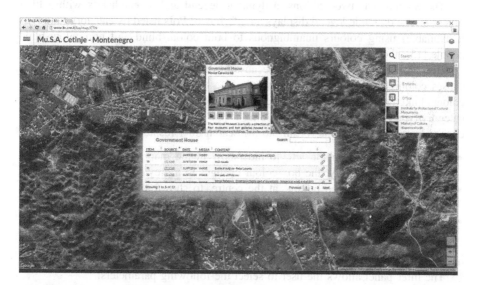

Fig. 9. 'Table' window activated by the 'Callout' component (only the 'Link' function to the multimedia content is available); in the 'Sidebar' (on the right side), the 'Historic Building' category, two types and 'Office' PoIs are listed [12]

The status icons report the physical accessibility level (through three emoticons: easy, uneasy and restricted) and special features, if available (qr-code, award plaque and rating).

Fig. 10. 'Tile' window activated by the 'Menu' component ('Link' and 'Locate' functions are available); the 'Advanced search panel' has been opened in the 'Sidebar' (on the right side) [12]

The Sidebar has two sections: a dynamic legend and a search box with a filter function. The dynamic legend displays an info box of PoIs listed by category (and type if available) using colours unambiguous to both colour-blind and non-colour-blind people [15]; these constraints limit to five the total number of different categories.

However, this is not a problem because having more than five colours at a time causes colour trouble (as in Fig. 2, where also the clustered markers have different colours linked to the number of grouped PoIs) instead of reducing ambiguity [16]. Each category/type box contains data according to the map status (i.e., each content could change from time to time according to the search/filter results):

- A 'marker button' on the left, to hide/show in the map all the markers for that category; subsequently, the box colour changes to a grey/default colour.
- A 'category/type name button' at the centre, to show/hide its group of PoI info boxes (containing an image and the name and address of each PoI).
- A display on the right showing the amount of PoIs available at that moment.

The search textbox allows the user to find PoIs according to the typed letters, updating the sidebar contents accordingly.

The filter panel allows the user to select the following parameters:

- Data (default field for text search: title; additional field: address and description).
- Accessibility (default: no filter; any combination of easy/uneasy/restricted available).
- Multimedia (default: no filter; any combination of gallery/sheet/video/3D available).
- Period (default: no filter; any period registered in the database available).

The multimedia type could be selected directly in the 'Folder' and 'Type' windows through a toolbar and in the 'Table' window through a menu.

3 The Multimedia Interactive Map Software

Keeping in mind the increasing number of older people (in 2025, 25 % of the people in the EU will be older than 65 years) and that old people tend to use more traditional mobile technology [17], we developed a mobile website, keeping the user interface as simple and intuitive as possible. This approach reduces the overall costs in respect to a mobile app, potentially resulting in a wider use for the following reasons:

- The development and maintenance are cheaper (a device operating system update could request a mobile app update).
- It is platform independent and easier to develop (PHP, HTML5 and CSS).
- The updating of the application and its content is independent of the app store's publication policies.
- It is not necessary to create contents specifically suited for mobile use.

The multimedia interactive map uses AJAX (Asynchronous JavaScript and XML or JSON, often used in the AJAJ variant), a simple JavaScript interface and the Google Maps API [18] for rendering geo-spatial data within a web browser and for accessing rich mapping features.

To simplify the publication of geo-referenced information, the application stores all data in a GeoJSON (Geographic JavaScript Object Notation) file rather than in a database, which would require the installation of a DBMS if not already present on the server hosting the system. GeoJSON is a specialisation of the JSON data interchange format that can manage geo-referenced data using a subset of instructions provided by the JavaScript language.

For the implementation of the editing environment, characterised by a high degree of interaction, we adopted the jQuery UI library, which is based on jQuery, a more general-purpose JavaScript library that provides a high level of abstraction for programming interaction and animation, advanced graphic effects and customizable event handling. This application is an example of a 'single-page application' (SPA), which is a different way of building HTML5 applications from traditional Web page development.

Instead of spreading the functionality of the multimedia interactive map across a collection of separate web pages with hyperlinks between them, it is possible to define a single root page where the users will land on and never leave as long as they are using the application.

This is a type of client-side logic that switches out the data and chunks of content within that page, allowing the users to navigate logical screens without leaving the page. This means that users never see a full-page refresh while using the application; instead, they see a change in a portion of the screen based on their interaction, and those changes can be done in a more fluid way with transitions to enhance the user experience.

SPA is almost like a client-server technology, where an HTML page is static and all dynamic changes occur in the browser. PHP, JSP, ASP, and HTML are mixed with server-side logic that is generated on the server, which makes it process more load. SPA separates the user interface (UI) library and the data (GeoJSON), and communicates with the server only through the JSON REST API (send/receive JSON using AJAX), allowing both parts to be independently developed and tested.

In computing, REpresentational State Transfer (REST) is an architectural style consisting of a coordinated set of components, connectors and data elements within a distributed hypermedia system, where the focus is on component roles and a specific set of interactions between data elements rather than on implementation details. Its purpose is to induce performance, scalability, simplicity, modifiability, visibility, portability and reliability [19].

The adoption of the REST architectural style is aimed at getting a 'stateless' solution software where each request from a client to the server contains all of the information necessary to process the request and the server does not store any session data on behalf of the client; instead, the client must store all session data. Indeed, the reliance of SPA on REST is perhaps the most immediately apparent characteristic of SPA.

To retrieve and manipulate data, SPA needs to make many calls to a server using means other than the traditional pattern of page refreshes.

SPA is fast, as most resources such as HTML pages, CSS files and scripts are only loaded once throughout the life span of the application and only data are transmitted back and forth, reducing the bandwidth usage, which is also a plus. SPA can use caching and local storage effectively. It is easy to scale, and it is easy to cache resources. SPA works and feels more like an application than a web page.

Furthermore, SPA is easy to debug with 'Google Chrome', which allows monitoring network operations and investigating page elements and the data associated with them. HTML5 enables a developer to write truly 'responsive' applications that resize automatically according to the browser and the screen size, and that automatically detect and change the UI according to the running platform and the orientation of the device.

HTML5 application performance is much different within the confines of a mobile web view in comparison to that within a desktop browser and requires a different approach to programming compared to a desktop setting, where resources are plentiful and fast.

A browser compatibility testing ensured that the application rendered without any errors using 'Google Chrome', the only web browser that we tested the application on because of its widespread usage.

4   Discussion

The use of WebGIS in cultural heritage (CH) presentation is growing, but, as in the four case studies presented, the majority of effort to date has been focused only on locating a PoI and on searching for its name, with poor attention given to the marker use.

Given the importance of 'showing' to catch the attention of users—who are potential visitors—an Internet-based multimedia interactive map was developed that allows users to choose the PoIs to visit and also preview its multimedia contents, using multi-shape markers with text icons and a set of colours unambiguous to both colour-blind and non-colour-blind people.

The interface shows the previews one by one in a sequence ('Folder'), all together in a scrolling window ('Tile') and as a list with search capabilities ('Table'), possibly selecting the multimedia type (gallery, sheet, video and 3D); a 'Print' function will be added soon.

Moreover, the 'Time slider' function allows users to filter the PoIs on the map according to the building period.

Search with aided completion and filtering—by category and type, century, physical accessibility and multimedia type—improves the system usability by allowing users to retrieve CH contents according to their specific interests.

Getting directions, social networking and collaborative features will be integrated into the mobile website, enabling the users to share specific content via social networks, to add PoIs with their information and to give PoI ratings.

The software components have been also illustrated, which contain information that is of potential benefit to other developers.

References

1. Petrescu, F.: The use of gis technology in cultural heritage. In: Proceedings of the XXI International CIPA Symposium, ISPRS Archives, vol. XXXVI-5/C53, Athens, Greece (2007). http://cipa.icomos.org/fileadmin/template/doc/ATHENS/FP114.pdf. Accessed 29 Aug 2016
2. Fu, P., Sun, J.: GIS in the Web Era. In: Fu, P., Sun, J. (eds.) Web GIS: Principles and Applications, pp. 1–24. ESRI Press, Redlands, CA, USA (2011). http://www.esri.com/news/arcwatch/1110/web-gis.html. Accessed 29 Aug 2016
3. http://www.visitmalta.com. Accessed 29 Aug 2016
4. http://geomatic.com.cy/visitcyprus. Accessed 29 Aug 2016
5. http://lakehavasu.micromaps.com. Accessed 29 Aug 29 2016
6. http://oswego.lunarcowimap.com/imap. Accessed 3 May 2016
7. Bedford, A.: Icon Usability. https://www.nngroup.com/articles/icon-usability. Accessed 29 Aug 2016
8. FGDC Homeland Security Work Group: Symbology Reference (2005). https://www.fgdc.gov/HSWG/index.html. Accessed 31 Aug 2016
9. Mollet, N.: Map Icons Collection. https://mapicons.mapsmarker.com. Accessed 31 Aug 2016
10. Artese, M.T., Biocca, L., Buono, P., Gagliardi, I., Lerario, A., Maiellaro, N., Paraciani, N.: 'MU.S.A. - must see advisor' project: a cultural heritage booster. In: Proceedings of the 6th International Congress on Science and Technology for the Safeguard of Cultural Heritage in the Mediterranean Basin, pp. 410–419. Valmar Ed., Rome, Italy (2014)
11. Maiellaro, N., Varasano, A.: Mu.S.A. Cetinje – Montenegro, 2014. http://www.itc.cnr.it/ba/map/CTN. Accessed 29 Aug 2016
12. Maiellaro, N.: A.I.M. - Advanced Interactive Map. In: 2015 Digital Heritage, Granada, pp. 205–206 (2015). doi:10.1109/DigitalHeritage.2015.7419494 http://ieeexplore.ieee.org/stamp/stamp.jsp?arnumber=7419494. Accessed 29 Aug 2016

13. Dollani, A., Lerario, A., Maiellaro, N.: sustaining cultural and natural heritage in albania. Sustainability **8**(8), 792 (2016). www.mdpi.com/2071-1050/8/8/792/pdf. Accessed 24 Aug 2016
14. Maiellaro, N., Varasano, A.: Mu.S.A. Cetinje – Montenegro, 2016. http://www.itc.cnr.it/ba/map/CTN3. Accessed 29 Aug 2016
15. Okabe, M.; Ito, K.: Color Universal Design (CUD). http://jfly.iam.u-tokyo.ac.jp/color. Accessed 3 May 2016
16. O'Daniel, M.: Psychology of Color. New Straits Times, Kuala Lumpur, Malaysia, p. 15 (2001)
17. Beasley, S., Conway, A.: Digital media in everyday life: a snapshot of devices, behaviors and attitude. In: Museums and the Web 2012, San Diego. http://www.museumsandtheweb.com/mw2012/papers/digital_media_in_everyday_life_a_snapshot_of_d.html. Accessed 29 Aug 2016
18. Google Maps for every platform. https://developers.google.com/maps. Accessed 29 August 2016
19. Fielding, R.T.: Architectural Styles and the Design of Network-based Software Architectures. University of California, Irvine (2000). https://www.ics.uci.edu/~fielding/pubs/dissertation/fielding_dissertation.pdf. Accessed 29 Aug 2016

Interactive Scalable Visualizations of Cultural Heritage for Distance Access

Sven Ubik[✉] and Jiří Kubišta

CESNET, Prague, Czech Republic
{ubik,Jiri.Kubista}@cesnet.cz

Abstract. Digitization of cultural heritage artefacts is now common. Creation of 3D models by various techniques is widespread. However, most spatial (3D) objects are still represented by photographs in portals such as Europeana. There is a significant potential of using 3D models for education, research, scientific collaboration and popularization.

We describe a web-based application that allows scalable visualizations of 3D models ranging from mobile devices to large LCD walls in classrooms and laboratories. Synchronized simultaneous access over a network enables distance learning and collaboration using such models.

Keywords: 3D models · Distance access to cultural heritage · Interactive visualizations

1 Introduction

Digitization of artefacts comprising our cultural heritage is now a widespread activity. The Europeana portal includes digital images of millions of artefacts. Most of them are represented by still photograph, a smaller part by 3D visualizations, mostly using 3D PDF format. An even smaller part uses external links to 3D visualizations, which can be displayed inside a user's web browser. A Sketchfab service is a popular solution.

Digital representations can document the current state of artefacts (which may deteriorate), allow study of artefacts without physical contact and my serve as a form of backup, to help restore precious artefacts, should a damage occur.

We foresee much bigger potential of digital representations of cultural artefacts for education, research, scientific collaboration and popularization, when some conditions are met. We concentrate on tangible three-dimensional objects, because we believe that this part of cultural heritage is now less well represented in digitalized forms than flat works, such as prints or paintings.

The rest of the paper is structured as follows. We identify the main requirements in Sect. 2. We discuss design options and describe a proposed architecture in Sect. 3. We present an experimental evaluation in Sect. 4. Finally, we draw conclusions and propose directions for future work in Sect. 5.

© Springer International Publishing AG 2016
M. Ioannides et al. (Eds.): EuroMed 2016, Part II, LNCS 10059, pp. 191–198, 2016.
DOI: 10.1007/978-3-319-48974-2_21

2   Problem and Requirements

Sketchfab[1] is a popular system for visualizations of 3D models, which is also used for cultural heritage artefacts. The problem is that the technology it is based upon does not support some scenarios requested by some researchers. Sketchfab uses a two-point communication between a server and a client (user's web browser) with client-side visualization implemented in Javascript and WebGL.

Laboratories and classrooms are now often equipped with a large visualization devices made from tiled LCD displays. Due to their decreasing cost, it is a convenient way to achieve large resolutions with high contrast, when compared to projectors. Researchers and teachers need to present visualizations of 3D models in scalable way, independent of the configuration of the LCD wall.

Students and researchers also need to discuss over presented models, pointing to some of their features. A local device, such as a tablet can be useful to navigate around the 3D models, if other users can see the model on the LCD wall and on their own devices synchronously. It can be also useful to extend this discussion across a computer network between institutions or classrooms for distance learning and collaboration. The model needs to be presented on each device in its own resolution.

Therefore, we identified two main requirements for visualizations of digitized cultural heritage of three-dimensional objects to be more useful for education, research and collaboration:

- Presentation on large LCD walls in a scalable way regardless of their configuration, which would allow to see both a "big picture" for context and small details at the same time, without the need to zoom or pan, enabling researchers to concentrate on the content
- Synchronous presentation among multiple devices over a computer network, ranging from small resolution mobile devices, to large resolution LCD walls

Museum institutions typically see two areas where 3D models can be useful. First, to enhance online presentations of their collectio. Second, as an addition to physical exhibitions, providing visitors with more information, hands on feeling of the exhibited objects and making the exhibition more attractive especially for young visitors.

It would be useful to allow collaboration between researchers and students in a laboratory or a classroom equipped with a large-scale visualization and a distant researcher who may have only a PC or a mobile device.

For distance collaboration and interactive feeling of remote object manipulation, the latency between commands and visualization changes should be as low as possible. An empirical evidence has shown that for the user to feel that a communication system is not affecting a workflow by its latency, the one-way delay should be less than 150 ms [4].

---

[1] www.sketchfab.com.

3   Related Work

Europeana[2] is a multilingual access point to Europe's cultural heritage in a digital form, allowing to search through millions of digital objects provided by European museums, galleries, archives, libraries and other institutions, whose objective is the preservation of cultural heritage. A number of museums in the world are also engaged in the Google Cultural Institute[3], which allows presentation of historical artefacts. Many countries also have their national databases of digital cultural heritage.

Digital heritage is in these databases are currently represented predominantly by still photographs, audio and video samples. A small number of models can be seen in 3D PDF documents specified in the Universal 3D (U3D) format. However, the interaction possibilities in 3D PDF are limited and it cannot be seen from within a web browser, a PDF viewer needs to be started externally.

Guarnieri et al. [1] describes a complete process of creating and presenting 3D models of cultural heritage using only open-source and free software. Models can be seen in a web browser, which however requires an X3D plugin and the solution is not scaleable to allow distributed rendering such as for LCD walls and remote access.

Scopigno et al. [2] stresses importance of tools beyond pure visualizations, which would help researchers to work with digitized cultural heritage, such as fragment restoration and shape analysis.

Sorin Hermon [3] suggests a process of creating 3D models in archaeology from multiple sources of information and using them to assist research work, such as reconstructions. This was confirmed in our talks with people in archaeological institutes.

Several free and paid web-based services are now available for storage and visualizations of 3D models using WebGL [5]. Sketchfab is now probably the most well know service, other examples include p3d.in, 3dvieweronline.com, a360.autodesk.com/viewer or sharemy3d.com. Sketchfab provides Data and Viewer Application Programming Interfaces (APIs) [6], which allows users to create their own visualization applications that can upload and use content stored in Sketchfab servers.

Visualisation laboratories and class rooms are now commonly equipped with walls from LCD panels of various sizes and configurations, thanks to their decreasing costs. To share such a wall by multiple visualizations and to utilize the total resolution of all LCD panels, some software for distribution of application visual output is needed. A commonly used system is the Scalable Amplified Group Environment (SAGE2) [7]. The SAGE2 system can drive LCD walls of different sizes and configurations in a scalable way, it is web-based using multiple web browsers running in a full-screen mode, stitched together to cover the LCD wall. Application functionality is divided into client and server side. The client side is implemented in JavaScript and runs inside web browsers that display the content. The server side can provide content to be streamed to the wall and exchanges synchronization messages between clients. The SAGE2 system can run on any web browser-based device, including tablets and mobile phones. SAGE2

---

[2] www.europeana.eu.
[3] www.google.com/culturalinstitute.

requires two web interfaces - one for applications in a full-screen mode and one for the SAGE2 controller (for starting new applications, etc.).

4 Architecture

4.1 Scalable Visualizations of 3D Models

The SAGE2 framework can be used to implement visualization applications scalable without the need to care about particular size and configuration of LCD panels. Although SAGE2 uses multiple web browsers to display content on LCD panels and Sketchfab is a web-based application, it is not possible to directly open Sketchfab models in SAGE2 web browsers and interact withit. One model can span multiple web browsers and the pan and zoom done in one web browser would not be shown in a synchronized way in other web browsers.

Therefore, we used the Sketchfab Viewer API to implement a SAGE2 Sketchfab Viewer application[4] that can present a Sketchfab model across multiple web browsers. Synchronization is done by exchanging SAGE2 messages through the SAGE2 server. Multiple instances of the SAGE2 Sketchfab Viewer application can be started and presented at the same time. Each window of any application instance can be freely moved and resized, while always keeping the full resolution across any number of LCD panels. The architecture is illustrated in Fig. 3.

Fig. 1. Presenting multiple interactive 3D models on an LCD wall

Some features provided by the web interface of the Sketchfab service (www.sketchfab.com) are missing in the Sketchfab Viewer API, such as automatic detection of the model visual centre for intuitive rotation. The Sketchfab Viewer API therefore assumes a rotation centre at the coordinates origin, which can be anywhere,

---

[4] https://bitbucket.org/sagelab_cesnet/sketchfab_viewer.

even outside the model. Presentations of multiple 3D models on an LCD wall using multiple instances of the application is illustrated in Fig. 1.

4.2 Integration of Mobile Devices

A user with a regular PC or a mobile device can connect to a SAGE2 server and display the content of the wall on her screen. However, given the smaller size of the PC monitor or or mobile device screen, it would be useful if a user can see a selected model separately and still be able to interact with the model in a synchronized way with other users. Also, rendering must be performed in a resolution of a particular user's device.

Therefore, we developed a Mobile extension to the SAGE2 server. It allows users to start a SAGE2 application directly in web browsers of their PCs or mobile devices. In order to utilize the smaller screen size, the browser can be switched into a full-screen mode. The user can then switch between multiple application instances even in a full-screen mode by a one-touch selection of the application in the upper left corner. It eliminates the need for a separate tab for the SAGE2 control page.

Touch control and gestures recognition are implemented using the Hammer.js library. The press and release, pinch to zoom and pan events are mapped to WebSocket messages, which are exchanged through the SAGE2 server with web browsers of other users, allowing all users to see the same application content. An example of sharing a model between a large LCD wall with high resolution and a mobile phone display is in Fig. 2.

Fig. 2. Sharing an interactive model between an LCD wall and a mobile device

The architecture is illustrated in Fig. 3. An LCD wall in the SAGE2 framework is driven by a set of servers, one per each column of LCD panels. Each server runs one web browser with one instance of the Sketchfab Viewer application implemented in Javascript using the Sketchfab Viewer API. There are also instances of the Sketchfab Viwer applications running on web browsers of user's with a mobile device and a laptop. When a user interacts with one instance of the Sketchfab Viewer or with the SAGE2 UI which arranges windows on the LCD wall, the visualisation changes are propagated through the SAGE2 server to other instances of the Sketchfab Viewer.

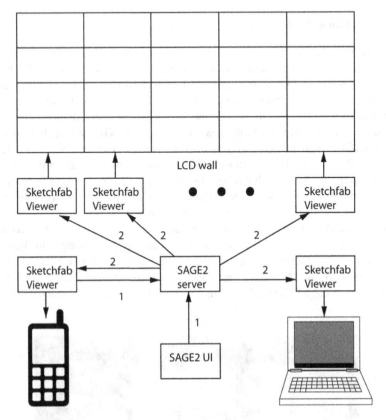

Fig. 3. Architecture of scalable visualization of 3D models including integration of mobile devices

For example, when a user moves a finger on a touch screen of a mobile device, the following sequence of events takes place to change the camera position of a 3D visualization for all connected users:

- A Hammer.js library inside the user's web browser detects the user's gesture
- The application calculates an offset from the previous position
- The application sends a pointerMove(x, y) or pointerScroll(wheelDelta) WebSocket message to the SAGE2 server to inform it about the change of the position of the user's pointer
- The SAGE2 server distributes this message to all user's web browsers
- Each application instance receives the message (including the original instance) and changes the model view accordingly. It is important that each application instance renders the model in a resolution of the user's devices, which can range from 300 × 200 pixels on a mobile phone to tens of megapixels on an LCD wall

- In order to change the model view, the application calculates the new position of the camera and its direction and then calls the setCameraLookAt function of the Sketchfab Viewer API:

```
api.lookat(
    [ 0, 13, 10], // camera position
    [0, 10, 0],   // target to look at
    4.3           // duration of the animation in seconds
);
```

5 Evaluation

We did several experiments to check scalability (R1), multiple model ability (R2) and low-latency distance sharing (R3) for various kinds of 3D models of cultural artefacts. We used a set of models created from three sources: (a) modelling applications Blender and 3ds Max, (b) photogrammetry software (Agisoft Photoscan and custom software used for the Langweil digitization project[5]) and (c) 3D scanner Creaform Go!Scan 50. We selected several models that differ significantly in the number of faces and vertices and in the size of textures. Characteristics of the selected models are summarized in Table 1.

Table 1. Models used for evaluation

Model name	Source	Size of textures	Number of faces	Number of vertices	Visualization update time
Amphora	Blender	1.2 MB	95 k	95 k	193 ms
Vessel	Blender	1.41 MB	56.1 k	56.1 k	200 ms
Langweil – 09	Photogramme try and modelling	35.4 MB	800	613	483 ms
Langweil – 27	Photogramme try and modelling	264 MB	29.3 k	17.1 k	551 ms
Cup	3D scanner (Creaform Go!Scan 50)	48 MB	273.3 k	136.6 k	177 ms

The last column in Table 1 shows the time from the user's request to change the camera position to the change of visualization measured by the timeline monitoring in the Google Chrome DevTools. The measurement was done a PC Dell 3610 with Xeon E5-1603 2.8 GHz, 8 GB RAM. We can see that the update time is more affected by the texture size than by the mesh size of the underlying 3D structure. For smaller textures, the response time is within the recommended limit (see Sect. 2). For larger textures, performance optimizations will be needed. A demonstration of synchronized interaction with a 3D model on an LCD wall, a PC and a mobile phone can be seen online[6].

---

[5] http://www.langweil.cz/index_en.php.

[6] https://youtu.be/Aj79dycaoYQ.

6   Conclusion

Technologies such as WebGL, SAGE2 and Sketchfab API allow creation of applications for visualizations of 3D models of cultural artefacts scalable from mobile devices to large LCD walls. These visualizations can be accessed in a distributed way, enabling real-time distance discussions, teaching and collaboration. Similar systems are already being used in industrial engineering. Their use for access to digitized cultural heritage can be useful for protection of collection items by minimizing physical handling, e-learning, research discussions and enliving museum exhibitions. In the future we plan to add support of WebRTC streaming to mobile devices for cases when the model intellectual property (IP) needs to be protected and server side visualization is therefore prefered.

References

1. Guarnieri, A., Pirotti, F., Vettore, A.: Cultural heritage interactive 3D models on the web: An approach using open source and free software. J. Cult. Heritage Elsevier **11**, 350–353 (2010). doi:10.1016/j.culher.2009.11.011
2. Scopigno, R., Callieri, M., Cignoni, P., Corsini, M., Dellepiane, M., Ponchio, F., Ranzuaglia, G.: 3D Models of cultural heritage: beyond plain visualization. Computer **44**(7), 48–55 (2011). http://doi.ieeecomputersociety.org/10.1109/MC.2011.196
3. Hermon, S.: Reasoning in 3D: a critical appraisal of the role of 3D modelling and virtual reconstructions in archaeology. In: Beyond Illustration: 2D and 3D Technologies as Tools for Discovery in Archaeology, BAR International Series, 36–45
4. ITU-T Recommendation G.114, 2003, Telecommunication Standardization Section of ITU
5. WebGL Specification, Khronos WebGL Working Group. https://www.khronos.org/registry/webgl/specs/latest/
6. Sketchfab Viewer API. https://sketchfab.com/developers/viewer
7. Marrinan, T., Aurisano, J., Nishimoto, A., Bharadwaj, K., Mateevitsi, V., Renambot, L., Long, L., Johnson, A., Leigh, J.: SAGE2: a new approach for data intensive collaboration using scalable resolution shared displays. In: 10th IEEE International Conference on Collaborative Computing: Networking, Applications and Worksharing (2014)

Differences of Field Dependent/Independent Gamers on Cultural Heritage Playing: Preliminary Findings of an Eye–Tracking Study

George E. Raptis[1]([✉]), Christos A. Fidas[2], and Nikolaos M. Avouris[1]

[1] HCI Group, Electrical and Computer Engineering Department,
University of Patras, Patras, Greece
`raptisg@upnet.gr, avouris@upatras.gr`
[2] Department of Cultural Heritage Management and New Technologies,
University of Patras, Patras, Greece
`fidas@upatras.gr`

Abstract. Based on a large number of different cognitive theories on information processing procedure, suggesting that individuals have different approaches in the way they forage, retrieve, process, store and recall information, this paper investigates the effect of field dependence/independence with regards to visual attention of gamers in the context of a cultural heritage game. Gaze data were collected and analysed from fourteen participants, who were classified as field dependent or independent according to Group Embedded Figures Test (GEFT), a cognitive style elicitation instrument. The collected data were analysed quantitatively to examine visual attention in terms of fixation count and fixation impact. The results revealed statistically significant differences in both fixation count and fixation impact towards interactive game elements. Statistically significant differences were also measured for specific types of game elements. Findings are expected to provide insights for designers and researchers aiming to design more user–centric cultural heritage games.

Keywords: Field dependence/independence · Cognitive style · Cultural heritage · Games · Eye–tracking · Visual attention · Game design

1 Introduction

In the past few years a lot of research on video games in the cultural heritage context has been conducted [2,7,10,17], since they can enrich visitors' experience and contribute towards a much desired learning outcome. To achieve this, game designers aim to include information processing tasks through game mechanisms that guide users to seek and comprehend information and to acquire and recall knowledge. Information processing is closely related to cognitive characteristics, therefore it seems worth investigating the impact of cognitive differences on game playing in cultural heritage contexts. The theoretical background

© Springer International Publishing AG 2016
M. Ioannides et al. (Eds.): EuroMed 2016, Part II, LNCS 10059, pp. 199–206, 2016.
DOI: 10.1007/978-3-319-48974-2_22

of this work is based on cognitive theories [15,26], suggesting that individuals have different habitual approaches in information seeking, processing and retrieval, which are related to their individual cognitive characteristics such as skills and abilities, e.g. visual attention. High–level cognitive processes, such as cognitive styles, have been the focus of many research endeavours explaining empirically the observed differences in information processing tasks [1,15,23,26]. One of the most well established, credible and validated [3,5] cognitive style is the Field Dependence/Independence style [26]. It is a single dimension model having the field dependence on the one side and the field independence on the other. According to this model, the individuals are classified as field dependent (FD) or field independent (FI). FD individuals tend to prefer a more holistic way when processing information, have difficulties in identifying details from information in complex schemes and perform better on inductive tasks [26]. On the other hand, FI individuals tend to prefer impersonal orientation, prefer a more analytical way when processing information, pay attention to details and easily separate simple elements and structures from the surrounding context [26].

2   Related Work

Several studies [4,18,19,24] have investigated the effect of cognitive styles in various application domains, such as e-learning, industrial engineering and marketing, using eye–tracking tools. Focusing on FD/FI cognitive style, research revealed a correction between the FD/FI style and eye movement and attention patterns, with FD users exemplifying a more disoriented and disorganised eye motion activity and generating a greater number of fixations and FI users following a more oriented and organised scan strategy when performing visual exploration and web search tasks [18,19]. Shinar et al. [24] examined the relationship between field dependence and on–the–road visual search behaviour and revealed that FD individuals require more time to process the available visual information and are less effective in their visual search pattern. Despite that a number of application domains has been researched, to the best of the authors' knowledge no other eye–tracking study has been reported on the gamers' cognitive differences on cultural heritage game playing.

3   Eye–Tracking Study

3.1   Methodology

Experimental Design and Procedure. We designed an eye–tracking experiment to investigate the effect of cognitive styles on visual attention during a cultural heritage game. To increase the validity of our study we recruited participants who were (a) engaged with online gaming activities more than twelve hours per week; (b) had no previous experience in playing Time Explorer; and (c) had never taken the Group Embedded Figures Test (GEFT) before. During the study session the players were firstly asked to complete a short demographic questionnaire; then they undertook the GEFT test; and finally they played the game. To test the study environment and instruments and make any adjustments, a pilot study was carried out prior to the main study.

Apparatus. The eye tracking experiment was performed on Tobii T60 Eye Tracker, integrated into a 17" TFT monitor (96 dpi) at a screen resolution of 1280×1024 pixels. We used the browser Google Chrome v.51 with a window size of 1040×996 pixels. Tobii T60 Eye Tracker has a tracking frequency of 60 Hz and an accuracy of 0.5^o of visual angle. The analysis of the collected gaze data was performed using the software Tobii Pro Studio.

Participants. Twenty one undergraduate students were recruited to take part in the eye–tracking study during the spring semester of 2016. However, only fourteen of them produced valid eye–tracking data, two females (14.3 %) and twelve males (85.7 %). They ranged in age between 18 and 23 years (M = 20.500, SD = 1.852). All the participants met the requirements discussed in Experimental Design and Procedure section.

Group Embedded Figures Test. To determine the participants' cognitive styles, the Group Embedded Figures Test (GEFT) [20] was used. The test consisted of three sections, and during each of them, the participants had to identify simple forms within complex patterns in a given time. The first section was introductory. The next two sections were the main ones and they consisted of nine items each; five minutes were allocated to each. The score is calculated by adding the number of simple forms identified correctly in the second and third section, thus the score range is between 0 and 18. During the administration and scoring of the GEFT, the directions about the materials, the test procedure, scoring and time limits described in the scoring template [27] were firmly followed. Participants' average score on GEFT was 11.714 (median = 12, SD = 2.894), distributed normally according to Shapiro–Wilk test (p = 0.471 > 0.05). The classification of participants into field dependent (FD) or field independent (FI) is based on a cut–off score, which however is not identified in the original work [20]. However, a number of classification procedures have been developed [8,16] and for the scope of this study the median score was adopted as the cut–off score, i.e. 12. The participants who scored 12 or lower were classified as FD, and those who scored 13 or higher as FI. Eight participants were classified as FD and six as FI. The users' scores on the GEFT test in our sample is comparably similar to general public GEFT test scores as shown in several studies which embraced individuals with different demographics [3,14].

Game. The game we selected for this study was Time Explorer; a well-known and multiple award winning game of British Museum, which requires players to perform several information processing tasks through game–play in order to complete their objectives. Time Explorer has four different levels, each related to an ancient civilisation. For the scope of this study, we used Aztec Mexico level. In order to complete the game successfully, the players had to rescue a mystical mosaic mask and deliver it to the tribe priest. To redeem the mask, the players needed to overcome challenges; solve problems; find and decode hidden messages. Hidden items and knowledge artefacts, e.g. bonus facts and objects, were scattered throughout the game, which would not only provide information about each civilization to the players, enhancing their knowledge, but they could also increase their score. In particular, the formula that calculates the final game score is formed by three main parameters: the total level completion time, the total in–game puzzle solution time and the number of hidden facts and objects collected. The hidden elements of the game are divided into two major types: helpful objects and bonus items (objects and facts). The collection of helpful objects is mandatory in order for the player to proceed in the game or complete it, while the collection of bonus items is optional, since they do not provide information crucial to game progress, but they provide general information about the Aztec civilisation.

Measures. For our analysis we wanted to know how visual attention on inter-active game elements is distributed among players with different cognitive styles. Therefore, we assigned gaze data to areas of interest (AOIs) on the interactive game elements. Twelve AOIs were identified for the Aztec level, representing all the interactive game elements. The collected gaze data are based on fixations, which were detected using the built–in algorithms of Tobii Studio. The algorithms generate a fixation if recorded gaze locations of at least 100 ms are close to each other (radius 35 pixels). Fixations assign the entire count or duration to the AOIs that contain the centre point of the fixation, and fixations projected on the foveal area of the eyes may be lost. Hence, we used a technique introduced by Buscher et al. [4], which takes into consideration fixations that are close to the fixation centre using a Gaussian distribution. We used two metrics:

– **Fixation count**: the number of fixations a participant has within an AOI, taking into consideration visits and re–visits to the AOI.
– **Fixation impact**: a modified version of fixation duration, introduced by Buscher et al. [4].

3.2   Results

Fixation Count. An independent–samples t–test was run to determine if there were differences in fixation count to any interactive object between FD and FI players. Fixation count for each group was normally distributed, as assessed by Shapiro–Wilk's test (FD: $0.227 > 0.05$ and FI: $0.590 > 0.05$), and there was homogeneity of variances, as assessed by Levene's test for equality of variances ($p = 0.169 > 0.05$). The FI players had a total greater fixation count (M = 47.167, SD = 17.291) than FD players (M = 24.625, SD = 9.303), a statistically signif-icant difference, M = 22.542, 95 % CI [6.973, 38.110], t(12) = 3.155, p = 0.003

< 0.05. Nonetheless, not all the interactive objects of the game were mandatory for the players in order to proceed in the game, as we discussed previously. Therefore, we investigate whether there are differences in fixation count regarding each type of interactive game elements. An additional independent–samples t–test was run for each element type to determine if there were differences in fixation count between FD and FI players. Regarding the helpful objects, fixation count for each group was normally distributed, as assessed by Shapiro–Wilk's test (FD: 0.184 > 0.05 and FI: 0.819 > 0.05), and there was homogeneity of variances, as assessed by Levene's test for equality of variances (p = 0.513 > 0.05). The FI players had greater fixation count to helpful objects (M = 5.167, SD = 3.656) than FD players (M = 2.875, SD = 2.997), but there is no statistically significant difference, M = 2.292, 95 % CI [−1.577, 6.160], t(12) = 1.291, p = 0.221 > 0.05. However, there is a statistically significant difference for both bonus items according to independent–samples t–test. In particular, the FI players had greater fixation count to bonus items (M = 42.500, SD = 13.172) than FD players (M = 20.500, SD = 7.910) a statistically significant difference, M = 22.000, 95 % CI [9.727, 34.273], t(12) = 3.906, p = 0.002 < 0.05. Fixation count for each group and each game element type were normally distributed, as assessed by Shapiro–Wilk's test, and there was homogeneity of variances, as assessed by Levene's test for equality of variances.

Fixation Impact. An independent–samples t–test was run to determine if there were differences in fixation impact to any interactive game element between FD and FI players. Fixation impact for each group was normally distributed, as assessed by Shapiro–Wilk's test (FD: 0.651 > 0.05 and FI: 0.145 > 0.05), and there was homogeneity of variances, as assessed by Levene's test for equality of variances (p = 0.488 > 0.05). The FI players had a total greater fixation impact (M = 25.422, SD = 8.484) than FD players (M = 16.708, SD = 5.909), a statistically significant difference, M = 8.714, 95 % CI [0.364, 17.065], t(12) = 2.274, p = 0.042 < 0.05. Likewise fixation count, we investigate the effect of cognitive style in the fixation impact of each game element type. Hence, an additional independent–samples t–test was run for each type to determine if there were differences in fixation impact between FD and FI players. Fixation impact for each group was normally distributed, as assessed by Shapiro–Wilk's test (FD: 0.057 > 0.05 and FI: 0.149 > 0.05), and there was homogeneity of variances, as assessed by Levene's test for equality of variances (p = 0.882 > 0.05). The FI players had greater fixation impact towards helpful objects (M = 3.283, SD = 2.462) than FD players (M = 2.428, SD = 2.845), but there is no statistically significant difference, M = 0.855, 95 % CI [−2.313, 4.022], t(12) = 0.588, p = 0.568 > 0.05. Regarding the bonus items, fixation impact for each group was normally distributed, as assessed by Shapiro–Wilk's test (FD: 0.250 > 0.05 and FI: 0.301 > 0.05), and there was homogeneity of variances, as assessed by Levene's test for equality of variances (p = 0.867 > 0.05). The FI players had greater fixation impact towards bonus items (M = 22.139, SD = 7.277) than FD players (M = 14.279, SD = 5.890), a statistically significant difference, M = 7.860, 95 % CI [−0.206, 15.513], t(12) = 2.237, p = 0.045 < 0.05.

4 Discussion and Interpretation

Eye–tracking analysis revealed significant differences between the game–playing approaches of FD and FI individuals. There was a significant difference on both fixation count and fixation impact towards the interactive game elements. FI players had greater fixation count and fixation impact than FD players, a finding that was anticipated as FI individuals tend to focus more easily on details and separate them from the background, whereas FD individuals are typically aware of the whole field, paying less attention to details [9, 26]. Therefore, the FI players looked more times and for longer time periods at the interactive game elements, and they interacted more times with them [21, 22].

Focusing on the different types of the game elements, no significant difference was found on the fixation count and fixation impact towards helpful objects. Since, the collection of such objects was mandatory in order for the players to proceed and complete the game, the fact that no differences between FD and FI players observed was anticipated. However, there was a significant effect regarding the fixation count and fixation impact toward bonus items. FD players observed less times and for shorter time periods the bonus items, as they tend to follow a more intrinsic approach and be less inclined in detecting details [26], having in mind to complete the game faster [22]. On the other hand, FI players tend to develop self–defined goals and be more analytical [26], and thus they observed bonus items more often and for longer time periods.

In both cases, the fact that FI players had greater fixation count and fixation impact towards bonus elements than FD players, would lead them to interact with these elements more often [21,22] and thus the game would provide them more information about Aztec civilisation. Therefore, FI players would more likely get involved in learning activities by acquiring information related to Aztec history, while FD players would process less information. Design wise there is a risk for game designers of unintentionally favouring players with specific cognitive styles. Therefore, cognitive differences should play a role in both the design and the play phase of the games. Our study reinforces the belief that FI/FD users develop different gaming strategies and suggests that research on players cognitive styles could reveal a lot about their interacting behaviour during game play. Hence, designing games that implicitly recognise the users cognitive style and adapts seem to be engraving a new promising path, especially in new emerging environments, such as augmented and virtual reality, where embedding eye-tracking mechanisms is feasible.

In terms of generalisability, we expect that similar effects will derive in different game genres as long as they involve information processing tasks. In cultural heritage contexts, given the large diversity of the visitors in terms of culture and the fact that there is a correlation between the culture and the different cognitive skills and styles [6,13], we believe that adaptive and personalising mechanisms should be proposed, to ensure better visiting experience for all audiences.

5   Conclusion

The aim of this study was to investigate the effects of FD/FI cognitive style on gamers' visual attention when playing a cultural heritage game. A main effect of cognitive differences on the fixation count and fixation impact towards interactive game elements was found. In particular, FI players had greater fixation count and fixation impact towards the total game elements and elements that were not crucial for completing the game. On the other hand, no effect was found regarding the fixation count and fixation impact towards objects that were mandatory to be collected by the players in order to proceed in the game. Our study had limitations such as the rather small sample and the non–varying participants' profiles. However, its distribution was normal towards GEFT scores, reflecting the general public distribution. The participants' age range was also limited, but taking into consideration that high–level cognitive characteristics rarely change throughout adult lifespan [25], the observed main effects of the eye–tracking study would possibly apply for other age groups. In our sample there was an imbalance in terms of gender distribution, which was not reflected to the GEFT scores as they followed a normal distribution. Researchers have argued for and against a correlation between the gender and the FD/FI classification [11,12]; the analysis of our results has not revealed any correlation between the two. Nonetheless more intensive research should be conducted in order to gain a deeper understanding on how cognitive factors are related to players' visual attention in games on a cultural heritage context.

References

1. Allinson, C.W., Hayes, J.: The cognitive style index: a measure of intuition-analysis for organizational research. J. Manage. Stud. **33**(1), 119–135 (1996)
2. Anderson, E.F., McLoughlin, L., Liarokapis, F., Peters, C., Petridis, P., de Freitas, S.: Developing serious games for cultural heritage: a state-of-the-art review. Virtual Real. **14**(4), 255–275 (2010)
3. Angeli, C., Valanides, N., Kirschner, P.: Field dependence-independence and instructional-design effects on learners' performance with a computer-modeling tool. Comput. Hum. Behav. **25**(6), 1355–1366 (2009)
4. Buscher, G., Cutrell, E., Morris, M.R.: What do you see when you're surfing?: using eye tracking to predict salient regions of web pages. In: Proceedings of the SIGCHI Conference on Human Factors in Computing Systems (CHI 2009), pp. 21–30. ACM, New York (2009)
5. Chapman, D.M., Calhoun, J.G.: Validation of learning style measures: implications for medical education practice. Med. Educ. **40**(6), 576–583 (2006)
6. Chiu, L.-H.: A cross-cultural comparison of cognitive styles in Chinese and American children. Int. J. Psychol. **7**(4), 235–242 (1972)
7. Coenen, T., Mostmans, L., Naessens, K.: MuseUs: case study of a pervasive cultural heritage serious game. J. Comput. Cult. Herit. **6**(2), 8: 1–8: 19 (2013)
8. Cureton, E.E.: The upper and lower twenty-seven per cent rule. Psychometrika **22**(3), 293–296 (1957)

9. Ehrman, M., Leaver, B.L.: Cognitive styles in the service of language learning. System **31**(3), 393–415 (2003)
10. Froschauer, J., Merkl, D., Arends, M., Goldfarb, D.: Art history concepts at play with thiatro. J. Comput. Cult. Herit. **6**(2), 7: 1–7: 15 (2013)
11. Hamilton, C.J.: Beyond sex differences in visuo-spatial processing: the impact of gender trait possession. Br. J. Psychol. **86**(1), 1–20 (1995)
12. Hughes, R.N.: Sex differences in group embedded figures test performance in relation to sex-role, state and trait anxiety. Curr. Psychol. Res. **1**(3–4), 227–234 (1981)
13. Joy, S., Kolb, D.A.: Are there cultural differences in learning style? Int. J. Intercult. Relat. **33**(1), 69–85 (2009)
14. Khatib, M., Hosseinpur, R.M.: On the validity of the group embedded figure test (geft). J. Lang. Teach. Res. **2**(3), 640–648 (2011)
15. Kirton, M.: Adaptors and innovators: a description and measure. J. Appl. Psychol. **61**(5), 622 (1976)
16. Maghsudi, M.: The interaction between field dependent/independent learning styles and learners' linguality in third language acquisition. Interact. Multimed. Electron. J. Comput. Enhanced Learn. **7**(5), 1–23 (2007)
17. Mortara, M., Catalano, C.E., Bellotti, F., Fiucci, G., Houry-Panchetti, M., Petridis, P.: Learning cultural heritage by serious games. J. Cult. Herit. **15**(3), 318–325 (2014)
18. Nisiforou, E.A., Laghos, A.: Field dependence-independence, eye movement patterns: investigating users differences through an eye tracking study. In: Interacting with Computers (2015). doi:10.1093/iwc/iwv015
19. Nisiforou, E.A., Michailidou, E., Laghos, A.: Using eye tracking to understand the impact of cognitive abilities on search tasks. In: Stephanidis, C., Antona, M. (eds.) UAHCI 2014. LNCS, vol. 8516, pp. 46–57. Springer, Heidelberg (2014). doi:10.1007/978-3-319-07509-9_5
20. Oltman, P.K., Raskin, E., Witkin, H.A.: Group Embedded Figures Test. Consulting Psychologists Press, Palo Alto (1971)
21. Raptis, G.E., Fidas, C.A., Avouris, N.M.: Do field dependence-independence differences of game players affect performance and behaviour in cultural heritage games? In: ACM SIGCHI Annual Symposium on Computer-Human Interaction in Play (CHI PLAY). ACM, Austin (2016)
22. Raptis, G.E., Fidas, C.A., Avouris, N.M.: A qualitative analysis of the effect of wholistic-analytic cognitive style dimension on the cultural heritage game playing. In: Proceedings of 7th International Conference on Information, Intelligence, Systems and Applications (IISA). IEEE, Chalkidiki (2016)
23. Riding, R.J., Cheema, I.: Cognitive styles-an overview and integration. Educ. Psychol. **11**(3–4), 193–215 (1991)
24. Shinar, D., McDowell, E.D., Rackoff, N.J., Rockwell, T.H.: Field dependence and driver visual search behavior. Hum. Factors J. Hum. Factors Ergon. Soc. **20**(5), 553–559 (1978)
25. Witkin, H.A., Goodenough, D.R., Karp, S.A.: Stability of cognitive style from childhood to young adulthood. J. Pers. Soc. Psychol. **7**(3), 291–300 (1967)
26. Witkin, H.A., Moore, C.A., Goodenough, D.R., Cox, P.W.: Field-dependent and field-independent cognitive styles and their educational implications. ETS Res. Bull. Ser. **1975**(2), 1–64 (1975)
27. Witkin, H.A., Oltman, P.K., Raskin, E., Karp, S.A.: Group Embedded Figures Test - Scoring Template. Consulting Psychologists, Palo Alto (1971)

The New Era of Museums and Exhibitions: Digital Engagement and Dissemination

Digital Technologies in the Museum: Same Old, Same Old?

Inge Kalle-den Oudsten[✉]

University of Amsterdam, Amsterdam, The Netherlands
i.kalle-denoudsten@uva.nl

Abstract. Digital technologies are often said to be open, democratic, social and participatory. These qualities are also associated with the concept of the post-museum. This paper explores the use of the digital in museums. It is argued that museums often employ new media to perpetuate traditional narratives rather than capitalise their transformative potential in order to change.

Keywords: Museum · Digital · Meaning · Ethnomethodology · Visitor studies

1 Introduction

Audio tours, tablets or large projections – it has become almost impossible to imagine a museum visit without digital technologies. Often, many advantageous qualities are attributed to these new media. Supposedly, they are democratic, open, social, participatory, and so on. These characteristics seem to relate closely to Hooper-Greenhill's vision of the post-museum, in which the authoritative narrative of the old modernist museum is replaced by an open, democratic, co-creative space. This might suggest that digital technologies are tailor-made to assist the museum in changing into a more democratic institution. The question that remains, however, is whether museums are, in fact, employing new media in such a way. Is the modernist museum transformed into a post-museum by using digital technologies, or is it simply being perpetuated, a new and flashy version of same old, same old?

2 The Post-museum

In *Museums and the Interpretation of Visual Culture*, Hooper-Greenhill compares two types of museums: the "modernist museum" and the "post-museum" [1]. The modernist museum emerged during the nineteenth century, and is still a powerful force today. This kind of museum is seen as an authority responsible for disseminating objective knowledge, whilst its visitors are cast as passive receivers of this 'Truth'. The modernist museum holds all the power, leaving no room for personal visitor meanings. Visitors are thought of as one homogeneous mass of "empty vessels waiting to be filled" [1]. Yet, during the second half of the twentieth century, changes begin to occur within the museum – a postmodern influence leads to new perspectives on visitors and their meaning-making processes [2]. The idea of the post-museum is born, and although it is still in development, its shape can already be perceived. It can be characterised most

© Springer International Publishing AG 2016
M. Ioannides et al. (Eds.): EuroMed 2016, Part II, LNCS 10059, pp. 209–213, 2016.
DOI: 10.1007/978-3-319-48974-2_23

clearly by a focus on its visitors. The post-museum will speak in a non-authoritative voice, through which it will acknowledge the constructed nature of its own narrative. This will open up the museum space to new, different, perspectives. Instead of offering the visitor the objective 'Truth' on a silver plate, the post-museum will function as a facilitator: it will encourage visitors to construct their own, personal, meanings [3]. Because each visitor brings a different set of preconceptions, many different meanings exist. The post-museum is an open space in which these varied meanings are seen as equally valuable [4].

3   The Digital

The post-museum is still a vision, it is not yet fully realised. How can we start moving towards this new kind of museum? Interestingly, there are some who argue that a solution is already present: digital technologies [5–10]. The rhetoric surrounding new media ("social, access, grassroots, empowerment, information, interactivity, 'new', collaboration, conversation, community, creativity, democracy, revolution, participation, choice, folksonomy") is very similar to the terminology used to describe the post-museum, suggesting a relationship between the two concepts [11]. The following paragraph is a brief exploration of that link between the post-museum and digital media.

One of the characteristics of the post-museum is its acceptance of a multiplicity of voices instead of one, authoritative, museum-voice. The modernist museum-voice was static, unchangeable, "a cultural freezer", but digital technologies are inherently open, dynamic, liquid – the exact opposite [12]. This is an essential quality of the internet, which is designed in such a way that information is never fixed, but forever open to further editing. These changes can also be made by anyone: there is a different distribution of authority. Wellington and Oliver note: "New media as a transformative power influences the hierarchies of knowledge, and contains the capacity to dissolve divisions between front- and back-of-house practice" [13]. This is very similar to what is envisaged in the post-museum, where the hierarchical distinction between visitor- and museum-meanings will fade. Another feature of the post-museum is its acknowledgement of the differences in their audience, and the way through which these visitors create personal meanings. In this case, digital technologies could offer more than one text label which contains "the watered-down lowest common denominator", and instead allow visitors to find information that will appeal to each of them personally [14].

Based on the above, and informed by the work of Henning, I would argue that new media have great *potential* for producing messages that are more open and democratic because of their inherent qualities [15]. In other words, the digital would be a suitable medium when aiming to transform the museum.

4   Keys to Rome

Do museums make use of these transformative powers of digital technologies? In an attempt to answer this question, a small case study was carried out at the Allard Pierson Museum, an archaeological museum in Amsterdam, the Netherlands. The main focus of this study was *Keys to Rome*, an exhibition which opened in 2014, created as part of the V-MusT Project, funded by the European Union's FP7 Programme. Accompanying the main storyline on the diversity of the Roman Empire are several iPads, incorporated into the showcases. These tablets are triggered by a key card, activated at the start of the exhibit, containing a personally-chosen 'guide'. In the project plan, written in preparation for the exhibition, the museum states "We want to use this project to enhance visitor participation through digital technologies", a goal that is in line with the ideas of the post-museum [16].

Between May and June 2016 a preliminary study in the *Keys to Rome* gallery was carried out, consisting of four accompanied visits of about 45 min. These accompanied visits, part of the ethnomethodological framework, are a particular type of contextual interviewing, in which the researcher follows a visitor through the gallery, whilst that visitor 'thinks aloud', giving the researcher opportunity to record these narratives on an audio device [17, 22]. Accompanied visits have been employed in a museum context before, in particular to study visitor meaning-making processes [18, 19]. Here, the aim is also to explore in what ways the participants make meaning, and, more specifically, whether the use of digital elements influences these processes. This exploratory study was done with only four participants, all in their twenties, in order to have a "deeper rather than extensive understanding" of how visitors make meaning [18]. The recordings of the visits were transcribed and then coded.

The results show different ways in which the participants attempt to create meaning during their visit to the gallery. These can be divided up in two main categories. Most of the time, participants associate what they see with what they already know. For example, upon reading a text sign that states that Romans ate flamingos, one of the participants retells her experience of eating similarly exotic foods while travelling in Namibia. Another participant, encountering a grave relief, tries to understand the practice by relating it to contemporary burial practices in which a photo of the deceased is often put on the coffin. The second way in which visitors try to make meaning is by imagining what the situation was like. In her attempt to comprehend several votive reliefs, one of the participants is imagining where they would be placed in an ancient home: in the bedroom, on the mantelpiece? Another is wondering whether Germania was very sunny, inspired by a text describing that clay bricks were baked in the sun. Interestingly, there seems to be almost no difference in these interpretive processes between the participants who used the digital elements and those who did not. There is one example where a participant interacted with a 3D scan to recreate the original position of an object, which was upright, rather than its horizontal position in the showcase. In this case, the digital element allowed that participant to create personal meaning. Other than that, the quantity and quality of the ways in which the participants created meaning were very similar for those who adopted the digital and those who did not.

These results suggest that the Allard Pierson Museum may not be truly transformative in their use of the digital. After further analysing the exhibit, some suggestions may be offered as to why this seems to be the case. At the start of the gallery, visitors are invited to choose a personal guide, which would suggest a multiplicity of voices. Yet these 'different perspectives' are simply the museum's voice, which, although disguised in three different personae, is quite traditionally authoritative. The three narrators have a slightly different way of speaking, but the information they provide is largely the same. Next to that, the museum seems to utilise the tablets as text signs. Although they contain some extra information (such as 3D scans and images), the text on the screen is precisely the kind of text that could be put on a traditional label. The museum is not employing the new media's ability to easily provide linked information, for example. Both Davies and Reading offer similar observations, giving examples of museums adopting digital technologies to present traditionally formatted information [20, 21].

5 Conclusion

It has been argued that digital media may be capitalised to transform modernist museums into post-museums. Yet, although many museums are already employing digital technologies, they do not always use these in ways that benefit this transformation. The small case study of *Keys to Rome* is an example in which the digital seems to be utilised to perpetuate traditional practices. Rather than adopting new media to convey a new kind of narrative, these kinds of museums are simply presenting a flashy version of same old, same old.

This brief example shows that, although museums might use digital technologies, the simple fact of incorporating them in exhibits does not lead to a transformation. Although such a statement might seem obvious to some, its importance is unquestionable. As was maintained above, a rhetoric exists in which digital technologies are continuously associated with transformative power. Such discourse leads museums to, almost thoughtlessly, incorporate the digital in their exhibitions, without being fully aware of their impact. Therefore, it is essential to study the relationship between digital technologies and museum exhibits. New media certainly possess particular qualities that have an affinity with the concept of the post-museum. This presents an exciting opportunity. Might the digital assist museums in achieving this transformation? In what ways *can* we use digital technologies to achieve the post-museum?

References

1. Hooper-Greenhill, E.: Museums and the Interpretation of Visual Culture. Routledge, London (2000)
2. Frazon, Z.: New Museology. Curatorial Dictionary Tranzit (2012). http://tranzit.org/curatorial dictionary/index.php/dictionary/new-museology/. Accessed 10 July 2016
3. Black, G.: The Engaging Museum: Developing Museums for Visitor Involvement. Routledge, New York (2005)
4. Doering, Z.H.: Strangers, guests or clients? Visitor experiences in museums. Curator: Mus. J. **42**(2), 74–87 (1999)
5. Fisher, M., Twiss-Garrity, B.: Remixing exhibits: constructing participatory narratives with on-line tools to augment museum experiences. In: Museums and the Web (2007)
6. Diamantopoulou, S., Insulander, E., Lindstrand, F.: Making meaning in museum exhibitions: design, agency and (re-) presentation. Des. Learn. **5**(1–2), 11–14 (2012)
7. Freedman, G.: The changing nature of museums. Curator: Mus. J. **43**(3), 295–306 (2000)

8. Jewitt, C.: Digital technologies in museums: new routes to engagement and participation. Des. Learn. **5**(1–2), 74–93 (2012)

9. MacKenzie, B.: Towards the sociocratic museum: how, and why, museums could radically change and how the digital can help. In: Rodley, R.S., Cairns, S. (eds.) CODE | WORDS. MuseumEtc, Edinburgh and Boston (2015)

10. Murawski, M.: Embracing a digital mindset in museums. In: Rodley, R.S., Cairns, S. (eds.) CODE | WORDS. MuseumEtc, Edinburgh and Boston (2015)

11. Kidd, J.: Are new media democratic? J. Cult. Policy Criticism Manag. **4**, 91–109 (2011)

12. Parry, R.: Recoding the Museum: Digital Heritage and the Technologies of Change. Routledge, London (2007)

13. Wellington, S., Oliver, G.: Reviewing the digital heritage landscape: the intersection of digital media and museum practice. In: The International Handbooks of Museum Studies: Museum Practice (2015)

14. Anderson, M.L.: Introduction. In: Jones-Garmill, K. (ed.) The Wired Museum. The American Association of Museums, Washington, D.C. (1997)

15. Henning, M.: New media. In: Macdonald, S. (ed.) A Companion to Museum Studies. Blackwell Publishing (2006)

16. Allard Pierson Museum: Keys to Rome: Projectplan, Amsterdam (2014)

17. Garfinkel, H.: Studies in Ethnomethodology. Prentice Hall, New Jersey (1967)

18. Chronis, A.: Tourists as story-builders: narrative construction at a heritage museum. J. Travel Tourism Mark. **29**(5), 444–459 (2012)

19. Hooper-Greenhill, E., Moussouri, T., Hawthorne, E., Riley, R.: Making Meaning in Art Museums 1: Visitors' Interpretive Strategies at Wolverhampton Art Gallery (2001)

20. Reading, A.: Digital interactivity in public memory institutions: the uses of new technologies in holocaust museums. Media Cult. Soc. **25**, 67–85 (2003)

21. Davies, R.: Overcoming barriers to visiting: raising awareness off, and providing orientation and navigation to, a museum and its collections through new technologies. Mus. Manag. Curatorship **19**(3), 283–295 (2001)

22. Heritage, J.C.: Ethnomethodology. In: Social Theory Today. Stanford University Press, Palo Alto (1988)

A Personal Tour of Cultural Heritage for Deaf Museum Visitors

Vaso Constantinou[1(✉)], Fernando Loizides[2(✉)], and Andri Ioannou[1(✉)]

[1] Cyprus Interaction Lab, Cyprus University of Technology,
30 Archbishop Kyprianou Street, 3036 Lemesos, Cyprus
va.constantinou@edu.cut.ac.cy, andri.i.ioannou@cut.ac.cy
[2] Emerging Interactive Technologies Lab, University of Wolverhampton, Wulfrana Street,
Wolverhampton WV1 1LY, UK
fernando.loizides@wlv.ac.uk

Abstract. This paper describes the first milestone and results of an ongoing project involving the implementation and pilot testing of an application aiming to promote cultural heritage and dissemination of information with the use of interactive small screen technology. The bespoke application was designed for deaf visitors to enable a museum experience without the support of a physical sign language interpreter. The application was pilot tested in the Pattichion Municipal Museum in Cyprus. Our findings showed high levels of user satisfaction and usefulness of the application in allowing deaf museum visitors to have an enjoyable tour, using their mobile devices as the only means of support.

Keywords: Museum · Cultural heritage · Small screen · Mobile · Deaf · Hearing impaired · Hard of hearing · Hearing disability · Accessibility

1 Introduction and Motivation

In the era of digital evolution, the use of interactive multimedia applications can change one's way of living and improve the quality of life. Deaf people are one such group of stakeholders that stand to benefit from the advances of ubiquitous technologies such as small screen devices. The objective of this work was to promote cultural heritage by improving the experience of deaf or hearing impaired museum visitors.

In the European Union 9 % of the total population, 44 million people, are deaf or hearing impaired [16]. In Cyprus, according to available data at the Ministry of Labor Welfare and Social Insurance, the number of people with hearing disability is currently approximated at 1000. In general, deaf people face many problems in daily life but also encounter obstacles related to their individual human rights. The impaired communication is the main reason for fewer educational and career opportunities. Reduced access to social services and communication difficulties cause social withdrawal, emotional problems and drop in self-esteem and confidence [3]. Despite the law (mainly in western world) complies with the relevant UN legislation and EU directives for the equal rights of persons with disabilities, the reality fails to meet the expectation. That is, deaf people have unequal treatment and encounter barriers in many issues like education and health

© Springer International Publishing AG 2016
M. Ioannides et al. (Eds.): EuroMed 2016, Part II, LNCS 10059, pp. 214–221, 2016.
DOI: 10.1007/978-3-319-48974-2_24

care, with effects on their social, emotional, and cognitive development [4]. They "often receive inadequate, inappropriate, and unethical health care" [6].

In this work, we acknowledge the growing need of utilizing technology to provide assistance to the individuals with disabilities such as deafness. The technologies can help us to enrich the lives of people with disabilities in allowing them to take part of common activities, such as tours within cultural heritage locations, without the need of specialist tour guides; which are too expensive or most commonly, unavailable. We present a bespoke application designed for deaf visitors to enable a museum experience without the support of a physical sign language interpreter. The application was pilot tested at the "Pattichion Municipal Museum - Historical Archives and Research Centre of Limassol" in Cyprus.

2 Related Work

There have been a few attempts to incorporate interactive technology in museums, in order to change how visitors interact with the exhibits, making the tours more person-alized and interesting. Researchers seem to agree that the integration of multimedia applications in museums can enhance the experience of the user, increasing their interest, knowledge transfer and entertainment. For example, Alexandri & Tzanavara [1] described how multimedia applications have helped to provide a more enjoyable museum learning experience. Similarly, Paternò & Santoro [12], presented how mobile devices equipped with appropriate applications allow users to obtain information about the exhibits and to use maps and games, enabling innovative ways to explore a museum. Mantyjarvi, Paternò, Salvador & Santoro [9] presented the interaction technique scan and tilt, and how it applied to a mobile museum guide in order to enhance user experi-ence. Studies focused on the deaf and their museums experiences are almost not existent. One example is the work by Proctor [13] demonstrating the effective use of handheld computers or PDAs to provide accessible interpretation for deaf museum visitors.

In recent years, there has been some effort to implement technology in real museum environment. In this direction is the implementation in National Sports Museum in Melbourne, carried out by the Australian Communication Exchange, a nonprofit organ-ization. The implementation consists of QR codes for each exhibit and an application for Android smart phones which reads the QR code and plays the information with captions in Auslan (Australian Sign Language) [2]. Similar implementations established in Fire Museum of Southeast Texas and to The Roald Dahl Museum - UK in cooperation with Deaf an organization for specialist visual and interactive deaf-friendly training [15]. In all cases, the goal was deaf and hearing-impaired people to gain easy access to the same information through a smartphone device with the use of QR code [7].

From a more theoretical perspective, Ruiz, Pajares, Utray & Moreno [14], used the MGA (Multimedia Guides for All) framework, to describe the required characteristics of a device in order to suit all users; the authors gave a series of recommendations for the selection, implementation, and content preparation. Signes de sens (France), Historic royal palaces (UK) and Norsk dovemuseum (Norway) joined a Grundtvig partnership project and provide a handbook of guidelines for the use of ICT in a way to make a museum Deaf-friendly [11].

As Lisney, Bowen, Hearn & Zedda [8], stated, the new technology can be a tool for the museums, in order to become accessible to all. The barrier to achieve that in most cases is not the cost, but the awareness and willingness. Echoing this view, in the present work we designed, developed and pilot tested a mobile application which targets hearing impaired individuals and allows for a personal experience of touring a museum via the use of their own mobile device.

3   Application Design and Development Processes

We followed a user-centered approach to the design of the application which involved three design cycles. The design process involved 68 participants in total, 49 male (72 %) and 19 female (28 %). The participants' varied in ages between 22 to 59 years. A total of 56 participants (82 %) were deaf (hearing loss 70 + dB HL) and 12 (18 %) were hard of hearing (hearing loss 20–69 + dB HL). To elicit user requirements, the participants completed a questionnaire after they were given a physical tour of the museum guided by a tour guide and a sign language translator. Based on the results of this questionnaire, a bespoke mobile application was designed to enable deaf visitors to have direct access to exhibits' information of the museum, using text (Greek and English), photos and videos with international sign language translation. The goal was for users to have the opportunity to become independent and to wander around the exhibits on site, without the presence of the museums' tour guide and the added need for a sign language interpreter.

We proceeded with the development of the application on the Android platform due to the large market share for the specific OS. According to Gartner, the rate of new devices running android in the first quarter of 2015 was 80.8 %, irrespective of manufacturer, with the second being iOS with 15.3 % [5]. The main aim of the application is to allow all user

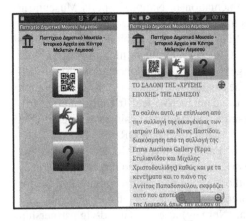

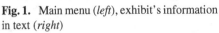

Fig. 1. Main menu (*left*), exhibit's information in text (*right*)

Fig. 2. Exhibit's information in international sign language (top), user instructions (*bottom*)

to create a self-paced guided tour of the museum. For each exhibit in the museum a unique QR code was created and positioned next to the exhibit in a prominent place. The user can scan the QR code, and information for the specific exhibit is displayed on the mobile device in the form of text and photos (Fig. 1). This information was translated in the international sign language and recorded on video (ISL video). Through the application menu, the user, can retrieve and see the ISL video on the mobile device (Fig. 2).

All data is stored on a server in the cloud which can be accessed through the application. With this structure the application on the mobile device is not heavily loaded with video and images. The communication between the app and the server is made by using the WiFi network that is available in all rooms of the museum. Furthermore, this cloud-based setup ensures expandability and scalability, making potential changes and additions easy. The menu appears in all pages of the application making the navigation easy and enabling the user to easily perform different options (Fig. 1). Instructions in the international sign language and can be called with a button located on the menu (Fig. 2). The current developed application is compatible with all Android-based operating systems Version 2.2 and above, which includes most tablets and mobile phones. The application is available free of charge. Visitors can also download it by scanning a particular QR code available at the entrance of the Pattichion Municipal Museum. The museum has purchased tables to provide for visitors who do not own a smartphone or a tablet.

4 Pilot Testing

The application was pilot tested at the "Pattichion Municipal Museum - Historical Archives and Research Centre of Limassol" in Cyprus. The Pattichion Municipal Museum is a newly established museum which aims to promote and spread the knowledge of the modern history and culture of the city of Limassol primarily from the 18th century onwards. The museum also hosts a research center where scientists and the general public have access to digitized archives of great historical value, as in Fig. 3. These archives contribute to the further promotion of Cyprus' history.

The pilot testing involved 28 participants, 16 male and 12 female, aged 22 to 59 years old. 24 (86 %) were deaf (hearing loss 70 + dB HL) 4 (14 %) were hard of hearing (hearing loss 20–69 + dB HL). Investigators carried out two rounds of measurements within a 1-month period from each other with the same participants. Participants were given the mobile application installed on their own devices without instructions for its use. There was no predetermined museum path that should be followed by the users, but instead, they were free to operate and browse the application (Fig. 4). Participants were expected to be able to tour the exhibits and retrieve the information, both in text and in ISL videos for each exhibit, with no other help other than the instructions in the application's options.

In terms of data collection, the participants' actions were recorded with a free-standing camera and the use of the application was also recorded in parallel using a Mobile Recording Device [10] attached to the mobile phone or tablet of the participant. A total of 250 min of video was recorded. At the end of each section participants responded to a short questionnaire.

Fig. 3. Exhibits within the Pattichion Municipal Museum

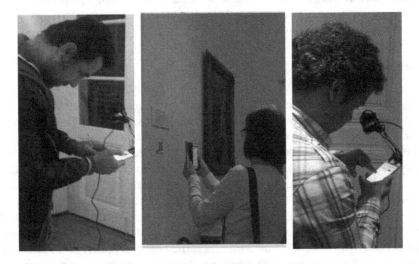

Fig. 4. Using the application in the user tests

5   Results

5.1   Learnability - Do You Remember How You Retrieved the Information in the Previous Exhibit?

Video analysis shed light to our investigation of the learnability of the application. By processing the video data, researchers recorded the time in seconds needed by the users to retrieve the information for each of the five exhibits.

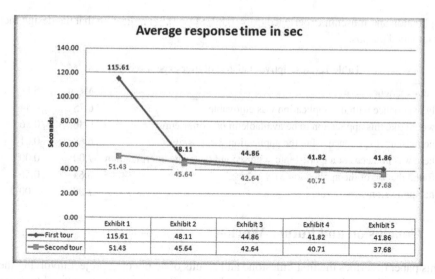

Fig. 5. Mean time needed by the participants to view each of the five exhibits during their first and second museum visits

Results showed that the time in seconds needed to retrieve information, decreased significantly between the first and second exhibit and remained low for the rest of the exhibits. There was statistically significant decrease (p < 0.001, n = 28) in the time needed to retrieve the information for the first exhibit (M = 115.61, SD = 26.70) compared to the time needed for the second exhibit (M = 48.11, SD = 15.52), which reflects a high level of learnability of the application. Figure 5 illustrates the mean time in seconds for retrieving the information for each of the exhibits during the first and second visits.

5.2 Memorability - Do You Remember How Your Retrieved the Information a Month Ago?

With regards to the memorability of the application, the researchers used the video measured to compare the time in seconds needed by the users to retrieve information for first exhibit during the first and second museum visits (one month apart). Results showed a statistically significant decrease (p < 0.001, n = 28) in the time needed to retrieve information for the first exhibit during the first visit (M = 115.61, SD = 26.70) compared to the time needed for the same exhibit during the second visit (M = 51.43, SD = 13.98), which reflects a high level of memorability of the application.

5.3 User Experience

Table 1, presents descriptive statistics of user experience, based on participants' responses to the short questionnaire. Rating was based on a 7-point ranging scale from 1 "Strongly Disagree" to 7 "Strongly Agree". The results showed a high level of satisfaction with the application and museum experience (M = 6.82, SD = 0.27) indicating that the design met its intended purpose.

Table 1. Descriptive statistics of user experience (N = 28)

User experience items	Mean	S.D
My experience with the application was enjoyable	6.75	0.44
I would like this application to be available in other museums	6.86	0.36
The museum experience using the application was positive	6.68	0.61
There was no need for a guided tour with second language interpretation	7.00	0.00
I found the use of the application easy	6.64	0.56
The application was useful	7.00	0.00

6   Conclusion and Future Work

This paper describes the first milestone and results of an ongoing project involving the implementation and pilot testing of an application aiming to promote cultural heritage and dissemination of information with the use of interactive small screen technology. We presented the first version of the released mobile application which was designed with the involvement of 68 deaf participants, following a user-centered design approach. Findings from a pilot study with 28 deaf participants using the application in the museum environment revealed high levels of user satisfaction. The application is easy to use and learn and allows museum tours for deaf, free from the need for support by specialized guides and interpreters. We close by concluding that the use of interactive media in museums not only should aim to provide a pleasant experience, but should seek to give access to everyone, including independence and freedom to disabled individuals.

The study showed that the use of the application revealed high levels of user satisfaction. As a next step and for the better understanding of the content, we need to add subtitles in all videos in sign language. Another future task may be the creation of a modular platform that would support all other museums on the island. The platform must be constructed and configured in a way so that it can cover any museum regardless of content, subject and size. Thus, the implementation of this technology in any museum could be done easily, with only the need the creation of the relevant videos in sign language.

Acknowledgement. Authors acknowledge travel funding from the European Union's Horizon 2020 Framework through NOTRE project (H2020-TWINN-2015, GA Number: 692058).

References

1. Alexandri, E., Tzanavara, A.: New technologies in the service of museum education. World Trans. Eng. Technol. Educ. **12**(2), 317–320 (2014)
2. Australian First in Museum Access for Deaf Australians at the National Sports Museum. http://travability.travel/blogs/nsm.html

3. Department for Social Inclusion of Persons with Disabilities - UN Convention on the Rights of Persons with Disabilities. http://www.mlsi.gov.cy/mlsi/dsid/dsid.nsf/dsipd08_en/dsipd08_en?OpenDocument
4. Fellinger, J., Holzinger, D., Pollard, R.: Mental health of deaf people. Lancet **379**, 1037–1044 (2012)
5. Gartner Inc.: Gartner Says Emerging Markets Drove Worldwide Smartphone Sales to 19 Percent Growth in First Quarter of 2015. http://www.gartner.com/newsroom/id/3061917
6. Harmer, L.: Health care delivery and deaf people: practice, problems, and recommendations for change. J. Deaf Stud. Deaf Educ. **4**, 73–110 (1999)
7. Lamar University Press – QR Codes opens museum experience to deaf. http://lamaruniversitypress.com/qr-codes-opens-museum-experience-to-deaf/
8. Lisney, E., Bowen, J., Hearn, K., Zedda, M.: Museums and technology: being inclusive helps accessibility for all. Curator **56**, 353–361 (2013)
9. Mantyjarvi, J., Paternò, F., Salvador, Z., Santoro, C.: Scan and tilt. In: Proceedings of the 8th Conference on Human-Computer Interaction with Mobile Devices and Services - MobileHCI 2006 (2006)
10. Noldus Mobile Device Camera. http://www.noldus.com/human-behavior-research/accessories/mobile-device-camera-mdc
11. Palaces, H.: Museums, Accessibility & ICT For Deaf people | Historic Royal Palaces. http://www.hrp.org.uk/accessibility/museums-accessibility-and-ict-for-deaf-people/#gs.7=LzYbQ
12. Paternò, F., Santoro, C.: Exploiting mobile devices to support museum visits through multi-modal interfaces and multi-device games. In: WEBIST (1), pp. 459–465 (2007)
13. Proctor, N.: Providing deaf and hard-of-hearing visitors with on-demand, independent access to museum information and interpretation through handheld computers. http://www.museumsandtheweb.com/mw2005/papers/proctor/proctor.html
14. Ruiz, B., Pajares, J., Utray, F., Moreno, L.: Design for All in multimedia guides for museums. Comput. Hum. Behav. **27**, 1408–1415 (2011)
15. The story of Signly. http://www.roalddahl.com/blog/2015/december/the-story-of-signly
16. Accessibility for People with Disabilities. http://www.eena.org/uploads/gallery/files/operations_documents/2012_01_13_112accessibilityforpeoplewithdisabilities.pdf

SigNet: A Digital Platform for Hellenistic Sealings and Archives

Stefano G. Caneva[1,3(✉)] and Branko F. van Oppen[2]

[1] Marie Curie Fellowship University of Padova, Padua, Italy
stefano.caneva@unipd.it
[2] Allard Pierson Museum, Amsterdam, The Netherlands
b.f.vanoppen@uva.nl
[3] Wikimedia Belgium, Brussels, Belgium
stefano@wikimedia.be

Abstract. The paper provides an overview of the SigNet Project with special attention to the implementation of a digital agenda fitting the dual purpose of promoting scientific research in the specialized disciplines of sigillography and numismatics and of bridging their gap with the broader field of cultural heritage. Focus is in particular on the role of interdisciplinary, open linked databases of big data and on the promotion of citizen science.

Keywords: Sealings · Numismatics · Archives · Hellenistic age · Iconography · Linked open data · Big data · 3D scan · Open source · Citizen science · Public engagement

1 Positioning Ancient History Research in the Digital Era: Big Data, Digital Cultural Heritage, and Citizen Science

SigNet is a project proposal for the study of Hellenistic seal impressions and coinage (*ca.* 330-30 BCE), currently under evaluation within the framework of a "Digging into Data" call for projects.[1] The project's aim is to develop digital tools for advancing research of the material as well as to make the material widely available for further study. Image recognition software, such as developed for numismatic analysis, will be used not only for the benefit of comparing hoards of sealings, but also for cross-referencing existing coin databases. Online resources, such as an umbrella website, blogs and open-access papers will facilitate the dissemination of the results of the research.

This collaborative project comprising of American, Dutch and French teams will be the first time that coins and sealings will be studied in conjunction rather than

---

[1] http://diggingintodata.org.

© Springer International Publishing AG 2016
M. Ioannides et al. (Eds.): EuroMed 2016, Part II, LNCS 10059, pp. 222–231, 2016.
DOI: 10.1007/978-3-319-48974-2_25

isolation.[2] The international and interdisciplinary SigNet Project brings together scholars in related fields of expertise, and is established to address several general and more specific questions about the interrelationship between seals and sealings on the one hand, and seals and coinage on the other. These small-scale or miniature artifacts carry images of various kinds – from gods to symbols of religious and administrative importance – which have never been compared systematically. Digital tools will be created and employed as aids in collecting, collating and analyzing the large data-sets at our disposal. State-of-the-art software will facilitate the cross-referencing within and across the (thus far first and only) digital image repository of seal impressions from selected Hellenistic archives and coin collections complemented with metadata available for statistical analysis. Such a tool will offer the potential of exploring and interpolating data in order to address a wide variety of research questions within the Humanities and Social Sciences.

Building on software created for coins by the American Numismatic Society and combining the existing databases and digital files of different hoards of sealings and multiple coin collections, the SigNet Project will address research questions relevant to the Humanities and Social Sciences in transformative and novel ways. The Hellenistic world involved a larger network of connections than previous eras. Interpreting overlapping networks on the level of iconography and archival practices will be significantly enhanced by employing large-scale, qualitative as well as quantitative data analysis. Combining sources of different – though related – nature overcomes the divide existing between highly specialized fields of research. As coins tend to be marked with a deducible year-date in which they were minted, numismatic evidence provides a firm chronological basis and can thus enable a more accurate dating of comparable sealings. Standardizing the data-sets of different miniature artifacts into a single repository, taking into account the option of future adjustments, by calibrating and correlating the source material will doubtless have invaluable consequences for increasing the scientific accuracy of the analyses.

The immediate pay-off of the project is to assist students in various areas of history, classics and archaeology, as well as (junior and senior) colleagues in related fields of expertise, such as iconography, numismatics, glyptics and of course sigillography itself. The research teams consist of a combination of senior and junior researchers, allowing younger scholars to develop new skills and improve their existing talents. The Dutch team will furthermore invite a post-doctoral fellow for performing statistical analysis and thus increase her or his experience. The collaboration of experts in various disciplines is expected to lead to mutually inspiring new insights.

---

[2] The teams constituting SigNet are led by Dr. Marie-Françoise Boussac (Université Paris Ouest), Dr. Sharon C. Herbert (University of Michigan, Ann Arbor) and Dr. Wim M.H. Hupperetz (Allard Pierson Museum, Amsterdam). Partners include experts associated with the American Numismatic Society (ANS, New York), Archéologies et Sciences de l'Antiquité (ArScAn, Nanterre), Histoire et Sources des Mondes Antiques (HiSoMa, Lyon), Fondation Gandur pour l'Art (Geneva), and the Universities of Louvain and Turin.

However, there is more. The SigNet Team believes that the combination of the chosen evidence and methodology provides suitable premises for developing cutting-edge tools as well as for innovative and replicable strategies for big data enrichment, standardization and quantitative as well as qualitative analysis both in the Humanities and the Social Sciences. Moreover, SigNet will offer tools for bridging the gap between specialized scholarship and the broader field of cultural heritage. In the following sections we will first focus on the basic features of the research, including the digital tools which will be specifically developed for the project; then discuss the research environment in which SigNet will develop and with which it will integrate; and end with some observations about how we hope to encourage the interaction with larger society. In this respect we intend to make our research results available to all levels of society. We support the application of all available methods, including open-access policy and citizen engagement, for the exchange of ideas between specialists and citizens. We thus align ourselves with the compelling vision arguing for the importance of disseminating scientific research as widely and effectively as possible.

2   Digging into (Big) Data: Archeology and Iconography

2.1   The Evidence: Archives of Hellenistic Sealings

The research planned by the SigNet Project focusses on the Hellenistic World, the territories conquered by Alexander the Great and held under Greco-Macedonian political control from *ca.* 330 to 30 BCE (Fig. 1). These territories stretched from the Aegean to Afghanistan, were ruled by different forms of government, and were inhabited by multiethnic populations. Following Alexander the Great's campaigns from Macedon to India, a substantial change in administrative practices occurred across the conquered regions. One common feature Hellenistic states shared was a commitment to record keeping and complex bureaucratic practices. States, including kings, confederacies and city-states, produced hundreds of thousands of documents written mostly on papyri in Greek, but others on parchment or cuneiform tablets and in various local languages. These documents were sealed with impressions from signet rings or stamps. They were stored in various types of archives [2–4] – ranging from the large official archive at Seleucia-on-the Tigris, Babylonia (25,000 + sealings) to the small household archive in Elephantine, Egypt (35 sealings).

Most of the documents have been lost to the elements, but many thousands of the sealings once attached to them do survive. These sealings were created by impressing signet rings, decorated with images, or seal stamps in clay or bitumen. They derive from the personal seals of private individuals, the official seals of cities and institution, the signet rings of the ruling dynasts or their officers – mainly those of the Seleucids in Syria and Asia Minor, and the Ptolemies in Egypt. These impressions therefore illustrate the choices individuals and institutions made in presenting their (often mixed) identity and status, the royal manipulation of local and imperial iconography, as well as the complexities of administrative procedures and the variety of archival practices used in different regions.

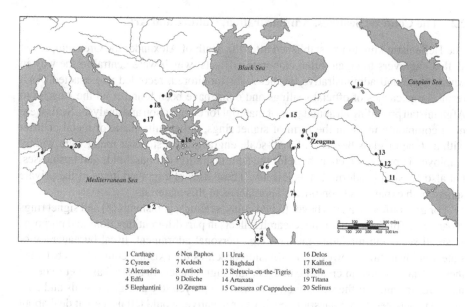

1 Carthage	6 Nea Paphos	11 Uruk	16 Delos
2 Cyrene	7 Kedesh	12 Baghdad	17 Kallion
3 Alexandria	8 Antioch	13 Seleucia-on-the-Tigris	18 Pella
4 Edfu	9 Doliche	14 Artaxata	19 Titana
5 Elephantini	10 Zeugma	15 Caesarea of Cappadocia	20 Selinus

Fig. 1. Map of the Hellenistic World with main sites of hoards of sealings

The hoards of sealings included in the SigNet project were found in the Greek island of Delos, the temple of Horus at Edfu as well as Elephantine in southern Egypt, Tel Kedesh in Israel near Tyre, and Seleucia in Mesopotamia near Babylon. It was also in the Hellenistic period that coinage was adopted as an official monetary and fiscal instrument across the Near East and in Egypt. The overlap in the iconography of sealings and coinage allows for a beneficial comparison for the intensity and extension of certain images. Conversely, differences in the typology of coins and seals offer insight in the regional significance of images.

Combining Hellenistic hoards of sealings found at different sites into a single research project – rather than studying series separately – will significantly improve scholarly insights into sealing and archival practices. Recent scholarship has made important advances in the study of archival practices and the buildings in which archives were housed. Some works encompass a wide geographical and chronological range following a cross-cultural and/or archeological approach, but many rely mostly on textual evidence. Researchers address a complex range of questions such as the gradual differentiation between archives and libraries, the significance of record-keeping, and the distinction between private and public archives. Hoards of sealings add invaluable information for interpretation as they are often the only remains directly linked to the archives, and provide information about the owners or users and thus the nature of the archive.

When studied in the systematic way proposed by the SigNet Project, Hellenistic sealings allow scholars to offer hypotheses on the nature of archives and their content, as well as to draw comparisons between archives and practices across distant regions and strata of the various societies. The study of surviving seal impressions is therefore imperative for the better understanding of ancient administration and the networks of contact between archives, as well as the political implications of the impressed images themselves.

2.2   The Context: Sealings, Administration, Culture and Art

The Hellenistic kingdoms established after the death of Alexander the Great employed skilled engravers to create often elaborate artifacts, which were central to the way in which fiscal and administrative business was monitored, recorded and enacted. As a result, large caches of official sealings and coins have been found from the Aegean to Afghanistan providing an abundance of material for comparison and analysis. Seals were most commonly made in the form of signet rings, either fully made of metal or inset with a stone or glass bezel [1]. Small-scale engravings in stone or metal were widely employed in private practice, both for the administration of households and businesses, but also for simple adornment as jewelry. These uses of engraved items in the private sphere both expand and complicate approaches to this material.

For generations scholars have studied coins, sealings, gemstones [5] and signet rings separately. This isolation of the research reflects in part different functions and purposes of small-scale and miniature media – e.g., personal adornment, fiscal bureaucracy or state administration. However, the division obscures the existing connections between these artifacts – e.g., in creation, imagery and significance. Scholars have yet to determine, for instance, if the same engravers were employed to carve gems, seals and coin dies. Any answer to that question, positive or negative, would tell us a great deal about interactions between public and private spheres, the organization of administrative practices, and artistic traditions.

At the administrative level, identifying links between seals, sealings and coins, could tell us much about the scope and scale of fiscal and managerial practices. No concerted effort to date has been made to study the broad spectrum of ancient engravings, in part because of the sheer abundance of the material and the interdisciplinary effort it requires. The results of such an endeavor are nonetheless sure to be transformative: new networks and interconnections between merchants, administrators, artists, and governments will be found.

The SigNet Project therefore aims to both broaden and deepen our understanding of the ancient world by testing this large set of interrelated evidence in terms of big-data analyses: key factors for this approach are aggregating multiple existing open databases, enriching and standardizing metadata, and developing digital tools to enhance machine-readable queries. The serial nature of the evidence is particularly suitable for this methodology. The following section explores more in detail the digital solutions foreseen by SigNet and their interaction with the existing ecosystem in the field of the digital analysis of miniature and small scale iconographic media.

2.3   Digital Tools Developed by the SigNet Project

There are two main digital tools that SigNet will use to organize existing sealing and coin databases. The first is software developed for the study of coin dies. This state-of-the-art computer technology will establish links between sealings, both within a single archive and between hoards from different – even distant – sites. The tool will moreover establish links between coins and seals or sealings. Digitization is performed through high definition 2D and 3D scanning techniques to reveal stylistic and artistic details – difficult to observe by the human eye – that could match similar types, recognize fragments from complete images, and even associate artifacts produced at the same workshop or by the same hand (Fig. 2). Overall, this computer-aided study will considerably speed up cross-referential analysis, as the process of establishing links between tens if not hundreds of thousands of items is painstakingly time-consuming – if not impossible – when done by individual scholars or even groups of experts.

Fig. 2. 3D scan of seal impression with the portrait of Cleopatra VII (APM inv. no. 8177-056)

The second tool within the SigNet Project is an open-access website that will allow users to cross-reference items within the selected hoards of seal impressions from Hellenistic archives and the numismatic collections. This overarching SigNet website will make the sharing and study of the source material more efficient. For, it will not only allow quick image comparison of impressions and coins, but will also provide metadata for analysis. The combined database will therefore improve our understanding of the relation between works of art and political propaganda, the circulation of iconographic types from different and distant centers of production, and thus the geographic diffusion of aspects of ideology and symbolism. In all, the repository will address questions about archival and administrative practices as well as the relations between artists and clients.

We expect that SigNet repository will provide an invaluable resource not only for the research of currently unpublished hoards of Hellenistic sealings, but also for advancing the scholarship on ancient seals, sealings and archives in general. Consequent advances in the study of ancient sealings will have its inevitable effect on the separate studies of contemporary coins, signet rings, seals and gemstones. The expected target groups therefore include experts in sigillography and related specializations, *viz.*, glyptic and numismatic studies; colleagues in more broadly related fields such as archaeology and ancient history, Egyptology and Assyriology, epigraphy and papyrology, classics and art history; scientific institutions; museums; and a larger audience of the interested general public.

3   The SigNet Research Ecosystem

3.1   Towards a Cross-Media Study of Sealings and Coins

The iconography of many sealings share features with the coin types of Hellenistic kingdoms and those produced by city-states. Like the sealings, coins were the product of an administrative process, perhaps in some cases related processes. Until now coins, seals and sealings have been studied in isolation by separate groups of experts. While the coins have been extensively studied and published, the sealings have been largely underexploited. One goal of this project is to form the first collaborative effort to bring these disparate groups of scholars together and shed light on the administrative practices of the Hellenistic world, as well as on the use of artistic media in these practices. Sigillography greatly benefits from comparative analyses of the imagery and styles of various miniature and small-scale media, such as contemporary coins, engraved gemstones, signet rings, seals and seal impressions from other sites and times. Such large-scale qualitative analyses provide useful information about specific aspects of the artistic milieus, administrative practices, political ideology and religious symbolism of the Hellenistic Mediterranean and Near East. Examining the influence of different local styles and traditions upon each other in the production of novel iconographic types will expose the complex interaction within the multicultural milieu of the Hellenistic period.

The data-sets available for the study of Hellenistic sealings and archives such as intended by the SigNet project are considerable and sizeable (Fig. 3). Of the roughly twenty archives of sealings of purely Hellenistic date, this project focusses on three of the largest, which were found in stratified excavations, and number well over 50,000 sealings. These include Seleucia's official archive (25,000+), a merchant's archive from Delos (*ca.* 27,500) and an administrative center in Tel Kedesh (2,000+). Included is also an important temple archive from Edfu (*ca.* 750) and the small household archive from Elephantine (35) in southern Egypt.

In addition, the project gains access to the American Numismatic Society's numismatic online database, which consists of over 25,000 coins of Hellenistic dynasts and nearly as many civic coins. All the sealings will have been digitized by the start of the project. All told, the combined objects from these collections amount to some 100,000 coins and sealings. Bringing together the information obtained from separate studies into a single platform of Hellenistic sealings and coins will offer new insights into

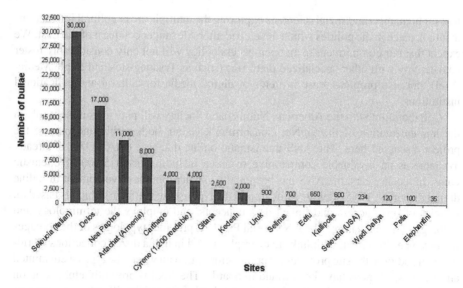

Fig. 3. Table of approximate numbers of sealings per hoard

questions of chronology, iconography, mass production and diffusion, archival procedures, as well as political and social history.

3.2 Interaction and Integration with Other Existing Platforms

The multifunctional SigNet portal will link information from the different existing datasets in a novel way. The website will adhere to, and contribute to the improvement of,
standards for open linked data, with reference vocabularies [6] and metadata compliant
with cultural heritage ontologies and semantic models, thus making the material much
more widely available for other research questions. The experience of leading actors in
the field of the digitization of cultural heritage, such as the Europeana Foundation[3] and
its partner project EAGLE (which has now turned into IDEA, International Digital
Epigraphy Association)[4], will play an important role in the implementation and fine-
tuning of the data-management model. Collaboration with these and other institutions
and networks will therefore be actively sought. With regard to reuse permission, a crucial
asset of the SigNet Project is that it directly involves the institutions owning the rights
of the selected hoards of Hellenistic sealings from Delos, Seleucia, Kedesh and Edfu.
These collections will therefore be accessible through a common licensing agreement
and available through open access – similar to the ANS platforms discussed below,
which have implemented a CC-BY-NC 4.0 International (Attribution-NonCommercial
4.0 International)[5] licensing policy for the pictures of coins. By making its data-sets
available over the internet to any user for free, SigNet will prove to be an invaluable

---

[3] http://www.europeana.eu.

tool for humanists and social scientists exploring the multiple cross-cultural interactions that took place in the polities which developed after Alexander conquest of the East. We expect that our commitment to an open-access policy will not only considerably foster connectivity with other specialized platforms (such as Trismegistos and Eagle Media-Wiki), but also promote reuse in fields of digital media for cultural and educational institutions.

Collaboration with the American Numismatic Society will play a prominent role in the implementation of the SigNet Consortium's vision, both within and outside the project discussed here. The ANS numismatic online database (MANTIS)[6] is already available as an invaluable comparative resource including about 50,000 Hellenistic coins. In recent years, the ANS has been at the vanguard in the development of online digital resources. ANS sites are built around the Numishare platform, which is based on policies of open access and linked data concepts, and employs the terminology and ontology of nomisma.org. The ANS portal PELLA[7] provides typologies of the coinages of Alexander the Great, with links to examples found in half a dozen collections world-wide. In addition, the site provides mapping information on where the types were minted and where specimens have been found in hoards. The ANS is presently embarking on a large-scale project involving Hellenistic royal coinage, which will result in a number of parallel portals each focusing on individual dynasties, *e.g.*, the Seleucids, the Ptolemies, etc. Information about provenance, date, type and so forth will be readily available for the SigNet portal, either through MANTIS or sister sites.

4   New Frontiers of Dissemination: Academic Research and Digital Cultural Heritage

The partners of the SigNet Project share the vision that stimulating collaborative, inter-disciplinary digital scholarship is an essential step to ensure significant advancement in research, cut down human and economic costs and make dissemination of research results effective. However, communication among experts and between related academic fields is not the only goal of the project. In compliance with current attempts of scientific research in humanities and social sciences to reach out to the larger society, SigNet recognizes the importance of promoting dissemination to the widest possible circulation. This effort consists of integrating the material as well as research into the broader field of cultural heritage, in order to make them available to the general public of cultural and educational institutions and organizations.

A readily and easily accessible web application available to the general interested public will allow a larger web community – well beyond the handful of scientific specialists – to become involved and share insights. Computer generated comparisons based on user search commands will analyze similarities within existing digital image

---

[4] http://www.eagle-network.eu.

[5] https://creativecommons.org/licenses/by-nc/4.0/legalcode.

[6] http://numismatics.org.

[7] http://numismatics.org/pella.

databases of seal impressions and coins. Such an innovative research tool will unquestionably lead to new insights. Registered users will be invited to add metadata to existing entries and/or upload similar artifacts. Thousands of engraved gems survive, mostly from undocumented excavations or old private collections. Evidence from sealing collections, archives and hoards will significantly benefit the study of ancient glyptics at large, which remains a highly speculative and under-documented field. Here too, adaptation to existing guidelines and good practices shared by leading international networks (*cf.* Europeana, Civic Epistemologies[8], RICHES[9]) will combine into an active collaboration among professionals from cultural and educational institutions who will share research insight through user engagement, digital storytelling and citizen science.

Collaboration will also be sought and promoted with Wikimedia[10] in order to develop outreach projects in schools and museums. A whole set of tools, from photo scavenger hunts to edit-a-thons and more structured Wikidata projects,[11] are available to engage students, museum professionals and interested citizens in a shared goal: making miniature iconographic objects convey their stories and contribute to the understanding of the multi-faceted life of the ancient world and, through comparisons, of the many other historical contexts – up to present day – in which coins and sealings play a role in everyday life.

In the future, the partners of the SigNet Project aim to establish an even larger consortium with the dual purpose of further augmenting and connecting the SigNet repository with similar databases across the world, and of coordinating and promoting individual initiative, group efforts such as edit-a-thons, and future subsidized projects concerning collections of ancient signet rings, engraved gems, seals and other collections of sealings. This commitment will assure that the web applications developed by the SigNet Project will keep on growing and facing the new challenges of research, museum engagement and citizen science for many years to come.

References

1. Boussac, M.-F., Invernizzi, A. (eds): Archives et Sceaux du Monde Hellénistique. École Française d'Athènes, Athens (1996)
2. Brosius, M.: Ancient Archives and Archival Traditions: Concepts of Record- Keeping in the Ancient World. Oxford University Press, Oxford (2003)
3. Coqueugniot, G.: Archives et bibliothèques du monde grec: Édifices et organisation, Ve siècle avant notre ère-Ier siècle de notre ère. Oxford University Press, Oxford (2013)
4. Faraguna, M. (ed.): Legal Documents in Ancient Societies. IV: Archives and Archival Documents in Ancient Societies. Edizioni Università di Trieste, Trieste (2013)
5. Plantzos, D.: Hellenistic Engraved Gems. Oxford University Press, Oxford (1999)
6. Szabados, A.-V.: From the *LIMC* vocabulary to LOD: current and expected uses of the multilingual thesaurus *TheA*. In: Orlandi, S., et al. (eds) Information Technologies for Epigraphy and Cultural Heritage, pp. 51–67. Università La Sapienza Editrice, Roma (2014)

---

[8] www.civic-epistemologies.eu.
[9] www.riches-project.eu.
[10] https://wikimediafoundation.org.
[11] www.wikidata.org.

Places Speaking with Their Own Voices. A Case Study from the Gra.fo Archives

Alessandro Pozzebon[1]([✉]), Francesca Biliotti[2], and Silvia Calamai[2]

[1] Department of Information Engineering and Mathematical Sciences,
University of Siena, Via Roma 56, 53100 Siena, Italy
alessandro.pozzebon@unisi.it
[2] Department of Education, Human Sciences and Intercultural Communication,
University of Siena, Viale Luigi Cittadini 33, 52100 Arezzo, Italy
{francesca.biliotti,silvia.calamai}@unisi.it
http://www.diism.unisi.it, http://www.dsfuci.unisi.it

Abstract. This paper proposes a novel approach for the fruition of cultural heritage based on the "Augmented Cultural Heritage" paradigm. This expression has been used to describe the improvement to the visit to a Tangible Cultural Site with additional Intangible Cultural Assets like audio recordings or oral testimonies. The proposed approach is applied to the area of the Montagna Pistoiese, Tuscany, Italy: in this case the visit to the site is enriched by providing visitors with oral material coming from the "Anna Buonomini" archive, a collection of audio recordings of high historical and cultural value. The audio files are geo-referenced and associated to a specific position in the area. The user is able to hear a recording only when he/she reaches the specific geographical point associated with the file. The audio is played adaptively with the distance to the point, so as to emulate a real voice coming from the place.

Keywords: Intangible Cultural Heritage · Oral archives · Smart devices · Storytelling · App

1 Introduction

Every space inhabited by men is the cradle of specific cultural products, such as folktales, folk music, gastronomic traditions, traditional crafts and practices. Such complex net of cultural products sheds a light on the identity of the people inhabiting the area and is a precious resource for the fruition of the area itself. In this respect, Intangible Cultural Heritage as described in the UNESCO Convention for the Safeguarding of the Intangible Cultural Heritage [1] (oral traditions and expressions, including language as a vehicle of the Intangible Cultural Heritage, performing arts, social practices, rituals and festive events, knowledge and practices concerning nature and the universe) appears to be an unexploited resource for tourism and travel that could offer a better understanding of the space/culture relation. Over the past decades, several oral archives have been

M. Ioannides et al. (Eds.): EuroMed 2016, Part II, LNCS 10059, pp. 232–239, 2016.
DOI: 10.1007/978-3-319-48974-2_26

created with the specific purpose of preserving and transmitting local speci-ficities. The project *Grammo-foni: Le soffitte della voce* (*Gra.fo*, grafo.sns.it), carried out by Scuola Normale Superiore and the University of Siena, funded by Regione Toscana (PAR-FAS 2007-13), discovered, digitized, catalogued and disseminated via a web portal nearly 3000 hours of speech recordings stemming from around 30 oral archives collected by scholars and amateurs in the Tuscan territory. Having preserved such a significant collection of oral documents (e.g. oral biographies, ethno-texts, linguistic questionnaires, oral literature), *Gra.fo* constitutes a precious repository of Tuscan memory and provides a first-hand documentation of Tuscan language varieties from the early 1960s [2,3]. Among the variety of possibilities offered by oral archives as for their description, analy-sis and reuse, their relation with space represents one of the most underinves-tigated perspectives. Such geographical perspective is at least twofold. In fact, some oral archives are collected for linguistic purposes: uncultivated speakers are asked to answer to linguistic questionnaires in order to document the linguistic repertoire of a particular linguistic community, which is represented as a point according to the geolinguistic lexicon and taxonomy. This is the case of archives such as that of *Carta dei Dialetti Italiani* and that of *Atlante Lessicale Toscano*, two major geolinguistic enterprises carried out in Italy in the 1960s and 1970s respectively [4]. Other oral archives are intimately connected with space and geography, in the sense that the speakers involved describe orally some partic-ular aspects of a site that they know and belong to. This is the case of other archives digitized and analyzed within the *Gra.fo* project, among which is the "Anna Buonomini" archive.

2 The Montagna Pistoiese and the Case of the "Anna Buonomini" Archive

Tuscany is world-famous for Renaissance Florence, Siena and the Tower of Pisa, but throughout the region there are other hidden treasures that deserve to be known and visited. Tuscany's beautiful, varied landscape, which is intimately related to and influenced by culture and traditions, allows the creation of alter-native itineraries also on those areas that are not affected by mass tourism. The so-called Montagna Pistoiese is among these hidden treasures. It includes the municipalities of San Marcello Pistoiese, Abetone, Cutigliano and Piteglio and occupies a vast area on the north and north-west of Pistoia, on the southern ridge of the Tuscan-Emilian Appennines. The area is endowed with exceptional natural riches: there are vast forests with plenty of drinking water, a rich under-growth and a varied fauna. The locals have always integrated perfectly with the landscape, taking advantage of all the resources available: they used cold temper-atures to produce ice, wood to produce carbon, hydraulic energy to manufacture objects made of iron, and they were involved in agriculture, farming, grazing and stone carving. In addition, the Montagna Pistoiese retains valuable historic, artis-tic, cultural riches and a vast repertoire of traditions, ancient crafts and local productions. The area under study is shown in Fig. 1. The Archive stems from the historical and ethnological research conducted in the area of the Montagna Pistoiese by Anna Buonomini, who, as for the IPR issues, signed a legal and ethical agreement with the *Gra.fo* project [5]. It contains 16 hours of recording arranged in three collections. One of these, "Cappel d'Orlando", is particularly important for the present study. It contains eight interviews collected in 1987 about the toponyms of the area of Cutigliano related to the legendary figure of Roland and retains precious testimonies of how *Orlando Furioso* by Ludovico Ariosto was received and transmitted [6]: the poem was known by heart and recited - together with Dante Alighieri's *Divina Commedia* and Torquato Tasso's *Gerusalemme Liberata* - by often illiterate shepherds and peasants during the so-called "veglie" (evening gatherings). The research also gives interesting information on the Tuscan tradition of oral improvised poetry (*stornello* and *ottava rima*) and on the figure of Beatrice di Pian degli Ontani, the shepherd poet whose talent was lauded by Niccolò Tommaseo.

3   The "Voice of the Places"

The solution described in this paper is based on the "Augmented Cultural Heritage" technological paradigm proposed in [7]. In order to provide tourists visiting specific sites with a multimedia support allowing them to improve their visit experience, technological features of common smartphones can be exploited to set up an innovative, immersive cultural experience [8,9]. The "Augmented Cultural Heritage" paradigm is based on the widely applied "Augmented Reality" concept. While in Augmented Reality the video streaming of a camera is augmented with an additional graphic layer providing 3D models, reconstructions, information and so on, in Augmented Cultural Heritage a Tangible Cultural Site is augmented by providing an additional layer of Intangible Cultural Assets. Like Augmented Reality, Augmented Cultural Heritage exploits technical features of common smartphones like GPS and Bluetooth to provide geo-localized multimedia content in real time. This approach is based on the philosophy that, when a tourist is visiting a cultural site, his/her attention has to be directed solely to the real site. For this reason, the interaction with the smartphone screen has to be reduced as much as possible. The automatic reproduction of an audio file meets this requirement: the user simply wears the headphones and waits for the audio file to be reproduced. While this approach could be compared to the one of common audio guides [10,11], some remarkable differences must be noticed:

1. While audio guides provide a simple description of a site, the audio files played in an Augmented Cultural Heritage scenario can be considered to all effects Intangible Cultural Assets. They can be for example narrations, ethno-texts, songs, folk tales, that can also be arranged to compose a story exploiting the concept of Storytelling [12].
2. Instead of using a top-down approach, a bottom-up approach is proposed: while the content of traditional audio guides is created ad hoc, in this solution the content consists in authentic testimonies.

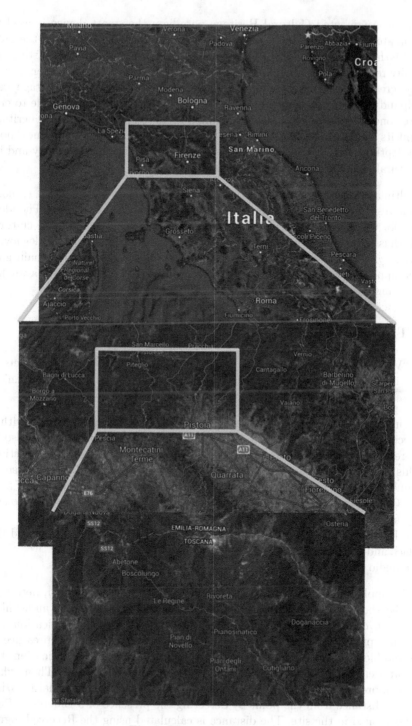

Fig. 1. The area under study

3. In the Augmented Cultural Heritage paradigm the smart device is used to emulate reality as much as possible. When approaching a speaker, the level of his/her voice grows with the proximity: this feature is emulated by dynamically reproducing the audio file according to the position of the user.
4. By creating immersive environments, Augmented Cultural Heritage can expand the attractiveness of certain cultural elements ("it is possible to create conditions that encourage and enable users to approach cultural heritage and its structures with less deferential, more dynamic, and sometimes more in-depth attitudes, which may cause users to bond with the territory and its cultural heritage in its broadest sense" [10]).

The ultimate goal of this approach is to give Voice to each specific Place exploiting the testimonies of people that have lived there through the years. The ideal target for this solution is represented by Italian speakers, with a good cultural level, thus interested in understanding the traditions and the cultural legacy of a territory. Only an English summary has been planned in that the main goal of the approach is to exploit real audio recordings that are obviously available in the language of the inhabitants of the specific territory.

4   The Mobile Application

The "Voice of the Places" approach is based on a mobile application that acts as a sort of dynamic audio player. This application exploits the following technical features of smartphones:

- an internal database storing the audio files to be played associated with a specific position identified by its GPS coordinates. The audio file could also be stored in a remote database and then streamed through Internet connection. This solution has been discarded in the proposed scenario due to the small number of audio files but could be set up in the case of a large number of files;
- the GPS, to track the position of the user and detect when he/she is approaching a place provided with its own Voice (i.e. an associated audio file);
- the Bluetooth LE 4.0 to detect the exact distance between the user and the Place and then to adapt the level of the audio to this distance;
- the audio player.

The application, when active, is able to track the user's position, detecting when he/she is approaching one of the points associated with the audio files. The width of the area covered requires the set-up of a push notification service, that provides a feedback to the user, notifying him/her the presence of an audio file associated with that specific point. Following the notification, the user can wear the headphones and wait for the audio to be played. Then, while he/she approaches the Place, the mobile application begins to calculate his/her accurate distance from the point by detecting the presence of a Bluetooth Beacon positioned in the site. The distance is calculated using the Received Signal Strength Indication (RSSI) of the Beacon: this value is then employed to set the

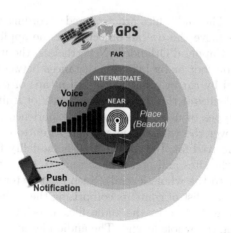

Fig. 2. The functioning of the application

Table 1. Sites list

Abetone
Cutigliano
Il Balzo della Monaca
Malpasso
Pian degli Ontani
Pian di Malarme
Pian di Novello
Prato della Peschiera
Torre del Fattucchio

volume of the audio player. The volume increases when the user approaches the Place where the Beacon is positioned, in the same way as the voice of a person appears louder when coming close to him/her. The functioning of the application is shown in Fig. 2. The audio file is perceived as a real Voice of the Place. The visit to a site is then turned into a multi-sensory experience, allowing the user to enjoy two different cultural assets associated to two different senses: the user sees the Tangible Cultural Site around him/her and listens to the Intangible Cultural Heritage represented by the audio material stored in the archive. The application is going to be customized on the scenario described in Sect. 2. For this purpose, nine sites have been identified where the Beacons will be positioned. The list of sites (Table 1) is clearly heterogeneous, as it includes different kinds of places: from wider areas (i.e. Abetone and Cutigliano) to smaller ones (e.g. Pian degli Ontani and Pian di Novello) to even more circumscribed locations (i.e. the Fattucchio tower). For each site, a linked audio file from the "Anna Buonomini" archive has been identified that constitutes a fragment of the legend of the

"Cappel d'Orlando". The audio files are arranged according to the Storytelling paradigm, so as to achieve the overall objective of the application: to tell the whole legend of the "Cappel d'Orlando". Nevertheless, the itinerary is not one that can be covered on foot or by bike: the distances between the sites require that the visitor travel by car or other motorized means of transport. Precisely because of the complexity of the itinerary, two levels of fruition are envisaged based on two ideal types of users: (a) the deep experience modality for those who are willing to cover the whole itinerary and listen to every extract in the place that it was conceived for; (b) the quick visit modality for those who visit only one or some of the sites and nonetheless want to listen to extracts related to the other sites (or to the whole legend). Such dual system of fruition allows the user to choose from a list of contents comprising the audio file associated to the specific place where he/she is, the audio files associated to the other sites and the file containing the whole legend. The audio files are fragments of longer interviews that need to be sophisticatedly edited for the purpose. Such work is demanding because of the nature itself of interviews: since spontaneous speech is authentic and mostly unmediated, it presents features that may appear problematic in the context of tourist guides (e.g. hesitations, filled pauses, silences, unfinished sentences, etc.). Nevertheless, it certainly makes visitors' experience significantly different from that of visitors using common audio guides. As far as the implementation costs are concerned, the development of the application is very simple and requires few weeks of work. As for the hardware, only the cost of the Beacons has to be taken into account: nevertheless, because each Beacon has a price around 20 euros, the installation of the whole infrastructure is cheap and every public administration could afford it.

5   Conclusion and Future Work

In this paper, an application of the "Augmented Cultural Heritage" paradigm has been presented. The augmentation of a Cultural Site through the reproduction of the Intangible Cultural Heritage represented by the oral documents stored in sound archives has been described, applying it to the case of the Montagna Pistoiese area in Tuscany, Italy, exploiting the audio material stored in the "Anna Buonomini" archive. Such solution is relevant on two levels: preservation and diffusion. On the level of preservation, embedding audio material taken from a historical archive allows the protection of an Intangible Cultural Heritage that, due to its immateriality, is intrinsically difficult to be safeguarded. On the level of diffusion the proposed application allows a wide range of users to access and enjoy a Cultural Heritage that cannot be usually accessed. The proposed scenario is expected to be deployed in the next months as a case study to prove the effectiveness of the "Augmented Cultural Heritage" paradigm. The final purpose of this work is the full exploitation of the audio material stored in the large number of sound archives available in Tuscany, in particular the ones already digitized within the Gra.fo project, to create a set of itineraries covering the least known areas of Tuscany, improving at the same time the number of tourists in these areas and the knowledge about a kind of Intangible Cultural Heritage that is often neglected.

References

1. World Heritage Committee: Convention for the safeguarding of the intangible cultural heritage (2003)
2. Calamai, S., Biliotti, F., Bertinetto, P.M., Bertini, C., Ricci, I., Scuotri, G.: Architecture, methods and purpose of the Gra.fo sound archive. In: Digital Heritage International Congress (DigitalHeritage), vol. 2, pp. 439–439, 28 October-1 November 2013
3. Calamai, S., Biliotti, F., Pesini, L., Bertinetto, P.M.: Building an open sound archive: the case of the Gra.fo project. In: Proceedings of the 6th International Congress on Science and Technology for the Safeguard of Cultural Heritage in the Mediterranean Basin, Rome, vol. 3, pp. 264–269 (2014)
4. Calamai, S., Biliotti, F.: Geolinguistic archives within the Gra.fo project: Carta dei Dialetti Italiani and Atlante Lessicale Toscano. In: Proceedings of the VII Congress of SIDG - International Society for Dialectology and Geolinguistics, Wien, 23–28 July 2012
5. Calamai, S., Ginouvs, V., Bertinetto, P.M.: Digital audio archives accessibility. In: Borowiecki, K.J., Forbes, N., Fresa, A. (eds.) Cultural Heritage in a Changing World, SpringerOpen (2016). Observation of strains. Infect Dis. Ther. **3**(1), 35–43, 37–54 (2011)
6. Buonomini, A.: Sul Cappel d'Orlando e su quanto si ricorda dei Reali di Francia in alcune localit dell'Appenino Tosco-Emiliano: repertori dei tradizione orale, in Anna Imelde Galletti & Roberto Roda (a cura di), Sulle orme di Orlando: leggende e luoghi carolingi in Italia: i paladini di Francia nelle tradizioni italiane. Una proposta storico-antropologica, Padova Assessorato alle istituzioni culturali, Centro Etnografico Ferrarese, Interbooks: 159–165 (1987)
7. Pozzebon, A., Calamai, S.: Smart devices for Intangible Cultural Heritage fruition. In: 2015 Digital Heritage, Granada, pp. 333–336 (2015)
8. Ioannidis, Y., Raheb, K., Toli, E., Boile, M., Katifori, A., Mazura, M.: Stories, One Object Many: Introducing ICT in museums and collections through digital storytelling. In: Digital Heritage International Congress (DigitalHeritage), vol. 1, pp. 421–424, 28 October-1 November 2013
9. Nordmark, S., Milrad, M.: Mobile digital storytelling for promoting creative collaborative learning. In: 2012 IEEE Seventh International Conference on Wireless, Mobile and Ubiquitous Technology in Education (WMUTE), pp. 9–16. IEEE, March 2012
10. Garau, C.: From territory to smartphone: smart fruition of cultural heritage for dynamic tourism development. Plann. Pract. Res. **29**(3), 238–255 (2014)
11. Dickinson, J.E., Ghali, K., Cherrett, T., Speed, C., Davies, N., Norgate, S.: Tourism and the smartphone app: capabilities, emerging practice and scope in the travel domain. Curr. Issues Tourism **17**(1), 84–101 (2014)
12. Floch, J., Jiang, S.: One place, many stories digital storytelling for cultural heritage discovery in the landscape. In: 2015 Digital Heritage, Granada, pp. 503–510 (2015)

Paintings Alive: A Virtual Reality-Based Approach for Enhancing the User Experience of Art Gallery Visitors

Stavros Panayiotou and Andreas Lanitis(✉)

Visual Media Computing Research Lab, Department of Multimedia and Graphic Arts,
Cyprus University of Technology, Lemesos, Cyprus
{sk.panagiotou,andreas.lanitis}@cut.ac.cy

Abstract. Visits to art museums are not appealing to a wide sector of the public, limiting in that way the exposure of art works to the wider community and especially the younger generation. In this paper we investigate the use of Virtual Reality (VR) for displaying animated artworks as a means for creating an enhanced user experience that could make visits to art-galleries more appealing. A key point of the proposed technique is the analysis of the art-works that enables the determination of a most appropriate setting and animation that best promotes the original message of the painter. The promise of this approach has been validated through an experimental user evaluation where users clearly indicated the benefits of using interactive virtual environments for presenting animated art paintings.

Keywords: Art paintings · Virtual reality · Interactive virtual environments

1 Introduction

Art-works constitute a significant share of the world's cultural heritage that needs to be exposed to the wider public. Unfortunately, the recent years the appeal of art-museums is decreased as members of the community, and especially the younger generation, show a strong preference to other activities than involve the use of technological gadgets. The aim of the work presented in this paper is to investigate whether the use of Virtual Reality (VR) for recreating and presenting artworks in interactive virtual environments could contribute to increasing the impact and appeal of artworks to the general public. As part of the proposed approach interactive animated 3D visualizations of art-works are created so that users have the ability to view, observe and interact with paintings providing in that way a contemporary way to acquire knowledge about art-paintings. A key point of the proposed technique is the prior analysis of art-works that enables the determination of a most appropriate setting, animation and soundtrack that best promotes the original message that the painter attempted to convey.

In our preliminary investigation, the attention is focused on two famous paintings by Pamplo Picasso: "The Three Musicians"[1] and "The Old Guitarist"[2]. An important

---

[1] https://en.wikipedia.org/wiki/Three_Musicians.
[2] https://en.wikipedia.org/wiki/The_Old_Guitarist.

© Springer International Publishing AG 2016
M. Ioannides et al. (Eds.): EuroMed 2016, Part II, LNCS 10059, pp. 240–247, 2016.
DOI: 10.1007/978-3-319-48974-2_27

aspect of our work involves a user evaluation where different aspects of the proposed methodology were evaluated. In particular, the aim of the evaluation was to determine whether: (a) The proposed application provides an enhanced user experience (b) The proposed application increases the learning outcomes obtained through observation of the exhibits and (c) If the proposed framework is suitable for extensive use in visualizing art museums.

2   Literature Review

The development and progress of virtual reality [1, 2] opened new avenues for artists to explore the potential of virtual spaces [3]. In essence art in Virtual Reality presents an illusion of the artist's reality, where it can generate "imaginary true", related to the inventiveness of art [4]. Furthermore, a strong point of displaying art using VR is the potential to reinforce the pedagogical value of artefacts [5, 6] and attract prolonged interest by visitors [7]. This argument is further reinforced by Dolinsky et al. [8] who argues that a photograph or video captures only a fraction of the experience when compared to VR-based experiences. The use of VR supports multiple iterations of the same scene at different locations simultaneously [9] increasing in that way the potential audience.

Among the most widely known attempts to present art-works in virtual environments is the Art Project by Google [10] that allows users to view on-line panoramas of different art galleries. A number of different approaches for presenting art-work in virtual environments were also recorded in an attempt to create interactive viewing experiences [3, 11]. Other approaches include the "The Living Canvas" [12], the "World Skin" [13] and the "Night Cafe" [14] or even projects that allow users to paint in virtual environments [15, 16]. Among the aforementioned applications the proposed approach shares more similarities with the award winning application "Night Cafe" [14] where animated works of Vincent van Gogh are presented in a virtual environment. However, an important aspect of our work involves the user evaluation that allows the registration of the views of experts and other participants, in an attempt to evaluate and improve the proposed framework.

3   Presentation of Art-Works in Virtual Environments

In this section the methodology adopted for representing the two selected paintings in a virtual environment is presented[3].

3.1   Three Musicians

"The Three Musicians" is an oil painting on canvas painted in 1921. The painting consists of the figures of a monk, a Harlequin with guitar, a Pierrot with a clarinet and

---

[3] Audiovisual material demonstrating the animated artworks is available at https://www.drop box.com/s/wfsmg6ihf7nol8n/animations.mp4?dl=0.

a dog. The Pierrot and Harlequin are characters in old Italian comic theater known as Commedia dell 'Arte, a familiar theme in Picasso's works. The composition table summarizes the style of Synthetic Cubism, the straight surfaces and the unshaded color, recalling the technique of collage. Through the analysis of the contents and meanings of the painting it was determined that the conversion of the painting to 3D should also adopt the use of straight surfaces and the unshaded color in order to achieve high consistency between the 2D and 3D representation.

The three-dimensional representation of the "The Three Musicians" was initiated with the design of the figures using simple surfaces and carried on by assigning volume and curved surfaces. All figures were animated so that the acts of playing musical organs is clearly conveyed to observers. The music-producing activity portrayed in the original painting was further enforced by the augmentation of a suitable soundtrack and the synchronization of the animation with the soundtrack. For the purpose of this animation an excerpt of the song Fibre De Verre[4] was selected. Figure 1 shows screenshots of the design process and the final representation of the painting in a 3D environment.

Fig. 1. The representation of "The Three Musicians" in a 3D environment

3.2 The Old Guitarist

"The Old Guitarist" is an oil painting on canvas that belongs to the Blue Period (1901–1904) of Picasso paintings, a painting period limited to a bleak and monochrome blue ballets and flat forms. An important aspect of Picasso's Blue Period is the emotional and psychological issues that represent the human misery and alienation encountered in social outcasts. In the "The Old Guitarist" Picasso portrays through an elderly and blind guitarist the timeless expression of human suffering. As a result of the analysis of the painting, it was determined that in this case it was important to incorporate a realism in the appearance of the guitarist in combination with the blue shadings, so that the message of the painting is better conveyed to the users.

The design process involved the creation of sketches of the front and side view of the guitarist (see Fig. 2) followed by the generation of the textured 3D figure using Autodesk Maya and Mudbox. The figure of the Guitarist was placed in a 3D environment displaying a local district including homes and streets with shades of dull blue (see Fig. 2).

---

[4] https://www.youtube.com/watch?v=I-gTQ1iY72w.

Fig. 2. Sketches of the guitarist, used as the basis for generating the 3D avatar and the resulting avatar placed in a 3D environment (Color figure online)

4 System Design

4.1 Virtual Environment Description

The integrated VR application was implemented using the Unity3D software where 3D models and soundtracks of the three-dimensional representations of the paintings "The Old Guitarist" and "The Three Musicians" were incorporated. The application environment contains the main area where a virtual visitor can view images of the original 2D paintings and assorted information panels (see Fig. 3). Behind each painting virtual spaces containing the animated art-works were placed.

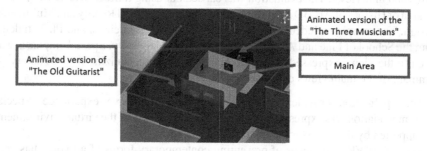

Fig. 3. An overview of the virtual environment containing the animated art-works

4.2 Scenario

According to the scenario of the application[5], after viewing a welcome screen, the user enters the main area where the two paintings are displayed. The user can 'walk through' a painting in order to be transferred to the 3D representation of each painting, and at the same time the corresponding soundtrack is activated. In the case of "The Three Musicians" the user is able to view the three animated musicians performing their act, from any viewing angle, and he/she can even take a place among the musicians. In the case of the "The Old Guitarist" the user can wander in the virtual district while watching the animated guitarist and listening to the soundtrack. An Occulus RIFT DK2 headset was

---

[5] A movie demonstrating the application is available at https://www.dropbox.com/s/hczkt 0l9t8oxyq5/demo.mp4?dl=0.

244 S. Panayiotou and A. Lanitis

used in an attempt to provide a highly immersive experience. The navigation in the virtual environment was based on both head trackers (incorporated in the Oculus Rift) in combination with a game controller.

5 Evaluation

The evaluation of the application was carried out in two phases. The first phase of the evaluation aimed to get the opinions of experts regarding the use of VR for presenting animated paintings whereas the second phase of the evaluation aimed both to assess the knowledge gain from using 3D representations of paintings when compared to the visualization of original paintings, and also to record user opinions regarding the use of this approach for presenting art-works.

5.1 Phase 1: Evaluation with Experts

Phase 1 of the evaluation involved only the 3D visualization of the 'Three Musicians'. During the evaluation users were able to navigate in a virtual environment containing the original painting and also they were able to enter the room with the 3D animated visualization of the painting. User opinions were registered using appropriate questionnaires and interviews. The evaluation was carried out using thirteen selected experts in the area of History of Art, 3D Modelling and Animation, Virtual Reality and Multimedia Design. The sample included Academic staff, Post-doc researchers, and PhD students from the School of Fine and Applied Arts of the local University. Special emphasis was given to the views expressed by senior Academic staff specializing in Art History. A summary of the main views expressed by the specialists were:

- The application provides a highly interesting immersive experience. Special commendation was expressed for the minimalistic design of the virtual environment, supported by the necessary animation and soundtrack.
- The use of VR as a means of presenting contemporary forms of artworks has very high potential.
- Almost all users considered the application as an interesting, pleasing and promising way of visualizing artworks. All users said that they will be very happy to use similar applications in the future.
- The visualization of both the original and the animated painting was highly commented, as it allows users to make a connection between the 'real' and 3D representation of a painting.
- The application itself offers an aesthetically pleasant application, but it could go further, intervening in paintings in order to give them a new symbolism and significance.

5.2 Phase 2: User Evaluation

During Phase 2 of the evaluation, users had the chance to use the integrated application that involves navigation in the main area and navigation in the two areas with the animated paintings (see Fig. 3). The evaluation was carried out with 32 volunteers, the majority of which were undergraduate and postgraduate students of the local School of Fine and Applied Arts. All volunteers were divided into two groups and each group followed a different procedure. The first group had the chance to first visualize the original 2D paintings in the main area and once this process was completed they were asked to answer six true/false questions related to the contents of the paintings (See Table 1). The participants then interacted with the 3D animated paintings and afterwards they were asked to answer the same set of questions. The second group followed the same procedure but in reverse order (i.e. they viewed first the animated paintings and then the original paintings) in order to remove any bias in the responses. According to the results of the observation experiment (see Fig. 4) in the case of the ''The Old Guitarist'' (questions 1, 2, 3) differences in the correct answers after viewing the paintings or the 3D representations are negligible, whereas in the case of the ''The Three Musicians'' (questions 3, 4, 5) superior observation performance is achieved after viewing the 3D representations. The results of a paired-sample t-test indicate that in the case of the ''The Three Musicians'' the improvement between the numbers of right answers after viewing the 3D representation of the paintings is significant at the 95 % level. The results indicate that when dealing with simple scenes (i.e. ''The Old Guitarist'') 3D representations do not provide a noticeable improvement in observation results. However, when dealing with complex scenes (i.e. ''The Three Musicians'') 3D representations enhance the observation power.

Table 1. The six observation questions that volunteers had to answer during the evaluation.

1	In the painting ''The Old Guitarist'' does the guitarist wear shoes?
2	In the painting ''The Old Guitarist'' does the guitarist wear hat?
3	In the painting ''The Old Guitarist'' is the guitarist blind?
4	In the painting ''The Three Musicians'' do the musicians' wear shoes?
5	In the painting ''The Three Musicians'' is there a bowl of fruit on the table?
6	In the painting ''The Three Musicians'' is there a dog?

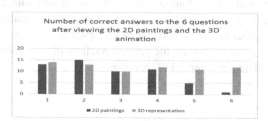

Fig. 4. The results of the observation experiment

After the completion of the observation test, volunteers completed a questionnaire in order to record their views concerning their overall experience and the future prospects of using this technology. The results indicate that users were satisfied with the immersion level, the experience and the overall application and as a result they are keen to use similar applications applied to different types of art-works. Participants were also asked to indicate the main feelings recorded while viewing each 3D animated painting. When viewing the animated painting "The Three Musicians", the most commonly encountered feelings of users were joy and pleasure, while enthusiasm and optimism, were also recorded. In the case of "The Old Guitarist" participants mainly felt sadness, loneliness and sadness, and also reported the feelings of fear, misery, isolation, injustice and coldness.

6 Conclusions-Future Work

The paper deals with the development and evaluation of a VR-application that allows users to view and interact with 3D representations of famous paintings. According to the results of a comprehensive evaluation, that included the registration of opinions of experts, the application provided an enhanced user and learning experience to the participants. Volunteers who took place in the experiments indicated that they are keen to experience similar deployments in the future for the presentation of art-works of different types. This type of applications could be incorporated in art galleries or museums in order to offer an enhanced experience in parallel to the observation of the 'real' exhibits.

Given the positive evaluations of our preliminary investigation, we plan to carry further work in this area guided by three main directions. The first direction involves the pedagogical impact of the animated artworks in relation to the symbolic nature of the paintings. Our ongoing work [6] on applying semiotic analysis to define an integrated framework for representing and reproducing artworks that convey symbolic meanings will be applied for defining a systematic framework for representing artworks in virtual enviroments.

The second future direction aims to overcome the dependency of the current implementation on an artist/3D modeler who is in charge to create the 3D representations using 3D modelling software. In order to facilitate the development of similar applications we plan to explore ways to develop appropriate toolboxes for automating the authoring process through the automatic generation of 3D animation-ready models from paintings [17] and by incorporating design rules related to different artefacts [18] in order to ensure the consistency of animated 3D representations with 2D paintings.

The third future direction involves the production of 3D animated stories of additional paintings and other artworks, and incorporate even more intensive levels of interaction. Extended evaluations among the general public will also going to be staged in order to further validate the potential of this approach.

References

1. Grau, O., Gustance, G.: Virtual Art: From Illusion to Immersion. MIT Press, Cambridge (2003)
2. Ryan, M.L.: Narrative as Virtual Reality 2: Revisiting Immersion and Interactivity in Literature and Electronic Media. JHU Press, Baltimore (2015)
3. Mitchell, B.: The immersive artistic experience and the exploitation of space. In: 1st International Conference on Ideas Before Their Time: Connecting the Past and Present in Computer Art, pp. 98–107. British Computer Society (2010)
4. Nechvatal, J.: Towards an immersive intelligence. Leonardo **34**(5), 417–422 (2001)

5. Economou, M., Pujol, L.: Educational tool or expensive toy? Evaluating VR evaluation and its relevance for virtual heritage. In: Kalay, Y., Kvan, T., Affleck, J. (eds.) New Heritage: New Media and Cultural Heritage. Routledge, Oxon (2006)

6. Voutounos, C., Lanitis, A.: A cultural semiotic, semiotic aesthetic approach for a virtual heritage project: part A: the semiotic foundations of the approach. J. Techné Res. Philos. Technol. **19**, 3 (2016)

7. Sung, D.: Abstract reality: why VR can learn from fine art (2015). http://www.wareable.com/vr/abstract-reality-what-art-can-teach-vr-976. Accessed March 2016

8. Dolinsky, M., Sherman, W., Wernert, E., Chi, Y.C.: Reordering virtual reality: recording and recreating real-time experiences. In: IS&T/SPIE Electronic Imaging, p. 82890H. International Society for Optics and Photonics (2012)

9. Fraser, M., Glover, T., Vaghi, I., Benford, S., Greenhalgh, C., Hindmarsh, J., Heath, C.: Revealing the realities of collaborative virtual reality. In: The Third International Conference on Collaborative Virtual Environments, pp. 29–37. ACM (2000)

10. Hart, K.: Art Project Powered by Google. The Charleston Advisor **13**(2), 16–20 (2011)

11. Wands, B.: Art of the Digital Age. Thames & Hudson, London (2007)

12. Dolinsky, M.: Blue Window Pane II. https://www.digitalartarchive.at/database/general/work/blue-window-pane-ii.html. Accessed 10 Jul 2016

13. Benayoun, M.: World skin, a photo safari in the land of war. http://www.benayoun.com/projet.php?id=16. Accessed 8 Jul 2016

14. The Night Cafe, An Immersive VR Tribute to Vincent van Gogh. https://vrjam.devpost.com/submissions/36821-the-night-cafe-an-immersive-tribute-to-vincent-van-gogh. Accessed 10 Jul 2016

15. Keefe, D.F., Feliz, D.A., Moscovich, T., Laidlaw, D.H., LaViola Jr., J.J.: CavePainting: a fully immersive 3D artistic medium and interactive experience. In: 2001 Symposium on Interactive 3D Graphics, pp. 85–93. ACM (2001)

16. Tilt Brush. https://www.youtube.com/watch?v=TckqNdrdbgk. Accessed 10 Jul 2016

17. Maronidis, A., Voutounos, C., Lanitis, A.: Designing and evaluating an expert system for restoring damaged byzantine icons. Multimed. Tools Appl. **74**(21), 9747–9770 (2015)

18. Michael, N., Drakou, M., Lanitis, A.: Model-based generation of personalized full-body 3D avatars from uncalibrated multiview photographs. Multimed. Tools Appl. (2016). doi: 10.1007/s11042-016-3808-1. Published as First online on 11 August 2016

Digital Documentation and Digital Prototyping of Sacred Artwork of Museum *Museu Mineiro* - Brazil

Altino Barbosa Caldeira and Silvio Romero Fonseca Motta[✉]

Pontifícia Universidade Católica – PUC/MG, Belo Horizonte, Brazil
altinocaldeira@gmail.com, silvio.motta@gmail.com

Abstract. The paper presents a research about digital documentation and digital prototype methods and techniques used for the artistic collection of the museum *Museu Mineiro*, Minas Gerais, Brazil. The *Museu Mineiro* collection is representative of the importance of Baroque art in Brazilian society and architecture. The choice of methods and techniques for digital documentation were based on methodological framework considering the following aspects *Scale, Purpose; Use*. The digital documentation baroque artwork was performed using hand 3D scanner and reproduction of the digital model was performed with 3D printing of polymeric material deposition. The research concludes that the digital documentation and manufacturing can contribute to the dissemination of the knowledge and information about the artistic and cultural heritage.

Keywords: Digital documentation of heritage · Prototyping of heritage · 3D scanner · 3D print

1 Introduction

The museum *Museu Mineiro* opened in 10 May 1982 and is subject to the Superintendence of Museums, one of the executive bodies of the cultural policy of the State of Minas Gerais. It is located in the central area of the city of Belo Horizonte, the capital of the state, and is installed in a eclectic architecture building It was first built to be-the official residence of the Secretary of State for Agriculture, then the Senate of the state and after the government pay-office. The building is listed by the IPHAN (National Institute of Historical and Artistic Heritage) and the museum has a collection of about 2,600 artworks, including paintings, sacred art, documents and objects of important historical and artistic expression that are kept on permanent display. This collection emphasizes the art of Minas Gerais state and is characterized by diversity. The museum objective is spread, disseminate and contribute to enhance the knowledge about the history, culture and citizenship.

The museum collection has symbolic and material aspects, representing the knowledge and imagination, according to Trinity [1].

The museum receives also third-party exhibitions in an annex building built especially for this, which must necessarily present a close link with the vocation of the institution, proposing themes that promote the dissemination and valorisation of cultural heritage.

© Springer International Publishing AG 2016
M. Ioannides et al. (Eds.): EuroMed 2016, Part II, LNCS 10059, pp. 248–255, 2016.
DOI: 10.1007/978-3-319-48974-2_28

In the early 2000s, the building was adapted, following the conservation, restoration and enhancement of the collection, consisting largely of a collection of sacred works that have been collected over many decades. In this sense, it values what- is more original and traditional in the artwork of Minas Gerais and is, currently, part of the Cultural Circuit of *Liberdade* Square, presenting activities and actions for the visiting public.

Among the museum's research, one of the more important is the Collection Inventory of *Museu Mineiro*. It is doing an acquisition database of the collection, promoting the museum's identity and allowing their specialized staff to operate with the new digital e information technologies.

It is the interest of *Museu Mineiro* provides new means of dissemination of sacred art collection, promoting educational practice, visitation and the dissemination of the knowledge about the art and culture of the State of Minas Gerais.

2 Objectives

This research aims to discuss and propose new means of communication and dissemination of sacred art collection of the Museum, by a digital collection and reproduction of these artworks in different scales and materials that could be executed in 3D modelling using precision tools that reproduce original detail. For that, it will be investigated digital information technologies and manufacturing. The fabrication of replicas is part of the museum's objective of provide information accessibility of the artwork's characteristics to many kind of people, like blind people, children, etc.

3 Method

The research is based on the characteristics and peculiarities of the Minas Gerais Baroque sacred artworks and its importance as decorative elements that add value to the historical architecture and cultural heritage, and artistic objects related to the architecture. The literature review that was conducted collaborates with the process of investigation, studying the variety of possible scanning techniques and digital manufacturing artefacts. From the analysis of the museum collection, it was chosen an appropriate scanning technique. Finally, it was performed a scan experiment and manufactured a replica of a baroque sacred piece.

4 Literature Review

4.1 Sacred Works of *Minas Gerais* and the Cultural Architectonic Heritage

From the 1920s, the Minas Gerais Baroque art and the craftsmen who produced it became considered very important for Brazilian art culture. The main responsible for this recognition was Brazilian Modernist Movement, whose members, travelling to Minas Gerais in 1924, made a journey through historic towns and focused in discovering a real Brazilian culture, identifying the uniqueness of the architecture of this cities, with a richness expression of baroque art, until that not valorised, and seeing in it reasons for exaltation of a genuine - Brazilian culture.

According to Julião [2]

"The appreciation of the colonial past and the reinterpretation of Baroque aesthetics have emerged an awareness of the need to preserve the historical and artistic heritage, arousing debates among different groups of the Brazilian intellectuals around the issues of memory, identity, heritage and nation"

Based on these ideas, protective measures were taken to the civil and religious architectural heritage with the creation of IPHAN that made cultural heritage preservation policies, opening museums for the collections and protect the creative memory of the Brazilian people. In this context, the *Museo Mineiro* came to be an official institution that protects the artwork for being threatened, vandalized or illegitimately usurped. Both national institutions such as the state are responsible to protect the cultural heritage of the Brazilian nation.

The sacred art collection of *Museo Mineiro* is the result of effort and care of many, whose legacy of baroque and modern art now occupies its rooms, revering the past and paving the way for the important recognition of the generations to come know this important heritage in the future.

4.2 Heritage Documentation and Digital Technologies

In the first century BC, *Marcus Vitruvius Pollio* wrote the first Architecture treatise, which describes the constructive and aesthetic characteristics used in buildings of the time. These records, in a sense, can be understood as the founders of systematic documentation of architectural heritage. The work of Vitruvius has not survived fully to the present, but, through his known records, we can understand some of the stylistic expressions of the buildings of the time. The records of the architectural styles of the classical orders, its proportions, its ornaments, its details, which are presented in *De Architectura* book, are fundamental information that complement and promote our knowledge of existing historic buildings.

For more than two centuries, the registration and the historical architectural heritage documentation is an important tool to obtain information for the preservation and promotion of our knowledge and culture.

The way that the records, documentation and data acquisition of the architectural heritage has been held since then, improves relatively slowly. Since the first documentation and somehow, until our day, the data and information acquisition of the architectural heritage are documented primarily through surveys using tools and traditional draw techniques.

Only in the nineteenth century, a tool brings news possibilities for data acquisition: the photography. The photograph was since its invention, used as a tool for documentation and data acquisition of architectural heritage [3]. The German architect Meydenbauer, developed special techniques of photography for building's data acquisition and documentation, establishing the photogrammetry discipline and creating the first photogrammetry Institute in 1885.

Since the nineteenth century, the documentation techniques using photogrammetry has been improving constantly, both in the equipment and in the procedures adopted [4, 5]. Digital photography was introduced in photogrammetry in the late twentieth century, replacing the optical-mechanical technology by digital technology. This substitution did not mean a change in the logic of traditional photogrammetry procedures, and did not incorporate new possibilities for recording, documentation and data acquisition of architectural heritage.

At the beginning of XXI century, new digital and information technologies become incorporated into the documentation of heritage. An important one is the digital technologies of 3D modelling. For the heritage documentation, the 3D digital technology that showed most interesting use was the laser scanning. Since its beginning, various researches and studies try to develop procedures that use the potential of laser scanning applied to the architectural heritage documentation [6–9].

Academic researches discuss the peculiarities of the use of laser scanning considering technical and methodological aspects. The laser scanning results a representation of the object by a cloud points. It is discussed issues such as accuracy, resolution and storage of the digital model. It is also discussed the new procedures and the interaction of the digital model with other information technologies like GIS, BIM, among others.

The main difficult techniques observed in academic researches are related to the adequacy of equipment for the characteristics of the cultural heritage. For example, the characteristics of different heritages require different scanning resolutions. Research also shows some technical advantages. The most important is the possibility of accurate records of the heritage without physical contact with it. This allows better security in preserving the heritage.

Another benefit showed in academic researches is the dissemination of cultural heritage in a variety of media. The digital model associated with GIS, BIM, Web, and other technologies, allows that heritage information could be access for a broad audience. It's extended the possibility of knowledge and dissemination of heritage, history and culture, strengthening the identity and memories of each nation.

5 Results

To define the scanning techniques and digital fabrication used in the experiment, it was made an analysis methodological framework.

The methodological structure has as basic fundamentals the following aspects: *Scale, Purpose; Use* (Fig. 1).

The aspect Scale evaluates the dimensional characteristics of the object considering the techniques possibilities. Böhler [10] studied the suitability of various techniques of topological surveys at different object ranges (Fig. 2).

The *Museo Mine*iro artwork collection has dimensions between 0.1 and 2 m, with a medium to high complexity. Considering the Scale aspect, the 3D scanning would be the most suitable techniques.

Fig. 1. Methodological structure to choose digital techniques. Source: authors

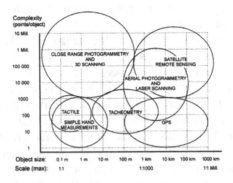

Fig. 2. Selection of appropriate surveying methods depending objet size and complexity [10]

The Purpose aspect tries to understand the objective of the heritage documentation. Patias [3] analysed some types of documentation and its suitability for its purpose (Fig. 3).

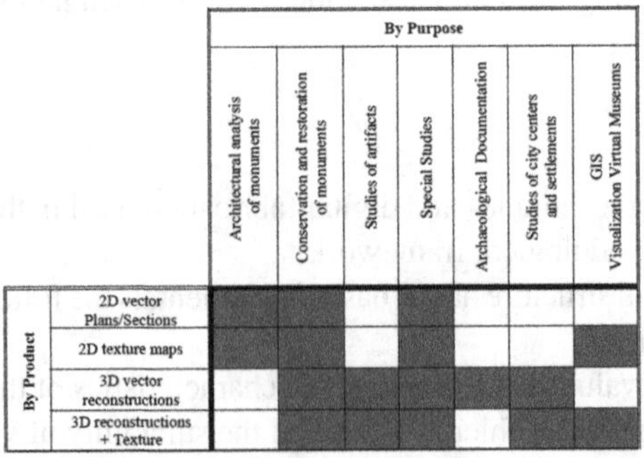

		By Purpose						
		Architectural analysis of monuments	Conservation and restoration of monuments	Studies of artifacts	Special Studies	Archaeological Documentation	Studies of city centers and settlements	GIS Visualization Virtual Museums
By Product	2D vector Plans/Sections	■		■	■			■
	2D texture maps			■			■	
	3D vector reconstructions	■	■			■	■	■
	3D reconstructions + Texture		■	■		■		■

Fig. 3. Classification of applications for heritage documentation [3]

The digital documentation of the *Museu Mineiro* collection has as main objectives to study the artwork and to present its collection virtually. Considering the aspect of Purpose, 3D modelling with texture would be the most suitable for the experiment.

The last aspect considered in the choice of digital documentation techniques was the Use aspect. To evaluate the use of digital documentation, we can consider the way that it, as data and information, will be managed. Letellier [11] proposes that the criteria involved in the use of heritage data management should consider the criteria of reliability, safety and accessibility (Fig. 4).

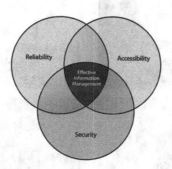

Fig. 4. Information management criteria [11]

One of the *Museu Mineiro's* objectives is to allow its digital documentation to be accessible to a various publics, such as blind people, children, etc. The production of replicas by digital manufacturing, with reliability and accuracy of the details of the documented heritage, allows the safe use by this various audiences.

Considering the methodological framework for choice of documentation techniques (Fig. 1), it was decided that the initial experiment would perform the 3D survey of the object using a 3D hand scanner. The digital model would be manufactured using a 3D print of deposition of polymeric material PLA.

Experiment. The objects chosen for the digital documentation experiment was a picture of St. Joseph (Fig. 5a) and a head of a procession statue (Fig. 5b).

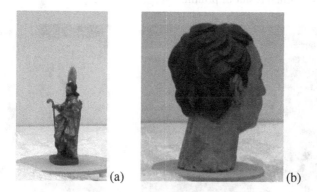

(a)   (b)

Fig. 5. (a) Picture of St. Joseph; (b) Head of a procession statue. Source: Sheila Mara Silva/*Museu Mineiro*

The Fig. 6 shows the scanning process of sacred artworks.

Fig. 6. Scanning processes. Source: Sheila Mara Silva/Museu Mineiro

Initially, to perform the scan, it was used a revolving basis to hold the artwork and a tripod to fixed the 3D scanner. However it was not possible to accurately get results for both artworks. Then, the scanner was manually operated, and this allowed to perform a digital model of head of a procession statue with appropriate resolution and accuracy results.

The scanned head of a procession statue was printed in 3D print (Fig. 7a). The Fig. 7b shows the final result of printing.

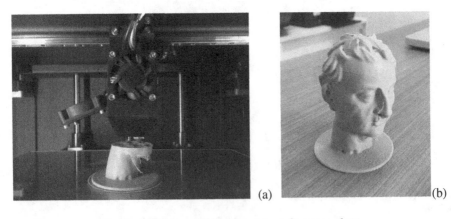

(a)   (b)

Fig. 7.   (a) Printing; (b) Final prototype. Source: authors

6 Conclusion

The digital documentation of sacred artworks of *Museo Mineiro* - Brazil, using techniques like 3D scanning and prototype, could bring opportunity for knowledge, dissemination and information about the history of Minas Gerais and Brazil to a large audience, including another part of the world. It can offer for those who do not have access for the collection, the opportunity to know the characteristics and details of the parts of Minas Gerais cultural heritage.

Acknowledgement. The researchers thank the Minas Gerais State Foundation for Research Development (FAPEMIG), and the *Museo Mineiro* for supporting the research.

References

1. Trindade, S.C.: Colecionismo Mineiro. Secretaria de Estado da Cultura, Belo Horizonte (2002)
2. Julião, L.: Colecionismo Mineiro. Secretaria de Estado da Cultura, Belo Horizonte (2002)
3. Patias, P.: Cultural heritage documentation. In: Application of 3D Measurement From Images, pp. 225–257 (27)
4. Atkinson, K.B.: Close Range Photogrammetry and Machine Vision. Whittles Publishing, Caithness (2001)
5. Carbonnell, M.: L'histoire et la situation presente des applications de la photogrammetrie a l'architecture. ICOMOS, France (1968)
6. Andrews, D., Bedford, J., Bryan, P.: Metric Survey Specifications for Cultural Heritage. Historic England, Swindon (2015)
7. Lucca, L.: Methods formalisms and tools for the semantic based surveying and representation of architectural heritage. Appl. Geomat. **6**(2), 115–139 (2014)
8. Bonora, V., Chieli, A., Spanò, A., Testa, P., Tucci, G.: 3D metric-modelling for knowledge and documentation of architectural structures (royal palace in turin). In: The International Archives of the Photogrammetry, Remote Sensing and Spatial Information Sciences, pp. 60–65 (2011)
9. HERIT, CIPA. CIPA Heritage Documentation (2011)
10. Böhler, W.: Comparison of 3D laser scanning and other 3D measurement techniques. In: Recording, Modeling and Visualization of Cultural Heritage, pp. 89–100 (2006)
11. Letellier, R.: Recording, Documentation, and Information Management for the Conservation of Heritage Places. The Getty Conservation Institute, Los Angeles (2007). Edited by Angela Escobar

Parian Marble: A Virtual Multimodal Museum Project

Marinos Ioannides[1], Pavlos Chatzigrigoriou[1], Vasiliki Nikolakopoulou[1],
Georgios Leventis[1(✉)], Eirini Papageorgiou[1], Vasilis Athanasiou[1],
and Christian Sovis[2]

[1] Cyprus University of Technology, 3036 Limassol, Cyprus
{marinos.ioannides,p.chatzigrigoriou,v.nikolakopoulou,
georgios.leventis,e.papageorgiou,vasilis.athanasiou}@cut.ac.cy
[2] 7Reasons, Hauptplatz 11, 3462 Absdorf, Austria
cs@7reasons.net

Abstract. This case study is about the cultural promotion and exploitation of the ancient quarries of Paros island in Greece, in a multilayered project which uses modern technologies attempting to "return" all the marble works that have been created from 7th to 5th century BC to their place of origin. Taking total advantage of the emerging technological affordances of 3-dimensional documentation of Cultural Heritage assets and Virtual and Augmented Reality, this case study's project is aiming at a curatorial concept of breaking the restrictions of geography and time and raising awareness by engaging stakeholders, policy makers and citizens of Europe in digitalization of heritage through virtual environments. Virtual Cultural Heritage along with Virtual Museums, being the current research advancement in the respective domain, propose the framework where broaden dialogues and intensified discussions among the people involved in the documentation of the past will take place, as well as fully contextualized educational practices and design studies for the development of new immersive experiences and innovative applications.

Keywords: Virtual Museum · Digital Heritage · Virtual reality · 3D objects

1 Introduction

Nowadays, many people during their daily routine come across remains of a world from another era, an ancient world, exquisite works carved from marble that may constitute parts of an ancient temple, a statue or a cultural monument. A number of these artifacts were made from a specific kind of marble called *Parian Stone*, as it was originated from the island of Paros in Cyclades complex, and constituted a priceless treasure for Paros offering wealth and fame on the island. In ancient times, the quarries of Paros produced distinct cultivars of marble that were standing out for their transparency degree, their size as well as their homogeneous shade [1]. This variety of marble was called 'lychnitis', because the local craftsmen used to extract the marble with the help of lamp lights. Due to its unique characteristics, lychnitis was used as the main ingredient for the craft of antiquity's greatest sculptures and monuments like the famous daughters of

© Springer International Publishing AG 2016
M. Ioannides et al. (Eds.): EuroMed 2016, Part II, LNCS 10059, pp. 256–264, 2016.
DOI: 10.1007/978-3-319-48974-2_29

Erechtheion - the Caryatids, Venus de Milo, Nike of Samothrace and the most ancient figurines ever found in Europe, the Cycladic idols (Fig. 1).

The commercialization of lychnitis, after a long pause in Byzantine times, experienced new growth in the Frankish period by the duke of Paros, Krousino Somarripa, who was responsible for the spread of Parian Stone resulting to its mass mining from the quarries. Since it was considered to be the most sought after of all raw materials for the construction of tangible cultural heritage masterpieces, it then constituted the medium of dissemination of Greek culture in the west civilization leading to its further export to European countries. Over the years, famous marble-made artifacts were exhibited away from their place of origin and set in museums like the Louvre, the Acropolis Museum, the MET and others.

Fig. 1. Famous sculptures made by Parian marble: (from left to right) Caryatid (By I, Sailko, CC BY-SA 3.0, https://commons.wikimedia.org/w/index.php?curid=17552891), Venus de Milo (Public Domain, https://commons.wikimedia.org/w/index.php?curid=1999049), Nike of Samothrace (By Shawn Lipowski (Shawnlipowski) - Own work, CC BY-SA 3.0, https://commons.wikimedia.org/w/index.php?curid=1034985), Cycladic idol (By Prof saxx - Own work, CC BY-SA 3.0, https://commons.wikimedia.org/w/index.php?curid=5093513)

Because of its huge network of quarries, Paros has unique global mineral deposit of great cultural significance. Today, this interrelated network of quarries constitutes an industrial archaeology monument with corridors, arcades and inscriptions of the ancient marble artists, while crude white marble pieces are scattered in nearby areas (Fig. 2). The cultural promotion and exploitation of the ancient quarries is a multilayered project, which uses modern technologies attempting to "return" all the marble works that have been created over the years to their place of origin. Although, this venture gives an optical illusion of returned marbles in a digitally constructed way, it shall act as a reference point towards the local growth of cultural, touristic and economic sectors, as visitors from all over the world will admire the greatness of the particular Parian Stone, acquiring this way a holistic immersive visual experience.

Fig. 2. Entrance to a marble quarry on the island of Paros in the Cyclades

2   Methodology

We are elapsing the era of Digital Culture accompanied by the technological break-through of smart devices, virtual environments and the supremacy of social media plat-forms. The technological advancement, that has been also brought in the field of the documentation of Cultural Heritage (CH), has resulted to its systematic and ever growing digitalization. On the one hand, the 3-dimensional (3D) models of CH assets produced using various techniques [2] (photo-generated 3D models, terrestrial laser scanning techniques etc.) and the presence of virtual 3D spaces on the other, have set the basis for the potential to shed light on Europe's rich and diverse mosaic of cultural and creative expressions, by bringing virtually together homogeneous works of art among the member nations of the continent.

Culture is the cornerstone that bonds together European countries. It has been formed by a great number of cultural perspectives illustrated in art, architecture, music, literature, and philosophy. Although the existence of diversified prospects and the multitudinous cultural roots, European culture constitutes what is frequently referred as "common cultural heritage", an essence that is shared among the citizens of Europe. It is our inheritance from previous generations and our testimony and legacy for the generations to come. It encompasses all the movable and immovable, tangible and intangible heritage, from natural and artificial monuments to literary and folkloric works. It tells of our origin, the story of Europe, the knowledge, the practices and the traditions of all European folks.

Museums in Europe are part of the dissemination process for several of the aforementioned elements of culture. They are institutions, private or public, that conserve, preserve and protect a collection of artifacts and other objects of artistic, cultural, historical, or scientific importance, and make them available, permanently or contemporary, for public viewing through exhibits [3]. Various works of art made from Parian Stone, such as sculptures and monumental marbles, from many regions of the world, are placed in museums across Europe. The challenge is to bring together such works of art in the place where their material was first created. It is a way for sustainable creation of links between cultural entities of Europe and the holistic view in the study and approach to a historic monument, the story behind its creation and the preservation of its memory which is far more significant (as of being a legacy) than its materialistic conservation.

The question raised concerns the possibility to physically bring together monumental works of art back to the place of origin. Policies and country regularities impede such endeavors making even harder, time and money consuming, to resort in these solutions. However, considering the technological state of the art and the emerging technologies of Virtual and Augmented Reality (VR/AR), the possibility of bringing them virtually together could be successfully feasible [4, 5]. Due to the extent growth of CH digitalization and production of numerous 3D models hosted in well-presented virtual environments, the notion of Virtual Cultural Heritage (VCH) and its relationship with the concept of Virtual Museum (VM) has become the current research advancement in the CH domain.

VCH is promoting the development of highly personalized, mixed reality and augmented e-services that add value to CH assets and make them re-usable in a wide spectrum of real-life applications such as advertising, leisure, film, game and creative industries, education and so forth. VR and AR market is expected to reach 150 billion USD in revenue by 2020[1] disrupting the mobile as well as TV markets[2], hence it is undoubted that this will not have an impact in reformulating VCH. With VR/AR being a redefined 'medium' and not just a product, the future of VCH experiences will be

---

[1] http://fortune.com/2015/04/25/augmented-reality-virtual-reality/.

[2] http://www.businessinsider.com/goldman-sachs-predicts-vr-will-be-bigger-than-tv-in-10-years-2016-1.

260 M. Ioannides et al.

shaped by instilling presence, the engaging *"feeling of being and doing there"* in the virtual world, and will be changing the present perspective of space and time travel.

On the other hand, VM, being part of VCH mediating tools, is now most usually defined as a digital entity that draws on the characteristics of a museum, in order to complement, enhance, or augment the museum experience through personalization, interactivity and richness of content on the World Wide Web (global approach). VM can perform as the digital footprint of a physical museum, or act independently, while maintaining the authoritative status as bestowed by ICOM in its definition of a museum, which is specifying its function, its role and the importance of communicating and exhibiting the tangible and intangible heritage of humanity and the related environment for the purposes of education, study and enjoyment[3].

Sustainability of VM is strongly linked with practical choices made by stakeholders concerning organizational structures for VM, technologies, cost and business plans, to justify the economic investment of public and private bodies in relevant projects. Their added value is also linked with the scientific accuracy and reliability of the methods of heritage preservation, digitization and presentation. Hence, it is of high priority to improve the design capacity of the actors involved in the VM project as well as to advocate and boost the support of local societies, citizens, policy makers, countries and the European Union, in a broader view.

As a result, the current project, has decided to follow the emerging approach of 'collective participation'. Crowdsourcing is undeniably the most efficient new business organization and development process in the Information Society as nowadays there is a tremendous number of users connected to others by sharing information and willing to help them in various ways. The project is aiming at the exploitation of the particular web affordance in order to engage both the stakeholders, in the domain of curation and museology, and the citizens around Europe that are getting in touch with the sculptures of Parian marble across all European museums. The concept is to unify the policy makers, of the related private and public sectors, with the public in an attempt to involve them in planning and evaluating Digital Heritage actions and policies which reconcile diverging aspects and interests, while at the same time sustained communication and interaction could be promoted.

In this way, raising awareness becomes an inseparable part of the project and can still gain ground as the people involved interact directly with the sculptures. Thus, it is proposed for the people to take part in the procedure of the unification of the dispersed sculptures, by taking images of them with their personal devices and then uploading them in order to create linked information. Policy makers of the hosting museums will be informed for the actions partaken and will have the opportunity to intervene and suggest methods and dissemination plans for the 3D reconstruction of the sculptures by the crowdsourced images. Technically, 3D reconstruction can be achieved through open source photogrammetry software, where the images are combined in order to generate the 3D model.

In this context, a VM is not transposed to the web, nor an archive or a database of virtual digital assets but a provider of knowledge and stories on top of being an exhibition

---

[3] http://icom.museum/the-vision/museum-definition/.

room, located online, in museums or on heritage sites. A VM is not competing with real-world exhibitions of museums, galleries or sites but tries to enhance the experience of the visitor by allowing them to explore the exhibits and interact with them as being a part of a bigger idea. In this phase of the project, the active users become actual creators of the virtual, 3D composed models and become acquainted with the history of the sculptures and their "birth" place; an Aegean island in Greece with tremendous historical and artistic significance for supplementing all the outstanding works of art of that time era.

Apart from the fully educational and sharing awareness context of the first phase of the project, the next phase concerns of the virtual representation of the united sculptures "returning to the place of their origin". VM can provide opportunities and services for people to access digital content before, during and after a visit in a range of digital 'encounters'. They are technologically demanding especially in terms of VR/AR, story-telling, creation of narratives and 3D experiences, located (or not) online. These forms of representation are a key to success in disseminating the content of VM. Computer vision can accomplish high attractiveness through sophisticated software and hardware solutions but must be balanced and adapted to the environment, behavior and experience of the user in order to be widely accepted.

Moreover, the potential VM to be developed should be able to combine available online databases of structured knowledge, such as digital encyclopedias, images and indexes as well as real time local or distant interaction technologies among visitors and exhibits and among visitors/curators themselves through the web. Furthermore, it should be in position to hold remote or local artistic events integrated with heritage and memory for the respective context; that of the history of the island, the Parian marble and its momentous offer to pieces of art from 7th until 5th century BC (from archaic till roman period). Last but not least, the proposed framework takes under consideration the handling of issues relevant with the evaluation of scientific integrity, copyrights of the digital assets, financial impact and feedback.

In conclusion, this project is addressed to the democratization of heritage, the sharing of awareness and common memories among the citizens of Europe. It is an attempt to create sustainable links throughout the old continent and promote the history of Greek civilization, the threat under which the marble quarry in Paros is at the present time, and the significance of virtually "revive" it by linking pieces of its history back together. Taking absolute advantage of the emerging technological affordances, we are aiming at a curatorial concept of breaking the restrictions of geography and time, broadening the educational context of museums and linking the aesthetics of that particular period of art, by enabling user's curiosity and contributing to a deeper understanding of CH in its widest standpoint.

3 Proposals

Since this project is focused on using and reusing crowdsourced images from tourists, experts, academics, or any user interested in the area of CH, the final outcome, besides the development of a VM, could be more specific and immediate.

3D printing is a revolutionary technology which is now more accessible to laboratories and individuals, as it has been evolving rapidly and thus resulting in cost reduction. Considering that completing this project a huge number of schools, universities, and laboratories around Europe will have access to numerous 3D objects, the ability to download 3D models in a 3D printing format will allow users to exhibit 3D representation of an object and disseminate knowledge and information with it. Furthermore, an actual physical Museum in Paros island, where the quarry is being placed, could offer 3D printing services and facilities and provide tourists and visitors with 3D printed models.

Along with the 3D printing proposal, VR could be another proposed medium, mediating the virtual representation of the sculptures and the history of the quarry. Nowadays, we have the opportunity to explore several software solutions that are capable of developing VR environments. These environments could provide users with immersive experiences and simultaneously disseminate knowledge and information. Unity is one of the most effective software for developing VR environments as it is cross-platform and can be used on mobile/tablet devices. The exploitation of Unity along with the content available from the VM, could create a concept of a cruise in the quarries of Paros and let the users witness the procedure of excavation of carved heritage and the minerals followed in ancient times. This interactive experience would be available as an application for mobile devices or could be downloaded through the project's webpage. In addition, the application could provide a conducted tour in ancient Paros, with a distinguished analysis of the process of excavation to the final product delivery. What is most positive is that the hardware will be of a low cost, since the users will use their own mobile devices and the optional VR headset, such as Google Cardboard.

4   The Virtual Multimodal Museum Project of Parian Marble

The key objectives of Virtual Multimodal Museum (ViMM) are, by building on the achievements, to date, to analyze and promote the role of VM as a strategic resource for Europe with cultural, social, environmental and economic value, building a widely-accepted 5-year roadmap for future activities and explore how the new encounters created can be evaluated to understand and define the models involved. ViMM will also broaden and intensify discussion among CH stakeholders and work towards necessary levels of consensus on key technical, legal and policy areas important for the goals and principles of VM, bringing together public and private stakeholders in partnership, taking full account of the main objectives, goals and interests of all EU stakeholders and International organizations actively involved in VCH and VM. It is certain that ViMM will gain high visibility through social media, TV, newspapers, publishers, professional associations, conferences and other forms of outreach among the stakeholder communities within Europe and internationally so that users of all types will benefit from the new possibilities to shape, access and study European Culture. Another objective of ViMM is to establish more accurately the exact nature of the key economic drivers for VCH and especially for VM and their added value for society, their economic impact and multipliers, taking into account the results of previous European investments and in the context of the current financial position in Europe, including the potential for both public and private investments.

ViMM will identify and improve awareness of the potential impacts of VM and develop understanding of the economic and social benefits and ways in which these can in reality be derived, including the ways different stakeholders influence sustainability and take up. The project will have the support and the inclusion of VCH and especially of VM in the move towards an integrated policy approach to Cultural Heritage for Europe, in readiness for the European Year of Cultural Heritage in 2018 and according to the latest EC, EU Parliament and EU Council Conclusions and Recommendations. Articulate communication and consultation with European and international organizations such as UNESCO, ICOM, ICOMOS, CIPA, ICCROM, Getty, Europeana Foundation, Wikipedia, in order to gain common understandings and establish positions of mutual support. Create a channel of communication with the EU Member States Expert Group (MSEG) on digitization and preservation and the EU DARIAH ERIC in order to stimulate consultations concerning future policy dialogues and mutual learning exercises and studies, including design studies for new infrastructures in the area of VCH and VM applications. ViMM will define and demonstrate the various functions and approaches of VM based on latest innovations and advances in the state-of-the-art in VR/AR, why different audiences need them to understand and interact with European CH, why and how VM are necessary to support the accessibility, conservation, use and re-use of CH. It will also define the way the CH data infrastructure exemplified by Europeana and the use of open data can reinforce the creation and sustainability of VM.

In this aspect, the VM of Parian Marble will be a case study that will offer to ViMM the opportunity to apply and evaluate the guide lines, the procedures and the communication channels of the project. The opportunity to build a VM based on ancient artifacts of exceptional value that are scattered today in different museums around the globe, is unique; it could be an example of excellency in the concept of ViMM. The material (Parian Marble) and the Virtual Multimodal Museum of the ancient artifacts made of it will lead to an original result that will involve major museums (Acropolis, Olympia, Archeological of Athens, Louvre, Boston, MET, and others) in a procedure that will raise awareness and promote the users to creators and curators.

Acknowledgements. 1. ITN-DCH (http://www.itn-dch.eu/) project has received funding from the European Union's Seventh Framework program for research, technological development and demonstration under GA no 608013.

2. INCEPTION (http://www.inception-project.eu/) has received funding from the EU's H2020 Reflective framework programme for research and innovation under GA no 665220.

3. Europeana Space (http://www.europeana-space.eu/) has received funding from the European Union's ICT Policy Support Program as part of the Competitiveness and Innovation Framework Program, under GA no 621037.

4. 4DCH (http://www.4d-ch-world.eu/) project has received funding from the European Union's Seventh Framework program for research, technological development and demonstration under GA no 324523.

5. Lo-Cloud (http://www.locloud.eu/) is co-funded under the CIP ICT-PSP program under GA no 325099.

6. ViMM (http://www.vi-mm.eu/) has received funding from the EU's H2020 framework programme for support and coordination actions under GA no 727107.

References

1. Schilardi, D.U., Katsonopoulou, D., Katsarou, S., Brenner, C.: Paria Lithos Parian Quarries, Marble and Workshops of Sculpture (2010)
2. Guarnieri, A., Pirotti, F., Vettore, A.: Cultural heritage interactive 3D models on the web: an approach using open source and free software. J. Cult. Herit. **11**, 350–353 (2010)
3. Fischer, S.: Museums in motion: an introduction to the history and functions of museums. Mus. Hist. J. (2013) (by E.P. Alexander and M. Alexander)
4. Carrozzino, M., Bergamasco, M.: Beyond virtual museums: experiencing immersive virtual reality in real museums. J. Cult. Herit. **11**, 452–458 (2010)
5. Lepouras, G., Vassilakis, C.: Virtual museums for all: employing game technology for edutainment. Virtual Real. **8**, 96–106 (2004)

Immersive Digital Heritage Experience with the Use of Interactive Technology

Marinos Ioannides[1], Vasilis Athanasiou[1]([✉]), Pavlos Chatzigrigoriou[1],
Eirini Papageorgiou[1], Georgios Leventis[1], Vasiliki Nikolakopoulou[1],
and Christian Sovis[2]

[1] Cyprus University of Technology, 3036 Limassol, Cyprus
{marinos.ioannides,vasilis.athanasiou,p.chatzigrigoriou,
e.papageorgiou,georgios.leventis,v.nikolakopoulou}@cut.ac.cy
[2] 7Reasons, Hauptplatz 11, 3462 Absdorf, Austria

Abstract. This paper presents alternative methodologies for disseminating information that derives from a holistic documentation of a monument with the use of interactive technologies. These technologies are incorporated within an interactive book, while the book's context is about the unique monument Panagia of Asinou church in Nicosia (Cyprus). The prototype of the interactive book has been developed at a previous stage as an experimental educational tool. In this phase the prototype will be further developed in order to incorporate all the multimedia data collected about the monument and demonstrate them in a user-friendly way. Moreover, it will be adequately evaluated by specific target groups of users and experts. The goal is to be installed at the church of Asinou and provide the visitors of the church with an amazing immersive experience.

Keywords: Interactive technology · Interactive books · Motion sensor · Kinect · Projection · Immersive experience · Education

1 Introduction

It is said that *"Between the pages of a book is a lovely place to be"*. One could imagine the potentials that derive from adding on a piece of paper digital content or even better combining both (written text and digital content). There is the opportunity to visualize the written content, making stories, enrich the written text, or compose an interactive narrative that concludes information from a holistic documentation of a monument. A monument includes data from its memory of the past, which produce diverse forms of multimedia such as: 3D model, images, video, audio and text. Transparent complex data can be filtered and presented, assembled into a form visible to human eye, through an installation that can be adapted and be functional for almost any group of users, acting as a rather personalized educational environment.

The installation includes multiple interactive pages which host multimedia content. Simultaneously, as a reference to the physical book, the interactive book has printed text in the same volume of pages as the conventional ones. This combination of the virtues of an analog book and of new digital technologies is more preferable as it keeps the traditional feeling of the book as a means of communication but also transforms it into a real time digital environment with a massive library of content.

© Springer International Publishing AG 2016
M. Ioannides et al. (Eds.): EuroMed 2016, Part II, LNCS 10059, pp. 265–271, 2016.
DOI: 10.1007/978-3-319-48974-2_30

2   Methodologies

A holistic representation of digital content is one of the main objectives of this project. The ability to bring together diverse representation media to create a holistic cultural depiction is a difficult task. Holistic documentation means huge amount of data in a multimedia form. For example, audio recordings are most suitable for capturing music or spoken language; rituals and dances are best captured in videos; physical artifacts are best captured by 3D modeling, 3D scanning, or photography. However, the complete significance of the artifacts in a digital depiction of heritage is brought out only if the artifacts are presented in the context of each other [1]. These will require data filtering, categorizing and abstracting in order to acquire the most valuable information that needs to be disseminate to the user as also a comprehensive way to present it in a user-friendly format.

2.1   Concept and Content Development

A book is a perfect gateway to impel fantasy to build one's own stories, environment and characters. Along that, since ancient times people commonly referred to books in order to collect knowledge, information or entertainment. In this case we research the Panagia of Asinou church which is included in UNESCO's world heritage list; the religion atmosphere and the history of books and libraries of Orthodox Church is a motivation to use this form of communication along with technology to provide an immersive interactive experience. With this installation there is both, analog and digital content creating a new engagement with the monument, which is not experienced by visiting the actual church. Since we are referring to a holistic representation of the monument the content should be analogous and the success of these initiatives is largely dependent on the richness of the digital representation utilized. The creation of an immersive installation requires extensive content creation, such as 3D modelling, video/image editing, visual design, and software development [1]. The content will be divided in analog and digital were analog will include the history and facts that are invariable and digital form content will get updated when is needed. According to [2] three different kinds of user groups should be targeted in order to cover the spectrum of typical cultural visitors: Foreign visitors, digital heritage enthusiasts and school children who visit the heritage.

2.2   Technical

For the development of the specific installation the technical side of the project is a key factor for a successfully implementation. The installation needs a good working equipment, the knowledge to set it up onside and advance programming skills.

The necessity of custom structure will be required as the projector will have to be on top of the book, a tripod for the tracking device which will be placed opposite of the book, speakers for the audio files, the actual book, an elegant surface or structure to accompany the book and act as a base and finally a dark area in the church were the installation will be sited (Fig. 1). The projector needs darkness if we want to get a sharp, bright output and the rest of the equipment needs to be somewhere safe from buglers, nature phenomenon's, humidity, animals etc.

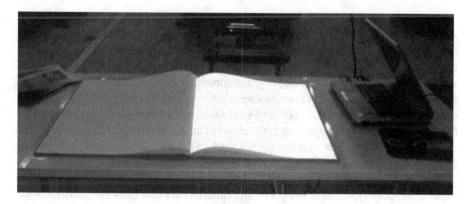

Fig. 1. A previous set up of the Interactive Book

Equipment is divided in the following categories (Fig. 2):

- Desktop PC: The PC will be the core of the equipment, is the system that will bring everything together. It will require an advance graphics card since it will handle 3D models, external hardware, video capture etc. Along with the graphics card a fast CPU and a decent amount of RAM will also be needed.
- Projector: Second asset of the hardware is a projector, the path to transmit the content from the PC to the book page. The projector needs at least an amount of 3200 Lumens or more.
- Web Camera: The use of the camera will be limited in recording the book until it tracks a mark which will be the sign of what content it should be projected on the page.

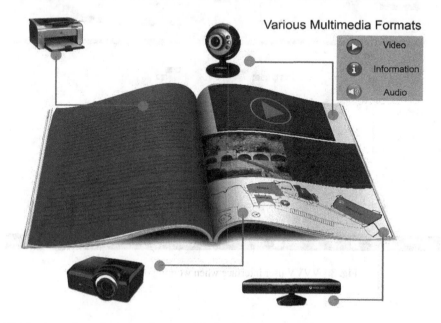

Fig. 2. A preview of an example page of the book along with the equipment that will be used

As for the software, VVVV multipurpose toolkit has been used for this installation. An open source graphical/textual programming environment which gives you the freedom and the possibilities to handle large media environments with physical interfaces, real-time motion graphics, audio and video that can interact with many users simultaneously [3]. VVVV has also a strong community which gives added value to the software. They help new users to start using effectively the software, with documentation of tasks, preparing tutorials, organizing workshops and a forum for Digital Arts called the Node. The forum is supporting the creation of an innovative and responsible movement by encouraging new collaboration, interdisciplinary exchange and open knowledge sharing.

The main goal of the forum is to empower individuals by encouraging them to experiment, prototype, and develop new algorithms, to ask new questions and to provide answers [4]. VVVV's job in this project is to combine all the areas together; receive the interaction coordinates from the sensor, filter them, process them, trigger actions, receive the input from the web camera and send the mapping content to the projector so it will be displayed only on the correct book page. Generally, is the extension of developer's thoughts and ideas into the computer (Fig. 3).

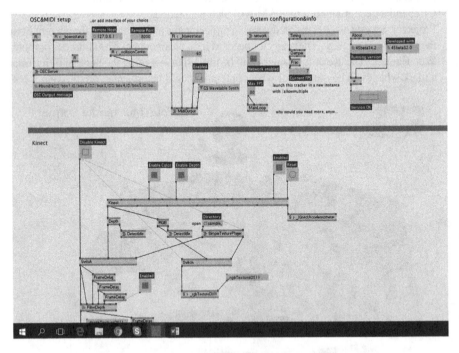

Fig. 3. VVVV user interface when working on the project

2.3 Gesture User Interface

The most critically part of this project is the interactivity; if the gesture user interface is not working flawlessly then the experience will not be as functional as it is supposed to be. The interaction can be achieved in various methods depending the equipment that one has available, the software and the "know-how". Until mow the use of Microsoft Kinect motion sensor was the best solution because of its low price and good results. The target was to track the hand movement which was the only part of the body that would engaged with the installation and by using Microsoft Kinect SDK in a VVVV environment along with the contribution from VVVV community (Kinect Nodes) gave us flexibility to track both hands simultaneously.

Furthermore, the part of the interaction that needed deeper research is the type of gestures that will be used and how the users will know them in order to interact with the book. Here the goal is simplicity but at the same time flexibility so users can receive an interesting, easy to interact installation. Considering that the page of the book will act as a screen, the gestures should be equivalent with the ones that are being widely used in all the other touch interfaces that people are using in their everyday life. The most common ones are: tap, double tap, drag, slide, hold/press, swipe, rotate, press & drag, pinch, spread (Fig. 4).

TOUCH GESTURES

TAP   DOUBLE TAP   DRAG   SLIDE   HOLD / PRESS

SWIPE   ROTATE   PRESS & DRAG   PINCH   SPREAD

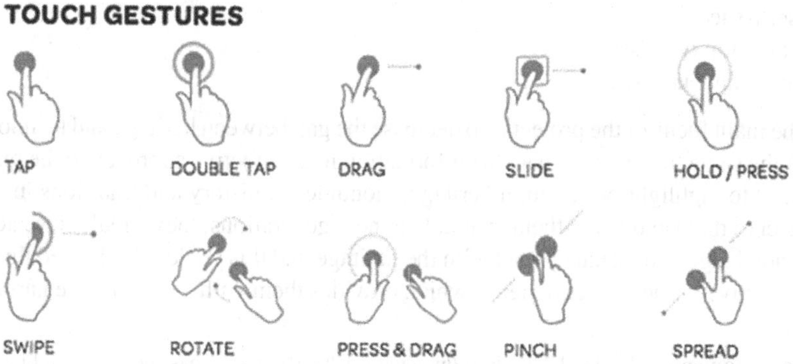

Fig. 4. Most common used touch gestures (Source: [5])

The challenge is to deploy hand tracking that Kinect provides and at the same time track the finger tips. Alternative option is to use the whole hand and basically skip the last two gestures: pinch and spread. Overall though the target is to use only: tap, drag, slide, hold, swipe and rotate as these are the most common gestures that a user -even one with no experience of touch technology- will easily pick up the gestures and engage with the installation. Furthermore, kids starting from age of two can use tap, drag and slide gestures, and when they reach the age of four another four gestures are added to their collection: drag&drop, rotate, pinch, flick, and spread [6]. Having the later in mind, the gestures that were adopted in the project are user friendly for younger and older people.

3 Future Work

As the technology evolves and the available choices are more, the upgrade of the previous installation to the latest technology becomes a necessity. There are plans on how to implement this installation in an alternative approach focusing into the interactivity area, replacing the Microsoft Kinect sensor with the use of touch foil technology. Touch foil is a transparent membrane that can transform any surface into an interactive touch screen. It is available in a variety of sizes and it is either single touch or multiple touch providing XY coordinates back to the software. This will give us the flexibility to use finger gestures which means a larger gesture library available, more accurate -since it doesn't track hands through a point cloud of data- and finally more elegant design of the installation as it won't be viewable to the public.

Additionally, the evaluation of the project needs to be planned specifically and carefully. As we previously mentioned our target groups are concentrated to foreign visitors, digital heritage enthusiasts and kids, so the evaluation will be attained on site. The concise overview provided by [7] mentions the following special characteristics of 3D user interface (3D UI) testing:

– Physical environment issues
– Evaluator issues
– User issues
– Evaluation type issues
– Miscellaneous issues

The main focus of the project is to decrease the gap between heritage and technology and at the same time disseminate the information in an effective approach to the public. We need to highlight our cultural heritage, monuments, history and traditions in order to preserve them and make them available to next generations; they should have access into knowledge and visual contact with the heritage and this could be achieved through an interactive immersive experience which provides them with an alternative narrative.

Acknowledgments.   1. ITN-DCH (http://www.itn-dch.eu/) project has received funding from the European Union's Seventh Framework program for research, technological development and demonstration under GA no 608013.

2. INCEPTION (http://www.inception-project.eu/) has received funding from the EU's H2020 Reflective framework programme for research and innovation under GA no 665220.

3. Europeana Space (http://www.europeana-space.eu/) has received funding from the European Union's ICT Policy Support Program as part of the Competitiveness and Innovation Framework Program, under GA no 621037.

4. 4DCH (http://www.4d-ch-world.eu/) project has received funding from the European Union's Seventh Framework program for research, technological development and demonstration.

5. Lo-Cloud (http://www.locloud.eu/) is co-funded under the CIP ICT-PSP program.

6. ViMM (http://www.vi-mm.eu/) has received funding from the EU's H2020 framework programme for support and coordination actions under GA no 727107.

References

1. Adabala, N., Datha, N., Joy, J., Kulkarni, C., Manchepalli, A., Sankar, A., Walton, R.: An interactive multimedia framework for digital heritage narratives. In: ACM MM 2010, pp. 1445–1448 (2010)
2. Reunanen, M., Díaz, L., Horttana, T.: A holistic user-centered approach to immersive digital cultural heritage installations. J. Comput. Cult. Herit. **7**, 1–16 (2015)
3. VVVV Group: Vvvv - a Multipurpose Toolkit. http://vvvv.org/
4. Node15: NODE15 Forum for Digital Arts April 27–May 3 2015 Frankfurt. http://node15.vvvv.org/
5. Moto, T.: gesture-icons-004 (2011). https://www.graffletopia.com/stencils/791
6. Abdul Aziz, N.A., Batmaz, F., Stone, R., Chung, P.W.H.: Selection of touch gestures for children's applications (2013)
7. Bowman, D.A., Kruijff, E., Laviola, J.J., Poupyrev, I.: Evaluation of 3D User Interfaces (2004)

Digital Cultural Heritage in Education, Learning and Training

Establishing a Remote Sensing Science Center in Cyprus: First Year of Activities of ATHENA Project

Diofantos Hadjimitsis[1], Athos Agapiou[1(✉)], Vasiliki Lysandrou[1],
Kyriacos Themistocleous[1], Branka Cuca[1], Argyro Nisantzi[1], Rosa Lasaponara[2],
Nicola Masini[3], Marilisa Biscione[3], Gabriele Nolè[2], Ramon Brcic[4], Daniele Cerra[4],
Michael Eineder[4], Ursula Gessner[4], Thomas Krauss[4], and Gunter Schreier[4]

[1] Remote Sensing and Geo-Environment Research Laboratory, Department of Civil Engineering
and Geomatics, Cyprus University of Technology, Saripolou str. 2–8, 3036 Limassol, Cyprus
{d.hadjimitsis,athos.agapiou,vasiliki.lysandrou,
k.themistocleous,branka.cuca,argyro.nisantzi}@cut.ac.cy
[2] CNR - National Research Council, IMAA- Institute of Methodologies
for Environmental Analysis, C. da S. Loya, 85050 Tito Scalo, Italy
{rosa.lasaponara,gabriele.nole}@imaa.cnr.it
[3] CNR - National Research Council, IBAM-Institute of Archaeological
and Monumental Heritage, C. da S. Loya, 85050 Tito Scalo, Italy
{n.masini,m.biscione}@ibam.cnr.it
[4] DLR - German Aerospace Center, EOC - Earth Observation Center,
82234 Oberpfaffenhofen, Germany
{Ramon.Brcic,Daniele.Cerra,Michael.Eineder,ursula.gessner,
Thomas.Krauss,Gunter.Schreier}@dlr.de

Abstract. ATHENA H2020 Twinning project is a three-year duration project
and its main objective is to strengthen the Cyprus University of Technology
(CUT) Remote Sensing Science and Geo-Environment Research Laboratory
in the field of "Remote Sensing Archaeology" by creating a unique link
between two internationally-leading research institutions: National Research
Council of Italy (CNR) and the German Aerospace Centre (DLR). Through the
ATHENA project, CUT's staff research profile and expertise will be raised
while S&T capacity of the linked institutions will be enhanced. In this paper the
abovementioned objectives are presented through the various activities accomplished in the first year of the project. These activities include both virtual
training by experts in topics such as active remote sensing sensors and sophisticated algorithms, as well as scientific workshops dedicated to specific earth
observation and cultural heritage aspects. During this first year, outreached
activities have been also performed aiming to promote remote sensing and
other non-destructive techniques, including geophysics, for monitoring and
safeguarding archaeological heritage of Cyprus. The ATHENA center aims to
serve the local community of Cyprus, but at the same time to be established in
the wider area of eastern Mediterranean.

Keywords: Cultural heritage · Remote sensing · Cyprus · Center of excellence

© Springer International Publishing AG 2016
M. Ioannides et al. (Eds.): EuroMed 2016, Part II, LNCS 10059, pp. 275–282, 2016.
DOI: 10.1007/978-3-319-48974-2_31

1   Introduction

ATHENA is the acronym of a three-year duration H2020 Twinning 2015 project, entitled "Remote Sensing Science Center for Cultural Heritage" (Proposal number: 691936), initiated at the end of 2015 [1]. Scope of the project is to establish a remote sensing science center in Cyprus for supporting the Cultural Heritage sector, by improving the capabilities of the local personnel involved in the project. National Research Council of Italy (CNR), by means of two institutes IMAA and IBAM, and the German Aerospace Centre (DLR) are acting as the leading research institutions aiming to provide this know-how and expertise through a variety of training activities and dissemination actions.

The project focuses on best practices for monitoring and safeguarding Cultural Heritage based on multidisciplinary collaborations and filling the gap between cross-disciplinary research and exploitation methods through different scientific domains such as history, archaeology, architecture, urban design, sociology, anthropology, engineering, science for conservation, and computer sciences through the use of remote sensing technologies. Such combination of innovative methodologies to enhance the understanding of European Cultural Heritage by means of remote sensing techniques will bring new knowledge, collaboration across disciplines, and social benefits. The innovative procedures [2, 3] and applications will enable remote communication and collaboration across the industry, professionals, experts, researchers and academia. ATHENA center is devoted to the introduction, development and systematic use of advanced remote sensing science and technologies in the field of archaeology, built cultural heritage, their multi-temporal analysis and interpretation and the distant monitoring of their natural and anthropogenic environment. As a starting point ATHENA exploits the current capabilities of the Remote Sensing and Geo-Environment Laboratory at the Cyprus University of Technology (CUT), both in terms of capacity as well of equipment, performing advance research and offering support to the CH sector. The Centre will be in close collaboration with both national as well international research institutes and stakeholders, providing integrated remote sensing services and solutions in the area of the Eastern Mediterranean. The new perspectives on archaeological and cultural heritage in the region will position ATHENA as a center of knowledge and a standard lab in the field of Remote Sensing Archaeology. This paper aims to present the overall activities carried out in the first year of the project in different levels: training, dissemination, outreach activities etc. The knowledge acquired during the first year will be used to maximize the impact of future work of the project and to promote the remote sensing capabilities for Cultural Heritage in the areas of Education, Research, Development, Technology and Industry. Similar activities are already planned for the next two years of the project with the participation of local stakeholders, as well as scholars.

2   Overall Strategy

The first year of ATHENA project was built upon a variety of training and outreach activities. The former includes workshops dedicated to specific topics of earth observation and remote sensing technologies, summer schools which were merged with in-situ visits to archaeological sites of Cyprus, researchers exchange between the Remote Sensing and Geo-Environment Lab of CUT and the two leading institutions (CNR and DLR) as well as virtual training courses. Outreach activities included amongst other, presentations to conferences and seminars, publications in scientific journals is the field of remote sensing and/or archaeology/cultural heritage, lecturing at schools, newsletters etc. ATHENA project was also presented to local stakeholders. Both activities aimed to "educate the educators" since remote sensing and earth observation technology is growing very fast, especially in the last decade. This link will enable current researchers working in the CUT to fill the gap between the existing technology used in the archaeological and culture heritage sector and the emerging technology arising in the next few years. In addition, ATHENA project will be exploited to promote in different levels (i.e. end-user, stakeholders, professionals, scientists) earth observation and remote sensing utility for Cultural Heritage.

3 First Year of Activities

3.1 Training

Virtual Training on Hyperspectral data and algorithms. The virtual training focused on hyperspectral data and algorithms was delivered by DLR using ordinary telecommunication platforms. The one-day training included an introduction to hyperspectral remote sensing followed by a seminar for band selection in hyperspectral datasets. As hyperspectral sensors measure the reflected solar radiation in up to hundreds different spectral bands, in practical applications it is usually desired to reduce the number of dimensions to speed up computations and increase the accuracy of the results.

The lecture included a discussion on statistics, building up to analysis based on mutual information starting from simpler concepts such as variance and Shannon entropy (Fig. 1). The training was concluded by a practical application on the detection of buried structures in an archaeological site in Europe.

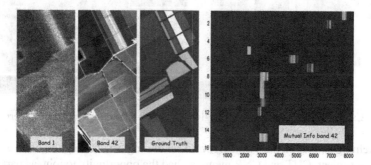

Fig. 1. Mutual information (M.I) for a variety of Bands from the case study of Carnuntum (see more [4])

Copernicus Workshop. A dedicated workshop for Copernicus entitled "Copernicus contribution to Cultural Heritage", was organized by DLR during "The Fourth International Conference on Remote Sensing and Geoinformation of Environment" conference held in Cyprus. The workshop was a one-day general introduction to the European Copernicus Earth observation program, focused on topics related to the H2020 ATHENA project: Establish a Center of Excellence in the field of Remote Sensing for Cultural Heritage. The ATHENA twinning partner DLR and guest speakers from European Space Agency (ESA) and the European Commission (EC) introduced the participants to the Copernicus mission and presented various aspects such as: Sentinel space segment; Contributing missions and access to their data; Core and collaborative ground segment; Data policy and access to the data and Core Services targeting those of relevance for ATHENA.

Amongst others, the following general issues have been raised during the discussion: (a) Access to Copernicus Data: The access to Sentinel data will be improved on a European scale by the new initiative of the European Commission to better coordinate and merge core and collaborative data access points. The initiative is name "integrated ground segment" and will start implementation in 2017; (b) There has been a growing interest in the use of satellite observation for monitoring cultural heritage, in particular seen the conflicts in the middle East and the difficulty in assessing damage in-situ; (c) Monitoring of Cultural Heritage - particularly related to damage assessment in conflict zones - is planned to be one of the services accessible through SEA (Support to EU External Actions) as from mid-2016. This is part of the civil security core services of Copernicus. Other actions for the future have been also defined in order to promote the use of remote sensing and earth observation for safeguarding and protection of Cultural Heritage (Fig. 2).

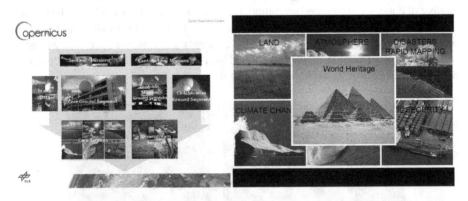

Fig. 2. Screenshots from the lectures given by DLR, presenting the use of Copernicus

Staff exchanges. Geophysics and Ground technologies: During the first year of the ATHENA project, CUT and CNR members had the opportunity to join, as part of staff exchange activity, a summer school organized by CNR IBAM and IREA, held in Pompeii. The summer school was entitled "Geophysics and Remote Sensing for Archaeology" and included lectures, practical field applications at the archaeological site of

Pompeii and processing. The course, provided a unique opportunity for researchers to be familiarized with the basics of data collection, processing and interpretation of geophysical techniques such as Ground Penetrating Radar (GPR), magnetic and Electrical Resistivity Tomography (ERT), as well as other passive and active remote sensing techniques, applied not only for detecting buried remains but also for investigating masonry structures and wall paintings in two important areas of Pompeii in accordance with the Archaeological Superintendence (Fig. 3).

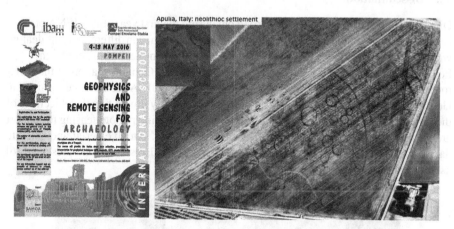

Fig. 3. Leaflet of the Summer School held in Pompeii (left) and example from the lectures given during the school indicating crop marks of a Neolithic settlement in Southern Italy (right)

Synthetic Aperture Radar (SAR) Principles and Applications Summer School.
Recent developments in space active remote sensing technologies have been presented during the summer school held in CUT premises by the DLR. The three-day course was focused on the fundamentals of both SAR and interferometric SAR. Targeted examples of interferometry, TerraSAR-X Data, SAR Sentinel-1 Data, ERS-ENVISAT-Data, SAR data availability for Paphos test site (Fig. 4) and SAR Data Evaluation were presented.

Fig. 4. Example of the TanDEM-X over Paphos district.

As evidenced during the training, several applications are now possible using SAR data, including oceanography sector, maritime security and ship detection, post-earthquakes, volcanic eruptions and flooding, as well as glaciology, geodesy, urbanization, agriculture and traffic monitoring. Finally, an in-situ visit to the archaeological site under investigation was also carried out.

3.2 Dissemination

Dissemination activities have been carried out during the first year of ATHENA project. Both posters and conference publications have been published in different events dealing with remote sensing and archaeology such as the SPIE Remote Sensing conference, the Fourth International Conference on Remote Sensing and Geoinformation of the Environment (RSCy2016), the ISPRS Congress, the GEOBIA conference, European Geosciences Union [5], a.o. The presentations were mainly illustrating the objectives of the ATHENA project and evidencing the importance of using remote sensing to support archaeological research and cultural heritage monitoring. Archive aerial and satellite datasets suitable for the case study of Cyprus have been also studied and presented [6] as demonstrated in Fig. 5.

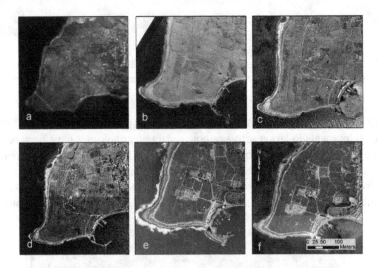

Fig. 5. Aerial images taken over the archaeological site of Nea Paphos: (a) aerial image of Cyprus before the Second World War (b) aerial image of 1945 taken from RAF; (c) aerial image taken in 1962; (d) aerial image of 1993; (e) aerial orthophoto of 2008 and (f) aerial orthophoto of 2014

Moreover, journal publications have been completed including the "Towards a spectral library of Roman to Early Christian Cypriot floor mosaics" [7]. The paper deals with the creation of a spectral library (see Fig. 6) in the range of 400–2500 nm for discrimination analysis of materials coming from ancient floor mosaics evaluated with linear constrained un-mixing techniques. The results were found very promising indicating that ground spectroscopy may be used for detection of dominant materials in floor mosaics tesserae.

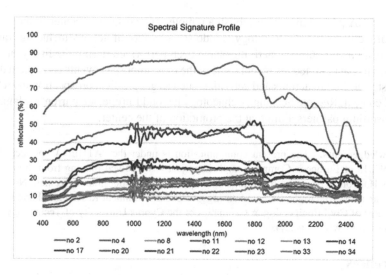

Fig. 6. Example of spectral signature profiles taken from the samples of floor mosaics acquired in the range of 350–2500 nm [8]

3.3 Outreach Activities

Educational activities during the Researchers' Night in Cyprus took place, demonstrating to participants of different ages the potential use of remote sensing to archaeology and the overall aims of the ATHENA project. In addition, lectures were given to undergraduate and postgraduate students of the Department of Civil Engineering and Geomatics of the CUT informing them about the running project and at the same time offering them the opportunity to learn about these new capabilities of Remote Sensing applications. Dissemination activities included the issuing of informational leaflets and press release in local newspapers. The most important events of ATHENA are also presented in the projects' website, which is continuously updated. At the website, informational and educational material can be downloaded, while a mailing list is kept to inform the users and other researchers regarding the progress of the project.

4 Conclusion

The up to date activities accomplished through the ATHENA project, have demonstrated the great possibilities of Remote Sensing technologies applied for archaeological research. New technological achievements of Remote Sensing science, such as the ameliorate of the spatial resolution offered by radar space sensors, provide new capabilities, acquisition of further data, as well as the exploitation of new areas of research interest.

The aforementioned achievements and the new knowledge acquired in local level (CUT), have been gained through the twinning to the partners from high performing European centers, experts on Remote Sensing and Archaeological Heritage (DLR and CNR) and by blending all necessary scientific expertise.

ATHENA project aims to establish a remote sensing science center in the areas of Cultural Heritage and Archaeology. To do so, a variety of actions including training, dissemination and outreach activities have been performed during the first year of the project. The paper aimed to present some of the most important events carried out during this first year. Future actions and activities, such as geophysical prospection in archaeological context, Remote Sensing Archaeology beyond Europe, are currently planned by the consortium partners aiming at the promotion of the center.

Acknowledgements. The present communication is under the "ATHENA" project H2020-TWINN2015 of European Commission. This project has received funding from the European Union's Horizon 2020 research and innovation programme under grant agreement No 691936. Thanks are also given to the Remote Sensing and Geo-environment Research Laboratory of the Department of Civil Engineering & Geomatics of the Cyprus University of Technology for the support (http://www.cut.ac.cy).

References

1. ATHENA website project. www.athena2020.eu
2. Lasaponara, R., Masini, N.: Satellite synthetic aperture radar in archaeology and cultural landscape: an overview. Archaeol. Prospection **20**, 71–78 (2013). doi:10.1002/arp.1452
3. Lasaponara, R., Masini, N. (eds.): Satellite Remote Sensing: A New Tool for Archaeology. Remote Sensing and Digital Image Processing, vol. 16, 364 p. Springer, Heidelberg (2012). 150 illus., 88 in color, ISBN 978-90-481-8800-0
4. Doneus, M., Verhoeven, G., Atzberger, C., Wess, M., Ruš, M.: New ways to extract archaeological information from hyperspectral pixels. J. Archaeol. Sci. **52**, 84–96 (2014). http://dx.doi.org/10.1016/j.jas.2014.08.023, ISSN 0305-4403
5. Diofantos, G., Agapiou, A., Lysandrou, V., Themistocleous, K., Cuca, B., Lasaponara, R., Masini, N., Krauss, T., Cerra, D., Gessner, U., Schreier, G.: ATHENA: remote sensing science center for cultural heritage in cyprus. Geophysical Research Abstracts, vol. 18, EGU2016-9191 (2016)
6. Agapiou, A., Lysandrou, V., Themistocleous, K., Lasaponara, R., Masini, N., Krauss, T., Cerra, D., Gessner, U., Schreier, G., Hadjimitsis, D.: Searching data for supporting archaeolandscapes in Cyprus: an overview of aerial, satellite and cartographic datasets of the island. In: Fourth International Conference on Remote Sensing and Geoinformation of the Environment (RSCy 2016), 4–8 April, 2016. Cyprus
7. Lysandrou, V., Cerra, D., Agapiou, A., Charalambous, E., Hadjimitsis, D.G.: Towards a spectral library of Roman to Early Christian Cypriot floor mosaics. J. Archaeol. Sci. Rep. (2016). doi:10.1016/j.jasrep.2016.06.029

The Contribution of Digital Technologies to the Mediation of the Conservation-Restoration of Cultural Heritage

Clément Serain[✉]

Paris 8 University, Saint-Denis, France
clement.serain@gmail.com

Abstract. This brief article presents some of the questions inherent to the thesis I am currently engaged in with the French Paris 8 University, in the field of Communication sciences. Entitled *Conservation and restoration of cultural heritage in regard to digital humanities*, that thesis aims at interrogating the impact of digital technologies on the managing, the conservation as well as the understanding and the appropriation of cultural heritage in terms of materiality. In other words, the goal is to question the importance of these technologies in the creation of new frameworks of memories, as well as in the establishing of a mediation of cultural heritage that would be the point of origin of the building and the vision of a singular history of art. To that end, this article proposes to analyze three digital devices from three different perspectives of the conservation-restoration of cultural heritage: research, restoration and diffusion.

Keywords: Conservation · Restoration · Digital technologies · Art · Cultural heritage · Museum · Research · Diffusion

1 Introduction

Gathering art historians, scientists, restorers or even curators, photographs and administrators, conservation-restoration is fundamentally interdisciplinary. More than a mere material safeguarding of the objects themselves, it is above all a reflection upon the different values encased within a work of art, might they be aesthetical, historical, but also ethical, political, cultural or religious. As a result, conservation-restoration is part of the discipline of art history because it provides us with a material history of our cultural heritage. Nonetheless, it is today considered as a full-fledged academic and scientific discipline in itself. Specialists such as Ségolène Bergeon Langle and Georges Brunel propose to define its constitutive elements with "a goal (the physical conservation of cultural goods), a methodology of work (interdisciplinarity for instance), the definition of the role of the different participants (scientists, historians or archeologists and restorers), the existence of a formation for them, the existence of a history of restoration and of a specific research, and finally a vocabulary which ensures the unity of the methodology and the transfer of knowledge" [1].

That definition allows for observing that conservation-restoration of cultural heritage is related to the three main missions of heritage institutions: conservation, but also

M. Ioannides et al. (Eds.): EuroMed 2016, Part II, LNCS 10059, pp. 283–289, 2016.
DOI: 10.1007/978-3-319-48974-2_32

research and diffusion. We can also note that these missions correspond to three forms of mediation of cultural heritage: research forms the "official speech" about art history, conservation has an impact on the aesthetical aspects of the works of art, and diffusion proposes cognitive and sensorial readings of these works to different publics within different institutions. In his book published in 1993, *La Passion musicale, une sociologie de la médiation*, the sociologist Antoine Hennion evokes the "stack of mediations". He explains that each one of these mediations contribute to the shaping of our perception of works of art.

As a result, if conservation-restoration is part of the museum's missions and if these same missions can be considered as three forms of mediation of cultural heritage, then we can hypothesize that conservation-restoration participates in the elaboration of the mediation of cultural heritage thanks to different systems of knowledge transferring.

Furthermore, it should be specified that the technologies of information and communication within the museums are more and more important. They diversify and enrich their missions, and they lead to the idea of virtual museum. Conservation-restoration was, as a result, naturally concerned by the upheaval induced by digital, and it renewed the methods of "material mediation" of cultural heritage. In that perspective, we can wonder how the use of digital technologies in conservation-restoration allows for reiterating the practices of the researches and professionals on the one hand, and how it allows for transforming our point of view on cultural heritage on the other hand. To answer that question, we will present three digital devices. The first one is used for research in conservation-restoration, and more specifically research in Human and Social sciences. The second one is used for the restoration of works of art, and the third one is used in the framework of the diffusion to a large public of the general knowledge in conservation-restoration.

2   The Rembrandt Database

Conservation-restoration of cultural heritage requires research in Human and Social Sciences (about history of restoration or techniques for instance), as well as research in Hard Sciences (notably about chemical composition of materials or the degree of alteration of a painting). Research, as a result, is the point of origin of the creation of history of art, which can be political, sociological, economical or material, as far as we are concerned. Of course, these different histories are complementary and they cross each other, especially for material history of art because the conservation-restoration is an interdisciplinary discipline as it was evoked earlier. As a result, research provides with a first reading of cultural heritage, a reading that we can qualify as "official". Concerning the digital technologies, they allow for the reiteration of the practices of researchers, and they transform the discipline within which they work. Consequently, the building of their object of study, that is to say works of art, is transformed, as well as the vision they have of it.

The online database *The Rembrandt Database*[1] [2] is part of the exemplary initiatives in this area. It is a project, which is supported by the Andrew W. Mellon Foundation in New York. It aims at gathering, as exhaustively as possible, the whole of the resources known about the paintings of the Dutch painter of the 17th century, Rembrandt van Rijn. Numerous institutions are collaborating together in the conception of that database. It is an initiative of the RKD Netherlands Institute for Art History and of the Royal Picture Gallery Mauritshuis in Hague, Netherlands. As for the content, it is provided notably by the European and American museums. Among these institutions, some are involved in the technical conception of the website and of its associated database. Thus, the participation of the whole of these institutions is a warranty of the reliability of information for the users of the database. Indeed, given the immense quantity of data on Internet network, the identification of sources is essential for experts since the quality of their research depends on it.

The Rembrandt Database, which has been opened since September 2012, is open access, and it contains 11083 documents about the 205 referenced paintings coming from 25 museum collections in the world. It is a research tool for specialists. It gathers a lot of documents about Rembrandt's paintings, yet it does not create any documentation. The provided documents are essentially related to the materiality of the paintings. As a result, the visitor can mostly find scientific images (infrared reflectographies, X-Ray radiographies, ultraviolet images etc.). Nonetheless, *The Rembrandt Database* is related to other databases which provide it with other types of documents, among them *The Rembrandt Documents Project*. The links between the different databases are particularly interesting for research because they allow for the crossing of data, and they lead to possible new interpretations. This is all the more interesting for conservation-restoration, which is composed with different forms of knowledge coming from several disciplines. As a result, the database allows for connecting these various forms.

That type of open access database also allows for a rapid and facilitated access to information, which is most important when the subject of study of a researcher deals with objects, which are located in another country as well as their documentation. There again, it is a significant advantage for conservation-restoration whose scientific images are still confidential and are still kept within the research laboratories that produced them.

At last, that kind of device conditions the building of Art History by researchers. The first goal of that database is to gather different documents and make them available to specialists, notably art historians that are interested in Rembrandt's paintings. Yet a significant part of these documents come from scientific laboratories of conservation-restoration. As a result, the privileged approach, whether it is conscious or not, is a material approach of the paintings. Consequently, it can have a significant influence on researchers' work, and thus induce new "official" readings on cultural heritage at the expense of more traditional interpretations such as iconography or about the artist's style.

---

[1] Consulted online on August 29th, 2016.

3   Renoir's True Colors

Conservation-restoration also corresponds to the theories and practices of the physical preservation of cultural heritage. It aims at ensuring the sustainability of the works of art, in order to bequeath them to the future generations. It is essentially composed with restoration techniques that necessitate direct interventions upon the work of art, as well as with preventive conservation techniques. These techniques refer to all the actions of controlling the environment surrounding the work of art (notably temperature and humidity). All these activities have consequences on the visible aspect of cultural heritage, and as a result, it transforms the vision we have of works of art. Indeed, contrary to research which gives us a cognitive, organized and intellectualized interpretation of cultural heritage, conservation proposes a sensorial reading of the objects (even though this is an unconscious process since the goal of conservation is not to propose an object that would satisfy aesthetical expectations, but to ensure its durability through time). Consequently, conservation can be seen as a second layer of cultural heritage mediation. Nonetheless, the intellectual and sensorial aspects in terms of perception of cultural heritage are not separated. Indeed, the appearance of an object is necessarily related to its history (material history for example), and to the way we chose to present it at a given time (the scenography of an exhibition as an impact on our senses, but it is defined in advance in an objective manner in order to produce a certain effect on the visitors).

There again, digital technologies do renew our sensorial vision of cultural heritage, which is reflected by the digital restitution of one of Auguste Lenoir's canvases by the Art Institute of Chicago, that is to say *Madame Léon Clapisson*. That restitution, carried out thanks to nanotechnology and specific softwares, shows the artwork as it could have looked when it came out of the artist's workshop, without any alteration. Besides, it was presented in the framework of a special exhibition, which was entitled *Renoir's True Colors* (see Footnote 1) [3]. Even though this was not a restoration strictly speaking but a restitution[2], that creation does raise questions. It interrogates the nature of these new "restorations", and the consequences they could have on our relationship with cultural heritage as well as on cultural heritage itself.

In the first place, that restitution reflects current evolution in the professional practices of cultural heritage restoration. Indeed, restoration necessitates new skills related to digital, and it creates new jobs. Besides, digital works of art do force restorers to diversy their practices. That technology also allows for the establishing of connections between the different actors of the discipline. Thus it facilitates the interdisciplinary reflections between research in Hard Sciences, and research in Human Sciences and cultural heritage restoration. Indeed, thanks to a new way of considering the restoration of an artwork, and thanks to research on the evolution of painting pigments, it is possible

---

[2] According to Ségolène Bergeon Langle and Georges Brunel, the restitution is an « operation which aims at virtually reconstituting an artwork or a building in its shapes and colors; it must be seen as a proposal which does not have any impact on the material reality of the cultural good » (La restauration des œuvres d'art. Vade-mecum en quelques mots. Hermann Editeurs, Paris (2014), p. 351).

for example to restitute an entire history of reception of the artwork according to its formal features changes through time.

In addition to enriching our knowledge and understanding of the artwork, that kind of digital restitution also transforms our global relationship with cultural heritage. The current restoration theories recommend avoiding intervening on the cultural objects. The goal is to avoid future alterations as best as possible, as well as to preserve all the values that have been attributed to the artwork throughout its life, without privileging any one of these values at the expense of another. Yet with that digital restitution, Renoir's painting is not a memory object that gathers all the eras it has been through anymore. On the contrary, it becomes an object that only has a value in the shape it takes at the precise moment of its creation. Indeed, while the exhibited object is doubly distanced from the public (due to the barriers and glass which make the object sacred as well as because of its temporal complexity), digital restitution allows for integrating Renoir's history into a specific period of time. As a result, it facilitates its comprehension and its appropriation by the visitors.

4 Focus on the Mona Lisa

At last, conservation-restoration of cultural heritage is also an amount of knowledge to be transmitted to a larger public than the specialists. According to the *Key concepts of museology* of the International Council of Museums, « mediation is defined as an action aimed at reconciling parties or bringing them to agreement. In the context of the museum, it is the mediation between the museum public and what the museum gives its public to see (…) mediation is an in-between, filling a space that it will try to reduce, creating a connection or even acceptance » [4]. Consequently, mediation aims at accompanying publics in the knowledge and understanding of cultural heritage, thanks to systems of knowledge transmission. Mediation for the larger public constitutes a possible third reading of cultural heritage. Indeed, it first necessitates a popularization of knowledge, which implies a different vision of cultural heritage from that of specialists. Then, sensorial perception of museum objects depends on the scenography, which organizes them. It should be noted that this third type of reading of cultural heritage is nevertheless conditioned by the two first readings we evoked earlier. As a result, the popularized approach of cultural heritage necessarily depends on the scientific approach (research), while the visual aspect of the objects presented in museums is also a result of the way they have been preserved (conservation).

Mediation devices also allow for documenting the iconography, the artist's style as well as the historical context in which the artwork is included. These devices, which facilitated the transmission of knowledge related to conservation-restoration, have been, until now, rarely present within exhibitions. The growing interest of the museums in the discipline itself and in its exhibition shows that the situation is changing. Indeed, we can evoke the guided tours within storage areas, as well as the restorations of artworks that take place within the exhibition spaces. Moreover, it should be noted that mediation devices deal with very diversified themes: restoration techniques, creation process of an artwork, analysis tools used by the scientists, the materials used by painters, or the use of preventive conservation.

The digital tools of mediation are increasingly used in museums and facilitate the mediation of conservation-restoration. They take the form of websites, of smartphones applications, of tactile tablets, or of augmented reality glasses One of the Louvre Museum's websites is dedicated to Leonardo da Vinci's masterpiece, *Mona Lisa* (see Footnote 1) [5]. In addition to the importance of communicating about the institution and its collections, that website allows the visitors to discover the secrets of that very emblematic painting of the 16th century. Opened in October 2014, that website is provided with several sections and features which participate in the building of a speech around the artwork's materiality. For instance, the high-resolution pictures and the zoom feature allow the visitor to actually see tiny details, and to have a more direct relationship with the paint layer. This is all the more interesting for an artwork such as *Mona Lisa*, which we can rarely approach because its success which attracts millions of visitors throughout the world. Furthermore, the website provides the visitors with several scientific images of the painting, which present views of the different paint layers of the artwork as well as its backside. These images are rarely presented to the larger public. Consequently, they give the visitor the opportunity to look at the artwork in an original, renewed way. It should also be noted that these images were born with digital. Consequently, their exploitation by mediation is obviously facilitated within the framework of digital devices. At last, the exchange of the contents of the website on social networks gives the institution the opportunity to indirectly raise the awareness of the visitors about the fragility of cultural heritage notably. It is a way of legitimizing the actions of conservation-restoration, and to remind everyone of the importance of these activities for the physical transmission of the artworks to future generations. As a result, conservation-restoration becomes a source of social link revolving around the idea of a common cultural heritage we have to preserve and share.

5   Conclusions and Openings

Digital humanities are a rather recent field of research, which questions the new practices of researchers in Human and Social sciences through their use of digital technologies. They aim at showing that technology is not a mere tool for researchers, but that it truly participates in the enriching of knowledge in Human and Social Sciences. Digital Humanities research, especially about cultural heritage is still little used. The questions that were discussed here about conservation-restoration tried to contribute to the filling of that particular gap. Indeed, that article reflects the numerous changes induced by digital technologies within the discipline itself, as well as the changes in terms of study, conservation and diffusion of cultural heritage.

While digital technology has been considered as a positive contribution for cultural heritage until now, for its conservation as well as for its restoration, it seemed necessary, in this conclusion, to also mention the potential risks and threats. Indeed, technology doesn't always appear as a solution, and sometimes it implies true constraints for the management, the knowledge and the understanding of cultural heritage: for example, the immateriality of technology often lets us forget about the obsolescence of supports as well as software. Otherwise, it is risky to consider that technology can produce authentic facts on which researchers can rely. Their conception always depends on a specific point of view of the object, a point of view that cannot be unbiased. As for the preservation of digital data in the field of conservation, it necessitates important infrastructures. Indeed, the processes of stocking and saving data have to face different threats, such as environmental and organizational. At last, the instrumentality of the power of images by digital technologies can be a danger for the transmission of knowledge to the general public. Indeed, scientific images for instance are very evocative, but they cannot be understood without specific explanation or a true dialog with the different publics. The digital tool should not only impress the visitors, but it must also enable them to understand what they see.

References

1. Bergeon, L.S., Brunel, G.: La restauration des œuvres d'art. Vade-mecum en quelques mots. Hermann Editeurs, Paris (2014)
2. The Rembrandt Database. http://www.rembrandtdatabase.org/Rembrandt
3. Art Institut of Chicago, Exhibition *Renoir's True Colors: Science Solves a Mystery.* http://www.artic.edu/exhibition/renoir-s-true-colors-science-solves-mystery
4. Desvallées, A., Mairesse, F.: Key Concepts of Museology, ICOM, Armand Colin, Paris (2010)
5. Focus on the Mona Lisa. http://focus.louvre.fr/fr/la-joconde

Author Index

Printed in the United States
By Bookmasters